Homophobic Bullying

Homophobic Bullying

Research and Theoretical Perspectives

IAN RIVERS

OXFORD
UNIVERSITY PRESS

OXFORD
UNIVERSITY PRESS

Oxford University Press, Inc., publishes works that further
Oxford University's objective of excellence
in research, scholarship, and education.

Oxford   New York
Auckland   Cape Town   Dar es Salaam   Hong Kong   Karachi
Kuala Lumpur   Madrid   Melbourne   Mexico City   Nairobi
New Delhi   Shanghai   Taipei   Toronto

With offices in
Argentina   Austria   Brazil   Chile   Czech Republic   France   Greece
Guatemala   Hungary   Italy   Japan   Poland   Portugal   Singapore
South Korea   Switzerland   Thailand   Turkey   Ukraine   Vietnam

Copyright © 2011

Published by Oxford University Press, Inc.
198 Madison Avenue, New York, New York 10016

www.oup.com

Oxford is a registered trademark of Oxford University Press

Library of Congress Cataloging-in-Publication Data

Rivers, Ian.
Homophobic bullying : research and theoretical perspectives / Ian Rivers.
   p. cm.
Includes bibliographical references.
ISBN 978-0-19-516053-6
1. Homophobia in schools—Great Britain. 2. Bullying in schools—Great Britain. I. Title.
LC212.83.G7R59 2011
371.5'8—dc22
2010046856

9   8   7   6   5   4   3   2   1
Printed in the United States of America
on acid-free paper

Rob, Tony, Arnie, Helen and, of course, Barney

Foreword

Homophobic Bullying by Ian Rivers documents in detail research findings on the phenomenon to date and provides a number of possible theoretical explanations. It charts the continuities and discontinuities across time in student behaviour at school, college and university, drawing on surveys of current experience as well as retrospective material. Relevant aspects of homophobic bullying in the workplace are also presented. This book is scholarly yet at the same time very readable. Each type of homophobic bullying is illustrated with case study material drawn from Ian Rivers' extensive research in the field. There are moving accounts of the emotional distress caused by the cruel taunting and social exclusion on the part of peers and the all too frequent indifference of adults. But at the same time we also read about the resilience demonstrated by some children and young people as they develop coping strategies to deal with such negative experiences. Their courage cannot be underestimated. Collectively over time these young people have seen a change in society's attitudes towards them. Ian Rivers' book not only documents the evident distress of being bullied for one's sexual orientation but also takes a longer-term, lifespan development perspective that records the resilience strategies of marginalised groups. He ends by reiterating the immense importance of social support in helping lesbian, gay and bisexual youth navigate their way through childhood and adolescence into adulthood. There is a clear message here for schools and all those who work with young people.

Helen Cowie
University of Surrey
August 2010

Preface

If truth be told I hoped that there would be no need to write this book. It has been 17 years since I began my research focusing upon the nature and long-term correlates of what has become known as *homophobic bullying*. In those early days of 1993, I presumed, as I think many other researchers on bullying have thought, that the capital we invest in young people's education would ensure that violence and discrimination would have come to an end, and schools would be safe places. However, this is not always the case and while some researchers have found evidence suggesting that, among older students at least, issues such as sexual orientation are no longer a matter for public ridicule, others continue to face daily harassment, sometimes as a result of an uncaring system that places conformity above individuality, and league tables above the exploration of knowledge.

In this book I refer to numerous studies that I have conducted over the last two decades. Some of that research is discussed in considerable depth and some of it is briefly described. I have been fortunate throughout my career in being able to discuss the implications of my research with some of the very best psychologists and sociologists working in the fields of education, and lesbian and gay issues. This book is not a polemic. It is not anti-heterosexual nor is it proselytising homosexuality. It is grounded in the belief that all young people regardless of background, culture, gender, religious belief, or sexual orientation should be educated in a safe and nurturing environment. Politics and the prejudices that underpin them have no place in schools. Similarly, religious beliefs, although important to many, are neither uniform nor universal, and there should always be respect for those who hold particular beliefs and for those who choose to challenge or ignore them. I firmly believe that all sides should be heard, and that no one side should have command over the other. While some faiths condemn homosexuality, there is little evidence to suggest that such condemnation translates into a condonment of the victimisation of lesbians, gay men and bisexual men and women.

In the end, *Homophobic Bullying: Research and Theoretical Perspectives* is my attempt to make sense of the school experiences of lesbians, gay men and bisexual men and women who were bullied at school and the impact bullying has had upon their adult lives. I have tried to use theories and ideas drawn from sociology, psychology, anthropology and zoology to understand the dynamics of homophobic bullying, sometimes using analogies drawn from studies of other forms of discrimination.

I am particularly keen to emphasise that there is much that has been done to support young people who are lesbian, gay and bisexual at school. Similarly there has been a great deal of work with students who are victims and perpetrators of homophobic bullying. In Chapter 6 I have included examples of some of the resources that have been developed or edited by me to support teachers who have found it difficult to challenge homophobic language and the underlying attitudes that permeat the classroom. Perhaps the most salutary lesson that I can provide to any teacher, administrator or governor of a school about the necessity of considering issues of sexual orientation comes from a conference presentation I did a few years ago with education providers within a local authority. The question I posed to each person in the audience was: 'do you have the children of gay or lesbian parents in your school?' Quite a few teachers and governors believed they did not. Based upon the data I had collected on behalf of the local authority I was able to demonstrate that every school had at least one child currently living with a same-sex couple.

As far as possible I have tried to make this book applicable to a wide range of readers in multiple countries. While its primary focus is on the experiences of lesbians, gay men and bisexual men and women living in the United Kingdom and the United States, there are parallels with the experiences of others living in European countries and in Australasia. I should also mention that this book sets the scene for another monograph by Mark McCormack, also published by Oxford University Press, which examines some of the more recent changes in the attitudes of young men towards homosexuality in senior school and college. This book is discussed in Chapter 8.

Finally, I have tried to write a book that is accessible. While there are references to statistics, I have also tried, wherever possible, to use qualitative data gathered from interviews to illustrate my findings. I have also included case studies and extracts from letters I have received during the course of my career to demonstrate the challenges and successes that young people and their families encounter when coming to terms with homophobic bullying. Undoubtedly there is much more to write on this subject, and this is my attempt to synthesise the data so far.

Ian Rivers
Brunel University, UK
May, 2010

Acknowledgements

I would like to take this opportunity to thank all of those people who have helped me finish this book. In particular I would like to thank the many participants from my various studies: their willingness to talk about their experiences of school and to build successful lives despite the lack of support they received when they were young is truly inspirational. I would also like to thank those colleagues with whom I have worked in gathering the data I present here. I am particularly grateful to Nathalie Noret and Andrew Richards who, as students and later as coworkers, gave of their time freely. I am grateful to Greenwood Praeger for allowing me to reproduce Table 6.1 in this volume. I am indebted to the Health Development Agency (now the National Institute of Health and Clinical Excellence) for allowing me to reproduce teaching materials I devised for use in primary and secondary schools in England and Wales. I would also like to thank Gay Youth UK for allowing me to reproduce "Letter from Aaron—Aged 16." I am also grateful for the support provided to me by Eric Anderson, Mark McCormack, and Richard Taulke-Johnson, whose work inspired me to reflect upon the messages I wished to convey and challenged me to complete this book. Finally I would like to thank Catharine Carlin, who allowed me to take an interminable amount of time to submit my manuscript.

Contents

Homophobic Bullying

I

Bullying: An Overview of Research

Bullying has been a feature of the educational experiences of young women and men for a great many years. Although it has been given different names such as "mobbing," "scapegoating," and "peer aggression," its meaning has rarely been misinterpreted. It has been the subject of novels, of plays, and of films, all of which have depicted the emotional impact such behaviour can have upon a young person within a closed institution.

In this chapter, I review key studies from 40 years of empirical research that has sought to define, categorise, and understand bullying behaviour at school. I discuss the early studies of "mobbing" conducted in Scandinavia in the 1970s, and then consider the various definitions offered by subsequent researchers, discussing both the similarities and differences in interpretation. I then consider some of the methodological issues researchers have encountered over the years in extending the range of behaviours we now describe as "bullying," whether physical, verbal, indirect, or relational in nature. Subsequently, I consider whether or not there are perceptible sex differences in such behaviour, and also whether or not there has been a shift in the pattern of bullying over the past 40 years. Finally, I provide a commentary on research addressing "cyberbullying" and discuss some of the conceptual and methodological issues researchers face today in tackling this new and expanding form of aggressive behaviour.

Early Research in Sweden and Norway

Though references to wilful acts of peer victimisation have been found in sixth-century Greek literature, wherein communities chose an individual—the *pharmakos*—upon whom they would transfer blame for their misfortune (Douglas, 1995), it was not until the late 1960s and early 1970s that a Swedish physician named Heinemann first questioned the acceptability of this form of behaviour, having observed it among a group of children in a school playground (Besag, 1989; Heinemann, 1972).

Although Heinemann's (1972) observational study is generally regarded as the first investigation of group aggression among schoolchildren—behaviour he described as "mobbing"—it was Olweus (1973) who developed this research further, exploring the nature, frequency, and long-term effects of "mobbing" in Scandinavian schools, culminating in a national study conducted in Norway in 1983 (Olweus, 1985, 1987, 1991, 1993a). Based upon the responses of some 130,000 Norwegian schoolchildren, Olweus determined that approximately 15% of those attending elementary and secondary/junior high schools (7–16 years of age) were involved in "mobbing" behaviours as either perpetrators or victims. When these results were broken down further, he found that 9% (52,000 pupils) were primarily victims while 7% (41,000 pupils) were primarily perpetrators (within these groups, 9,000 pupils were found to be both perpetrators and victims). He also found that over 50% of pupils reported being victimised by someone older than themselves.

Later, in his intensive Bergen Study (1983–85), which comprised 2,500 schoolchildren, Olweus reported that there were both age and gender differences in the nature and frequency of "mobbing" at school. Not only did he find an age-related decline in the frequency of such behaviour, he also found that physical acts of aggression (hitting, kicking, etc.) declined with age (Olweus, 1993a, 1994). When he compared gender differences in "mobbing," he found that boys and young men reported far more incidents of physical aggression, whereas girls and young women reported less obvious methods of intimidation (e.g., name-calling, being locked indoors, etc.). He also noted that, generally, acts of aggression against both boys and girls were perpetrated by boys (80% for boys and 60% for girls; Olweus, 1994), suggesting that such behaviours, particularly hitting, kicking, and punching, were primarily a male phenomenon.

Defining Bullying

In their early research both Heinemann (1972) and Olweus (1973) used the term "mobbing" (Norwegian/Danish) or its Swedish/Finnish equivalent "mobbning" to describe wilful acts of aggression perpetrated by one or more peers against an individual or group (Olweus, 1993a). However, outside Scandinavia the collective noun "mobbing" is used only when referring to the activities of a group rather than those of an individual. Similarly, the verb "to mob" has been and continues to be used to describe specifically the uncontrollable acts or behaviours of a disorderly crowd rather than those orchestrated deliberately by a group or individual against another group or individual (Allen, 1992). For this reason, research published outside Scandinavia in languages other than Danish, Swedish, Norwegian, or Finnish has referred to acts of peer aggression as "bullying" whether they are perpetrated by an individual or a group.

Building upon the work of Heinemann (1972) and Olweus (1978, 1987), in their surveys of peer aggression in the United Kingdom (U.K.), Ahmad, Whitney, and Smith (1991) and Whitney and Smith (1993) extended the scope of the behaviours under investigation to include less obvious methods of intimidation such as rumour-mongering, social isolation, and the destruction/loss/theft of personal property. By extending the parameters of what constituted bullying for children and young people at school, these researchers provided us with an opportunity to examine more closely the nature of the gender differences first noted by Olweus in his Bergen study (particularly the prevalence of subtle methods of victimisation) and, perhaps for the first time, they were able to offer us a taxonomy of such behaviour. However, while such an extension in our knowledge was to be welcomed, it also resulted in a reduction in the ability of the researchers to compare accurately the findings from their studies to those of the Norwegian national survey and, more importantly, the intensive Bergen study.

According to Olweus (1993a), "mobbing" occurred when a person was "exposed, repeatedly and over time, to the negative actions on the part of one or more other students" (p. 9). A similar definition was provided by Roland (also from Norway), who described it as "the long term and systematic use of violence, mental or physical, against an individual who is unable to defend himself [sic] in an actual situation" (Besag, 1989, p. 3). In both cases, as I indicated earlier in this chapter, the term "mobbing" was used to denote the aggressive actions of either an individual or a group. In the U.K., however, Smith and Sharp (1994) described "bullying" as "the systematic abuse of power" (p. 2). As they said:

> There will always be power relationships in social groups, by virtue of strength or size or ability, force of personality, sheer numbers or recognised hierarchy. Power can be abused; the exact definition of what constitutes abuse will depend upon the social and cultural context, but this is inescapable in examining human behaviour.
> If the abuse is systematic—repeated and deliberate—bullying seems a good name to describe it. (p. 2)

As Smith and Sharp's (1994) definition of bullying demonstrates, the imbalance of power between perpetrators and victims may not necessarily be one of number; it can also be founded upon the greater size, strength, ability, or force of personality of an individual.

In the United States (U.S.), the National Conference of State Legislatures has defined the term "bullying" as any behaviour that constitutes harassment, intimidation, taunting, and ridicule. Bullying may be motivated by ignorance or fear, or hate, or bias. It may be reinforced through cultural norms, peer pressure, and in some cases the desire to retaliate against another person. Bullying also includes initiation rituals, and it includes experiences of gendered or sexualised harassment.

Unlike much of Europe, researchers in the U.S. have found it difficult to agree upon a single definition of bullying. However, comparable with researchers in other countries, the majority agree upon a few common factors in defining bullying behaviour. For example, a consistent pattern of victimisation should be discernable. The intention of the perpetrator should be to inflict injury or discomfort upon one or more victims. In addition, there should be an imbalance of power between the perpetrator and the victim such that one student is able to dominate the other. Indeed, 24 states have passed anti-bullying laws (Limber & Small, 2003). By passing these laws, state legislatures have attempted to provide a clear definition of bullying that schools can use in establishing policies and codes of conduct for students. However, this task has been made all the more difficult for those states' legislators as a result of federal laws that require school boards and authorities to consider the individual circumstances of some perpetrators (particularly those with special needs) when deciding upon a course of action. Thus, it is impossible to legislate for blanket sanctions and penalties (Rivers, Duncan, & Besag, 2007).

Methodological Issues in Early Research

As I noted earlier in this chapter, in his intensive study of mobbing in Bergen schools (N = 2,500 pupils), Olweus found both age and gender differences in the nature of peer aggression (see Olweus 1993a, 1994). While the majority of his initial findings (particularly those relating to the frequency of physical acts of aggression among boys at primary or junior/middle school) have been replicated by various other European researchers (see Ahmad & Smith, 1994; Ahmad, Whitney, & Smith, 1991; Björkqvist, Ekman, & Lagerspetz, 1982; Björkqvist, Lagerspetz, & Kaukiainen, 1992; Lagerspetz, Björkqvist, & Peltonen, 1988; Rivers & Smith, 1994; Whitney & Smith, 1993), there has also been a degree of discord between these studies, particularly the association between gender and types of bullying behaviour. For example, whereas Olweus (1994) has clearly suggested that bullying was primarily a male phenomenon and had argued that "relations among boys are by and large harder, tougher, and more aggressive than among girls" (p. 1177), other researchers (Rivers & Smith, 1994; Whitney & Smith, 1993) have shown that, in the U.K. at least, rates of direct verbal bullying do not vary greatly between boys and girls at both primary school (41.3% and 39.1% respectively) and secondary school (23.1% and 24.4% respectively).

Undoubtedly, one of the difficulties in comparing and contrasting the findings from more recent studies of bullying to those of Olweus lies in the fact that there exist a number of versions of his survey instrument which, as I indicated earlier, have incorporated extended definitions of "mobbing" or "bullying" at school. It has already been suggested that such revisions have made it difficult for researchers to draw accurate comparisons between their studies and those of Olweus, and, as a consequence, this has produced a number of analytic problems for those wishing to determine the effectiveness of intervention programmes similar to those employed in Norway in the late 1980s. For example, in more recent versions of the survey instrument, researchers have provided students with examples of indirect or relational bullying to assist them in understanding the more subtle forms of behaviour that may be construed as aggressive. However, in the original survey instrument students were provided with only five behavioural categories in response to the question *In what way have you been bullied at school?* The response options were: *(A) I haven't been bullied this term; (B) I have been called nasty names about my race or colour; (C) I have been called nasty names in other ways; (D) I have been hit or kicked; (E) I have been bullied in other ways (for example, threatened or locked indoors); describe how.*

Although in this first version of the survey students are given the opportunity to provide further examples of behaviour which they perceive to be bullying under option E, it is questionable whether or not they would understand that mobbing or bullying includes activities such as social isolation and rumour-mongering. As Rivers and Smith (1994) demonstrated in their study, in the original survey instrument Olweus used a separate question when considering social isolation, and this question appears in an unrelated section of the survey: *How often does it happen that other students don't want to spend recess with you, and you end up being alone?* Response options for this item include: *(A) It hasn't happened this term; (B) It has only happened once or twice; (C) Now and then; (D) About once a week; (E) Several times a week.*

The inclusion of the above question in the survey instrument (which incidentally preceded the section asking pupils about their experiences of bullying) suggests that participants may not have made an association between being alone in the schoolyard or playground and mobbing or bullying. Indeed, it is noteworthy that the lengthy definition provided by Olweus later in the survey instrument does not mention any indirect forms of bullying—although, as Arora (1996) recalled, he has previously acknowledged its subtlety, describing bullying as "harassment physical or mental" (Olweus, 1978, p. 35).

It is also questionable whether the location of the item on social isolation would have elicited accurate or truthful responses from participants, especially when the previous question asked pupils to estimate the number of friends they had in their class. Where a pupil indicated that he or she had two or three good friends in his or her class and was being bullied by others, the potential for misreporting would seem to be high, as the response to the first question may not reflect positively upon that of the second. As Olweus (1977, 1978, 1994) has pointed out, peer nomination strategies were required to assess the reliability of pupil self-reports, and although correlation coefficients are quoted as being between

.40 and .60, these were drawn from composite scoring procedures (3–5 items on the self-report survey), which do not necessarily provide an accurate estimate of the variance in observer/participant ratings. In addition, as Olweus later found, the bullies in his survey tended to be older than their victims and, therefore, were unlikely to be in the same class or year group. Therefore, friendships formed with classmates could, in principle, be maintained by pupils without the knowledge of the bully (although it is recognised that peer pressure would invariably affect the longevity or success of such friendships). Finally, in the Norwegian studies no attempt to determine whether or not the friendships pupils wrote about were enacted within or without the school grounds: a pupil who was being bullied by older pupils may have retained contact with classmates either in the evenings or at weekends. Indeed, it is worth noting that there has been little research focusing upon the impact of friendships formed outside school upon the socialisation skills and self-perceptions of victims of bullying. Inevitably, concerns surrounding the lack of clarity provided by the survey instrument in terms of so-called indirect or relational bullying, and the revisions made it over the years, is likely to have had an impact upon others' ability to demonstrate a 50% reduction in school bullying, as reported by Olweus (1991). Rivers and Smith (1994) found only a fair association between their measure of indirect bullying (*"no one would talk to me"* and *"I had rumours spread about me"*) and that used by Olweus. Nevertheless, today the Olweus Bully/Victim Questionnaire and the associated intervention package, the Olweus Bullying Prevention Program, are the most widely used resources for assessing and combating bullying in the world. The questionnaire provides educators with accessible data on the prevalence of bullying in their schools and, following training to deliver and run the program, its effectiveness in reducing such behaviour.

The Emergence of Gender Differences

Following on from Olweus' work in Norway, in the early 1980s a group of Finnish researchers embarked upon an examination of aggression among students in their schools, particularly the frequency of indirect behaviours such as social isolation and rumour-mongering (particularly among girls). In their study, Lagerspetz et al. (1988) argued that early research examining the nature of male and female aggression had demonstrated a qualitative difference in the reactions to provocation of boys and girls. They cited a review of literature by Frodi, Macauley, and Thome (1977) in which the authors concluded that while females reacted to provocation just as much as males, they did not display unprovoked aggression to the same degree. For example, in an earlier study, the Finnish researchers had already noted that there was a palpable difference between aggressive boys and aggressive girls in their desire for power over others. They found that aggressive boys wished to dominate other boys, whereas aggressive girls wished to be less domineering, and they argued that this difference was a result of the belief among boys that domineering behaviour was something expected of them within Western culture (see Björkqvist et al., 1982). Based upon this observation, Kirsti Lagerspetz and her colleagues hypothesised that "if direct aggression is discouraged by society for females more than for males, females possibly will make greater use of indirect forms of aggression instead" (p. 404).

Developing the above findings further, Björkqvist et al. (1992) conducted a subsequent study with Finnish schoolchildren in which they examined both age and gender differences in the expression of direct physical aggression (hitting, pushing, kicking), direct verbal aggression (name-calling, labelling, threatening), and indirect aggression (telling tales, spreading rumours, persuading others not to associate with a particular person). In this study, they compared boys and girls from three age groups: 8, 11, and 15 years. Whereas in a previous article (Lagerspetz et al., 1988) the authors had argued that indirect aggression was more likely among girls than boys, here they extended their hypothesis to argue that the use of indirect aggression in bullying behaviour was reliant upon both maturation and the ability of young people to manipulate peer relationships successfully. Their results demonstrated that while indirect aggression was used by girls as young as 8 years of age, it did not develop as an alternative to direct forms of aggression (physical and verbal) until 11 years of age. They also found that levels of direct physical aggression declined with age for boys and girls, while, contrary to Olweus' beliefs, direct verbal aggression rose steadily.

Using Whitney and Smith's (1993) data set collected from 7,000 primary, junior/middle, and secondary school pupils in the U.K., Rivers and Smith (1994) compared their data to those of Björkqvist et al. (1992)

to determine whether or not a similar pattern of age and gender differences in the nature of bullying behaviour could be found. Comparable with Björkqvist et al.'s findings, an age-related decline was found in the frequency of direct physical bullying (hitting, kicking, etc.) among both boys and girls and indirect bullying (rumour-mongering, social isolation, etc.). However, Rivers and Smith also found a decline in direct verbal bullying (name-calling, labelling, etc.). While these results supported Olweus' (1993a, 1994) general finding that bullying decreased with age, interestingly they also demonstrated that pupils did not necessarily substitute one form of bullying behaviour for another as they grew older, as Björkqvist et al. had intimated.

According to Rivers and Smith (1994), while their comparison with Björkqvist et al.'s (1992) study provided constructive validation of the generality of both age and gender differences in the types of aggressive behaviour experienced at school, the reported reduction in all types of bullying with age requires some consideration. As Rivers and Smith pointed out, despite the relative similarity of the behaviours under investigation (i.e., physical, verbal, and indirect), Björkqvist et al. had used peer nomination strategies to determine the bully/victim status of the pupils in their study, whereas Rivers and Smith's study was based solely upon pupils' self-reports. Given that Björkqvist et al.'s study relied upon peers identifying others who had either been perpetrators or victims of bullying, it may be argued that their estimates of the number of pupils engaged in direct physical and direct verbal bullying were, potentially, much more likely to be accurate because of the objective nature of data collection, but the accuracy of reports relating to indirect or relational bullying remained questionable. In Rivers and Smith's study, much of the self-report data relied upon individuals' subjective interpretations of their bully/victim status. While this was not particularly helpful in determining the reliability of pupils' responses in relation to direct physical and direct verbal bullying, in the case of indirect bullying (which, as the researchers pointed out, is not only subjective but often hidden from teachers or classmates) it can be measured only by self-reports (ideally validated through a process of test–retest reliability). Therefore, the accuracy of such reports was at least comparable to those of Björkqvist et al. Having said that, a caveat must be appended to this discussion: in Rivers and Smith's study, despite the fact that pupils received a clear definition of behaviours that constituted direct physical, direct verbal, and indirect bullying, from the perspective of the participant, it is worth considering whether, similar to the Norwegian studies, a pupil who had experienced physical or verbal aggression previously at school would necessarily consider or identify himself or herself as a victim if he or she was isolated from peers during break time or lunchtime. Indeed, although Whitney and Smith (1993) found that there was an association between being bullied at school and being alone in the schoolyard or playground during break time or lunchtime, the nature of that association was not explored further, and, as a result, it is unclear whether social isolation has been used by students as a method to escape bullying or harassment as well as a means to bully others.

More recently, in their study of over 15,000 students attending both public and private schools in the U.S. (grades 6–10; 11–16 years), Nansel Overpeck, Pilla, Ruan, Simons-Morton, and Scheidt (2001) found that 30% of their respondents reported moderate to frequent involvement in bullying, with the majority of such behaviour occurring in sixth, seventh, and eighth grade (i.e., middle school). Comparable with the earlier studies by Björkqvist and colleagues and Rivers and Smith (1994), this data suggested that there continues to be a decline in bullying behaviour with age. However, they also found that victims were more likely to report feeling lonely and, as a consequence, found it difficult to make friends or interact successfully with classmates.

While the rates of bullying behaviour reported by Nansel et al. (2001) are higher than those reported by earlier studies conducted in Scandinavia and the U.K., a cross-national study of violence in adolescence found that rates of bullying in U.S. schools are similar to those found by researchers working in the Republic of Ireland, Israel, Portugal, and Sweden (Smith-Khuri, Iachan, Scheidt, Overpeck et al., 2004), with up to 40% of students reporting involvement in bullying once or twice a week to several times a week. Other studies have also found rates ranging from 25% to 39% (see Juvonen, Graham, & Schuster, 2003; Smith, Morita, Junger-Tas, Olweus, Catalano, & Slee, 1999). In addition, gender differences in bullying behaviour have not been found to change dramatically with the passage of time. Comparable with the findings of Björkqvist and colleagues in Finland in the 1980s, and Smith and colleagues in the U.K. in the 1990s, Price (2004) found that American boys were more likely to report using direct physical bullying, while American girls were much more likely to report indirect or relational methods of aggression.

Bullying: A Complex Social Process

In the intervening years numerous researchers have continued to study bullying behaviour. It continues to be described as a form of aggression different from any other. Its definition includes antisocial behaviours such as teasing, name-calling, group exclusion, hitting, kicking, and punching (Poteat & Rivers, 2010). While some researchers have argued that it can be distinguished from more extreme forms of aggression and antisocial behaviour (see Espelage & Holt, 2001), it is increasingly being criminalised. While bullying is still popularly perceived to be an exchange between two people (the bully and the victim, with some consideration being given to those students who occupy both roles), it is very much grounded in the social worlds of children and young people and societal expectations of conformity and the pursuit of culturally avowed goals (see Ball, Arseneault, Taylor, Maughan, & Moffitt, 2008; Ma, 2001; Solberg, Olweus, & Endresen, 2007). Indeed, several studies conducted in recent years have shown that bullying often involves groups of students rather than individuals (Atria, Strohmeier, & Spiel, 2007; Espelage, Holt, & Henkel, 2003; Henry, Cartland, Ruchross, & Monahan, 2004; Salmivalli, Lagerspetz, Björkqvist, Österman, & Kaukiainen, 1996; Salmivalli & Voeten, 2004). The frequency and severity of such behaviour can vary dramatically across different contexts (Atria et al., 2007; Espelage et al., 2003; Henry et al., 2004). Using peer nomination strategies, researchers have also shown that students with the same degree of aggressiveness tend to cluster together, and that these students' behaviour can intensify over time through social reinforcement by peers (Espelage et al., 2003; Werner & Crick, 2004; Xie, Cairns, & Cairns, 1999).

Several researchers have commented on the pivotal role that witnesses and bystanders can play in challenging bullying behaviour; however, only a handful of studies have been conducted looking at this issue (Craig & Pepler 1997; Frey, Hirschstein, Snell, Edstrom, MacKenzie, & Broderick, 2005; Hawkins, Pepler, & Craig, 2001; McLaughlin, Arnold, & Boyd, 2005). For example, Smith and Shu (2000), in their study of 2,308 students attending 19 schools in England, estimated that approximately 66% of a school's population has a primary (perpetrator and/or victim) or secondary (bystander) role in bullying behaviour. But what exactly is the role of bystander and how is it enacted with bullying behaviour?

Perhaps the earliest work to consider the pivotal role that bystanders can play in bullying interactions was conducted by Christina Salmivalli and her colleagues in Finland (Salmivalli et al., 1996). They identified a number of secondary or subservient roles that incorporated observer and bystander behaviour (Salmivalli, Huttunen, & Lagerspetz, 1997). Using both self-reports and peer nominations, Salmivalli and her colleagues found that those students whom they identified as bystanders took on a number of different roles within bullying episodes: *assistants* aided perpetrators in bullying others; *reinforcers* provided positive feedback to perpetrators; *outsiders* kept away and watched from a distance; and *defenders* attempted to intervene to protect the victim.

Salmivalli et al.'s (1996) study was a significant stepping-stone in our understanding of bullying behaviour within the whole school context. However, while the *assistant* role clearly referred to a student taking on an active but secondary role when another person was being bullied, some of the roles identified by Salmivalli were, on closer inspection, less well defined (see Rivers, Poteat, Noret, & Ashurst, 2009). Salmivalli and her colleagues had devised a questionnaire that included items that identified each of the bystander roles. Students were assigned to their respective roles according to the answers they gave to the questionnaire. Items relating to the *reinforcer* role incorporated statements such as, *Comes around to see the situation* and *Is usually present, even if not doing anything,* along with more active statements relating to encouraging the perpetrator on (Salmivalli et al., 1996, p. 15). However, those who took on the role of the *outsider* included those students who responded positively to statements such as, *Goes away from the spot, Doesn't take sides with anyone,* and *Pretends not to notice what is happening* (p. 15). The *defender* role (found primarily among girls) included positive responses to items related to consoling the victim or being supportive, in addition to what might be described as active items demonstrating direct intervention or help-seeking behaviour. Salmivalli et al.'s work demonstrated that there was sometimes a very subtle distinction in the roles students undertook in bullying episodes, and that these roles were not easy to unravel.

Building upon Salmivalli et al.'s (1996) observations, Rivers et al. (2009) undertook a study to explore further participant roles in bullying behaviour, but using an adapted version of the widely available Olweus Bully/Victim Questionnaire (Olweus, 1994). Students were offered the opportunity to answer questions relating to whether or not they had experienced, perpetrated, or witnessed bullying behaviour in their school. In effect, each question was asked in three different ways (i.e., from the perspective of a victim, a perpetrator, and then a witness or bystander). Overall, Rivers et al. found that approximately 20% of the 1,990 students they surveyed reported being perpetrators of recent bullying, and that approximately 34% had been or were victims. Sixty-three percent of students said they had witnessed peers being bullied. When Rivers and colleagues began to look at the combinations of roles students took at school during bullying episodes, a very complex picture of social interaction emerged. Only 27.6% of students said they were completely uninvolved in bullying behaviour. Only 1.4% were solely perpetrators, 6.7% solely victims, and 30.4% solely witnesses in recent bullying episodes. A further 1.3% identified themselves as "bully-victims." In contrast, 6.7% said they had been perpetrators in some incidents and witnesses in others, while 15.2% said they had been victims in some incidents and witnesses in others. Finally, 10.7% admitted having been perpetrators in some situations, as well as victims and witnesses in others. Thus, comparable with the findings of Smith and Shu (2000), bullying was part of the daily lives of the majority of students in this study, with many of them taking on one or more roles.

Cyberbullying: A New Challenge?

Inevitably, with every advance we make, there is always a less desirable corollary. In the past decade, developments in mobile technology and Internet connectivity have revolutionised the way in which we communicate with one another. However, as we have learned the benefits of communicating instantaneously with others, so too have we learned of the dangers of mass mobile communication. As personal computers, Internet connectivity, and mobile/cellular telephones became commonplace, so too did the "cyberbully." Technology is now the new friend of the bully. Anonymous telephone calls, e-mails, instant messages, and postings to websites, newsgroups and bulletin boards are the tools the cyberbully uses to assault his or her victims. Comparable with more traditional forms of bullying, cyberbullying is the "willful and repeated harm inflicted through the medium of electronic text" (Patchin & Hinduja, 2006, p. 152). Others have described cyberbullying as:

> The use of information and communication technologies such as email, cell phone and pager text messages, instant messaging, defamatory personal Web sites, and defamatory online personal polling Web sites, to support deliberate, repeated, and hostile behavior by an individual or group, that is intended to harm others (Li, 2007, p. 1779, reporting the definition used by *www.cyberbullying.ca*).

In the U.K., researchers Smith Mahdavi, Carvalho, Fisher, Russell, and Tippett (2008) have defined cyberbullying as "an aggressive, intentional act carried out by a group or individual, using *electronic forms of contact*, repeatedly and over time against a victim who cannot easily defend him or herself" (p. 376). While all of these definitions stress that cyberbullying has to be repeated (just like conventional bullying), the media through which such bullying is perpetrated is diverse.

As Figure 1.1 shows, of the 19 major studies that were conducted on cyberbullying between 2000 and 2008, the majority researched e-mail,

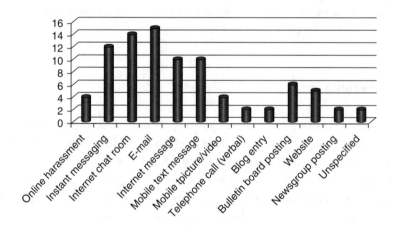

FIGURE 1.1   Cyberbullying: Inclusion criteria for studies conducted between 2000–2008

SMS/text messages, and instant messages as means of bullying others. However, other researchers have explored other media (see Rivers & Noret, 2010, for a review). For example, Smith et al. (2008) have included verbal abuse conducted via mobile/cell phone as a form of cyberbullying. Other researchers (but not all) have studied the prevalence of bullying in Internet chat rooms (see Finkelhor, Mitchell, & Wolak, 2000; NCH, 2002; Li, 2005, 2006; Hinduja & Patchin, 2008; Kowalski, Limber, & Agatston, 2008; Patchin & Hinduja, 2006; Smith, Mahdavi, Carvalho, & Tippett, 2006; Smith et al., 2008). Some have asked perpetrators of cyberbullying if they have uploaded images onto websites or distributed embarrassing images to others using mobile/cell phones (Smith et al., 2006, 2008). Others have asked about posting messages on bulletin boards or newsgroups (Hinduja & Patchin, 2008; Patchin & Hinduja, 2006). As a result of the different ways in which cyberbullying has been perpetrated and recorded, incidence rates have varied dramatically between studies— ranging from 4% to 36% (Rivers & Noret, 2010).

Although incidence rates have varied considerably, cyberbullying shares many similarities with more traditional forms of bullying. For example, Kowalski, Limber, and Agatston (2008) found very significant gender differences among the 3,767 students they surveyed: 25% of girls and 11% of boys had received hurtful e-mail, SMS/text messages, or instant messages, been subjected to chat room abuse, or had something hurtful posted on a website at least once in the previous two months. In contrast, Li (2007) found that boys were more likely to report being perpetrators of cyberbullying than girls (22.3% and 11.6% respectively). Both these findings were supported by an online survey conducted by Hinduja and Patchin (2008). In their study of 1,378 young Internet users (under the age of 18 years), the researchers found that victims of cyberbullying were more likely to be girls (36%) than boys (32%). Their results showed that girls were more likely than boys to report being bullied by computer text message (19.8% vs. 17%), e-mail (13.0% vs. 9.7%), and mobile/cell phone text message (4.7% vs. 4.0%). However, in terms of bullying others, boys were more likely than girls to bully others in chat rooms (9.6% vs. 7.3%) and on bulletin boards (3.4% vs. 2.4%).

Hinduja and Patchin (2008) also looked at the relationship between cyberbullying and other behaviours offline. Their findings indicate that cyberbullying is associated not only with issues such as truancy and cheating on examinations, but also with other forms of bullying, fighting, and alcohol or marijuana use. Williams and Guerra (2007), in their study of 3,339 youths in grades 5, 8, and 11 attending U.S. public schools, further explored the offline correlates of Internet bullying. They found that while Internet bullying is relatively infrequent among 5th-grade students (4.5%; 10 or 11 years of age), it peaks in 8th grade (12.9%; 13 or 14 years of age) and then declines by 11th grade (9.9%; 16 or 17 years of age).

The findings of Hinduja and Patchin (2008) and Williams and Guerra (2007) mirror the age and gender differences reported by researchers in their early studies of bullying behaviour. In addition, Smith et al. (2008) found that the victims of cyberbullying in their study were also victims of bullying in other contexts (i.e., offline), and that perpetrators of cyberbullying were also perpetrators of bullying in other contexts. Williams and Guerra also found that all three of the types of bullying they measured (physical, verbal, and Internet) were associated with students' beliefs about being able to bully others (i.e., their approval of it), their negative appraisal of their school's climate, and poor peer support. Taken together, these findings demonstrate that cyberbullying is intrinsically linked to other forms of bullying and, as such, is an extension of those traditional behaviours that are frequently witnessed by others in classrooms, on playing fields, and in playgrounds and schoolyards.

Summary

In this chapter I introduced some of the early pivotal work that took place in Europe in the late 1960s and early 1970s. Building upon these early studies, researchers have demonstrated that there remain significant age and gender differences in the types of bullying that children and young people are exposed to at school. In the following chapter I discuss some of the issues surrounding students who are perceived to be different. Some come from different ethnic or cultural backgrounds, some have a different skin colour, some have special needs, and some are perceived to be different because they do not display those stereotypical characteristics or traits that society attributes to masculinity and femininity. It is this last group of students who are the primary focus of this book.

2

Students Who Are Different

Although both the Norwegian and British studies described in the previous chapter incorporated a general index of racial bullying ("I was called nasty names about my name or colour"), until the early 1990s there had been no systematic investigation relating to the victimisation of children and young people from minority groups. To date, there have been only a few studies that examined the role of ethnic/cultural influences upon children's and young people's aggressive behaviour in school. By the same token, there have been only a few studies that have explored the school experiences of children with learning and/or motor disabilities. In this chapter, I provide data from a number of studies that suggest that children who are perceived to be "different" (whether it is on the grounds of their colour or cultural background, religious beliefs, ability, or learning/motor disability) have experienced and continue to experience harassment at school. Finally, I turn my attention to homophobia in educational contexts and review the research that led to the series of studies I conducted for this book.

Bullying and Young People of Colour

In his qualitative study of prejudice among British schoolchildren, Davey (1983) asked a group of African-Caribbean, Indian, and White European children what colour they would prefer to be, and without exception he reported that they all replied that they would prefer to be white. The stigma children attach to a person's colour can be seen clearly in Cohn's (1988) discussion of multicultural teaching. In this study Cohn catalogued the various pejorative terms used in everyday speech by children and young people when referring to cultural minority groups. Among 13- to 17-year-old pupils, she recorded 60 abusive terms that were racist; among the under-13s, she recorded no less than 40. Several recent studies of bullying (conducted in the U.K. and the U.S.) have indicated that, in terms of its nature at least, there are discernable differences in the school experiences of young people of colour when compared to those described as White European, reinforcing the view that race and ethnicity remain strong antecedents of bullying behaviour (Boulton, 1995; Espelage & Swearer, 2003; Kelly & Cohn, 1988; Malik, 1990; Moran, Smith, Thompson, & Whitney, 1993; Spriggs, Ioanotti, Nansel, & Haynie, 2007).

In one early study in the U.K., Kelly (1988) surveyed 902 Black (African-Caribbean and Asian) and White (European) students from a Manchester school who were asked to complete a questionnaire focusing upon their personal experiences of teasing and bullying (especially name-calling and fighting), and their observations of the behaviour of other pupils. Each pupil was asked to list three names that made him or her angry or miserable, and to list those names he or she had heard most frequently in the schoolyard or playground (Troyna & Hatcher, 1992). Of the 2,706 potential responses received from pupils relating to names that made them angry or miserable, only 154 were racially abusive (the greatest number of responses, 440, were names that were "anal or sexual" in origin). However, of those names pupils heard most frequently at school, Kelly reported that 72% related to ethnicity, race, or religious beliefs:

According to Troyna and Hatcher (1992) these results confirmed the view that racially abusive name-calling is part of "the repertoire of children's discourse" (p. 35), and, as the data demonstrate, it increased with age rather than decreased—a view shared by Cohn (1988) in her study of name-calling among 569 secondary school pupils. While Kelly's study provides a valuable resource for exploring the nature of name-calling in U.K. schools, the study itself left a number of important questions unanswered. First of all, it did not determine the frequency of racially abusive name-calling at school across a term or year. Secondly, it did not determine what proportion of ethnic/religious minority students experienced this form of abuse when they were at school. Finally, it did not seek to determine what proportion of the student population actively participated in racial name-calling and abuse.

In contrast to Kelly's (1988) study, Boulton (1995) explored the nature of both intra-group and inter-group bully/victim problems among 156 schoolchildren aged between 8 and 10 years, of whom

53 were described as Asian and 103 as White (p. 280). In this study, students were interviewed by the researcher, who asked them to nominate peers whom they perceived to be either bullies or victims. Each student was then asked to indicate the race of a preferred partner when engaged in a shared activity (e.g., to have on his or her team for a game). Using Davey's (1983) method of eliciting racial stereotypes, the students were also asked to ascribe positive traits (e.g., "works hard," "friendly," "clean") and negative traits (e.g., "lazy," "tells lies," and "dirty") to photographs of unfamiliar children from different ethnic backgrounds. Finally, a subset of 60 pupils (30 Asian and 30 White) were asked about the different types of bullying behaviour they had experienced at school.

While Boulton (1995) found that there was some intra-group bullying occurring among Asian and White children (9.5% and 10.3% respectively), significantly more bullying was perpetrated by those he described as "other-race school mates" (p. 287). Of those students bullied at school, White children received significantly more abuse about the colour of their skin (80%) from other-race school mates than Asian children (33%). On the other hand, Asian children reported much more social exclusion (53%) than their White counterparts (17%). Interestingly, no significant differences were found between the groups in terms of being hit, kicked, or pushed or being teased.

Although Boulton's (1995) findings are in general agreement with those of Kelly (1988), both studies were drawn from inner-city schools with catchment areas serving large communities from the Indian sub-continent, Africa, Asia, and the Caribbean. Given the sampling frame and the fact that students were likely to have been exposed to cultural variation from a relatively early age, the data collected by these researchers may have been skewed towards an underrepresentation of the problem (i.e., in less diversely populated areas, students from ethnic minorities may experience greater harassment as a consequence of peers' lack of exposure to cultural/racial/religious variation).

As mentioned above, Kelly's (1988) study left a number of questions unanswered, particularly that relating to the frequency of racial name-calling at school. While Boulton (1995) provided an index of the number of students involved in racial name-calling (as well as providing much-needed information about other forms of racial abuse), it was unclear how often such behaviour occurred in school. In one piece of qualitative research conducted by Moran et al. (1993) with 66 children (33 Asian and 33 White) attending primary school, although rates of racial name-calling were found to be very low indeed (6/33 for Asian children and 0/33 for White children), overall 38% of this sample reported being bullied "sometimes" or more often—a markedly higher percentage than expected. While this figure included the 6 Asian students who reported being racially bullied, the authors argued that the higher rate they found (when compared to those quoted by Ahmad et al., 1991, or Whitney and Smith, 1993) was significant, and may have been due not so much to the ethnic background of students, but to the fact that 18% of the children they interviewed who were bullied at school (12/66) also held statements of special educational needs.

In contrast, in the U.S., Nansel et al.'s (2001) study of 15,000 students indicated that Hispanic-American youths were more likely to report being involved in bullying behaviours when compared to African-American students. Bullying among Hispanic-American youths has been the focus of a great deal of research in the past few years, with researchers focusing on the link between perceptions of safety in local communities, youth culture, and their respective impact upon school engagement and good behaviour (see Garcia-Reid, Reid, & Peterson, 2005). This is a view supported by Spriggs et al. (2007), who found that the African-American students in their study reported significantly lower rates of victimisation than both White and Hispanic students. They also found that school satisfaction and academic performance were negatively related with bullying involvement for White and Hispanic students, but were unrelated to bullying for Black students.

These studies show that problems that occur outside of the school environment (i.e., within families, peer groups, or the community) have a significant impact upon these young people's engagement with school, and this is exacerbated by teachers' lack of understanding or experience of working with youth of colour. Thus, those bullying behaviours perpetrated or experienced by young people of colour are often not addressed effectively by teachers, and because they do not understand the experiences of these youths outside of school, often the fears these youths experience and the protective measures they take also occur within the school building.

Special Educational Needs and Bullying

According to Whitney, Nabuzoka, and Smith (1992), children with special educational needs are at particular risk for bullying behaviour. This point of view was supported by research conducted in the U.K. (Nabuzoka & Smith, 1993; Thompson, Whitney, & Smith, 1994; Norwich & Kelly, 2004) and the Republic of Ireland (O'Moore & Hillery, 1989), Spain (Ortega & Lera, 2000), and the U.S. (Van Cleave & Davis, 2006). In one study, Nabuzoka and Smith found that children with moderate learning difficulties were four times more likely to be nominated by their peers as victims of bullying behaviour (33%) than those children without such difficulties (8%). A similar pattern was found by O'Moore and Hillery (1989) in their study of bullying in Dublin schools: children who attended remedial classes were nearly twice as likely to report being victimised regularly (once a week or more) than children in the mainstream (12% and 7% respectively).

Nabuzoka and Smith (1993) have argued that one of the reasons why children with special educational needs experience much more bullying than their non-statemented peers relates to the fact that they have few social support networks. According to Martlew and Hodson (1991), in their study children with special educational needs were more likely to be left alone in the playground during lunchtime and break time and had made fewer friends compared to non-statemented children. In addition, as Nabuzoka and Smith found, children with learning difficulties tended to be rated as less popular and more rejected by their peers than more able children, a finding mirrored by O'Moore and Hillery in Ireland (1989).

While Nabuzoka and Smith's (1993) study suggests that children with special educational needs are bullied much more frequently than children in the mainstream, research focusing upon children with physical or motor difficulties or disabilities who attend integrated schools has been less emphatic. Although in one early report Olweus (1978) commented that 75% of those children he identified as victims of bullying behaviour suffered from motor coordination problems (so-called "clumsy children"), the nature of their motor coordination difficulties was not discussed any further. Indeed, little consideration was given in the text to the definition of the term "clumsy," and little mention was made of the method of assessment used to determine the children's level of motor ability. As far as it is possible to determine, Olweus (1978) drew heavily upon the fact that male victims (who he described as "whipping boys") were physically weaker than their aggressors, which, together with "a certain sensitivity and anxiousness, lack of assertiveness and self-esteem" (p. 140), he believed contributed to their social rejection at school. However, such a profile does not necessarily equate with motor deficiency. It could also be argued that children, especially boys, who are physically weaker than their peers, and are anxious in social situations, are more likely to fail or, at the very least, are likely to be perceived as being unable to compete effectively with their peers in activities such as sports where good eye–hand coordination is required. If one takes this hypothetical scenario to its logical conclusion, such a negative appraisal by peers and, correspondingly, by teachers could result in a boy being relegated or otherwise passed over in sporting activities, which would not only promote the popular perception of his poor coordination skills, but also deny him the opportunity to practise those skills and thus improve upon them. Such a scenario would have notable ramifications for a researcher using peer or teacher nomination strategies as a means of identifying both the perpetrators and victims of peer rejection at school. In this respect, it would seem that Olweus has inadvertently bought into a self-fulfilling prophecy, one that has existed on the sports fields of many schools for a number of years.

Overall, Olweus' (1978) observation about the motor ability of the victims he identified in his research is more diversionary than informative, and does not provide evidence relating to whether or not children with physical or motor difficulties or disabilities are bullied at school any more or less frequently than their able-bodied peers.

In one early study conducted by Anderson, Clarke, and Spain (1982), young people with motor disabilities were asked to describe their experiences of attending both integrated and special schools. Overall, 119 teenagers were sampled (89 were diagnosed as having cerebral palsy, while 30 suffered from spina bifida). According to Anderson et al., many of the young people who were interviewed reported feeling unhappy, worried, and isolated from their peers. Very few who attended state schools with able-bodied teenagers reported sustaining friendships outside the classroom, and most said that "watching television" was their only recreational activity. Overall, 30% of those young men and women who attended integrated schools reported being teased because of their motor difficulties, while others said that peers imitated their gait in the playground during lunchtime and breaks. Surprisingly, Anderson et al. argued that the young people they interviewed were likely to have been more sensitive about their disabilities and, as a result, they may have over-estimated their experiences of being bullied because they felt very "different" from their able-bodied peers.

Within special schools, Anderson et al. (1982) found that 12% of participants said they had been bullied. For example, one young woman who suffered from cerebral palsy reported being physically assaulted by a group of pupils; another, who was confined to a wheelchair, reported that her transistor radio had been placed out of reach by a peer who chided her for being too slow. Although within integrated schools the authors did not believe that physical disability increased participants' likelihood of being bullied by able-bodied peers, they acknowledged that when bullying did take place, it was the nature of the disability that attracted the perpetrators rather than the victim's behaviour or personality. However, within special schools (where all the pupils suffered from some form of learning or motor disability), they argued that the converse was true: the disability had little or no significance, and the perpetrators were attracted by the child's or young person's personality.

Anderson et al.'s (1982) conclusions are contentious: they suggest that the disabled children who participated in their study overreacted when they were being teased by their able-bodied peers, and that those who attended special schools were no more likely to be bullied than any other child or young person. Yet without appropriate data for comparison (i.e., rates of bullying experienced by able-bodied students who attend schools that have a policy of integrating disabled students into the classroom) there would seem to be little substance to their first conclusion. If one takes, as an example, Whitney, Smith, and Thompson's (1994) study of the experiences of 93 students with special educational needs (including children with physical disabilities and visual and hearing impairments) who were matched with 93 mainstream peers, their results demonstrated that those students with statements of special educational needs experienced much more bullying at junior/middle school (62%

and 48% respectively) and secondary school (59% and 16% respectively) "sometimes" or more often. In secondary school particularly, Whitney et al. found that students with special educational needs were almost three times more likely to be bullied regularly (once a week or several times a week) than their mainstream peers (30% and 11% respectively). While this finding does not provide conclusive evidence of the inappropriate nature of Anderson et al.'s conclusion, it does suggest that children who have learning difficulties or physical impairments are much more likely to be the victims of peer aggression than their able-bodied mainstream counterparts. This position was supported by Norwich and Kelly (2004) in their study of 101 students attending both mainstream and special schools.

Anderson et al.'s (1982) second conclusion—that those students who attended special schools were no more likely to be bullied than any other child or young person—also requires consideration. In their discussion, Anderson et al. cited the child's or young person's personality as being a key factor in the determination of his or her victim status. However, where they used the term "personality," in effect they were describing "temperament"—a factor that Olweus (1978, 1993b, 1994) has also linked with victim status (and one that he has also intermittently described as "personality"). In their study Norwich and Kelly (2004) found that girls in special schools were much less likely to be bullied than girls in mainstream schools; however, there were no significant differences among boys. What Norwich and Kelly did find that is significant is that students with special needs preferred to receive learning support away from mainstream students, and were more likely to be bullied by students from other mainstream schools, reinforcing the argument that perceived "difference" and poor integration are key drivers for bullying perpetrated against students with special needs.

Temperament and School Bullying

The temperamental correlates of victim status have already been alluded to briefly in the discussion of "clumsy children." In two key studies, Olweus (1978, 1993b) has discussed the impact of temperament upon the social status of children in school. He has characterised victims

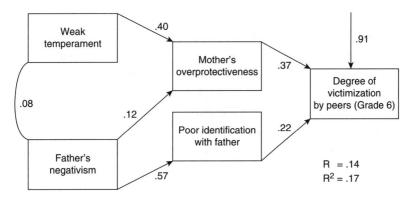

FIGURE 2.1   Path diagram for determinants of degree of victimisation by peers at age 13 (N = 76)
(SOURCE: Olweus, 1993b, p. 323)

of bullying as having a "weak temperament" (Olweus, 1993b, p. 321), a disposition he described as "quiet, calm and placid" (p. 321), and one that he correlated with particular parental attachments (an overprotective mother and a distant, negative father). Evidence for this association was provided via two path models that were based upon an analysis of data collected from two samples of young men aged 13 years (Fig. 2.1) and 16 years (Fig. 2.2).

Although, at best, both models accounted for approximately 20% of the variance in the degree to which an individual was victimised by his

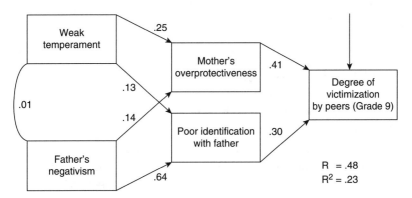

FIGURE 2.2   Path diagram for determinants of degree of victimisation by peers at age 16 (N = 51)
(SOURCE: Olweus, 1993b, p. 324)

or her peers, Olweus (1993b) has argued that the similarities he found between them (in terms of variable loadings) are illustrative of the general validity of the model. Based upon this analysis, he has argued that a "weak temperament" in a boy or young man results in his mother's overprotective behaviour and, to a certain extent, his infantilisation. At the same time, the boy's temperament also results in a negative appraisal from his father, and later contributes to the inability of father and son to find some common ground upon which to build or maintain their relationship. Ultimately, the lack of identification a boy or young man feels towards his father will reinforce the bond he has with his mother, and, according to Olweus, may result in him experiencing difficulties in asserting himself in "traditionally boyish or masculine ways" (p. 324).

While a number of other researchers have found similar temperamental characteristics among the victims of bullying in their various studies (see Björkqvist et al., 1982; Boulton & Smith, 1994; Farrington, 1993; Lagerspetz, Björkqvist, Berts, & King, 1982; Perry, Kusel, & Perry, 1988), as Olweus has conceded, "it is reasonable to assume that such tendencies toward overprotection (on the part of a mother) are both a cause and a consequence of bullying" (Olweus, 1994, p. 1179). Hence, it remains unclear whether or not the "weak temperament" of a child or young person is an antecedent rather than an outcome of bullying behaviour. More recent research among former victims of bullying conducted by Gladstone, Parker, and Mahli (2006) suggests that childhood factors associated with later anxiety and depression include parental over-control, illness, disability, and an inhibited temperament.

Gender Roles, Sexuality, and Bullying

In Kelly's (1988) study of racism in a Manchester school (discussed above), she described the most common form of name-calling that made pupils either "angry or miserable" as "anal or sexual" (Troyna & Hatcher, 1992, p. 33). Despite the higher prevalence of racist names (72% of the total number of names reported), pupils were nearly three times more likely to say that they had been hurt by an "anal" or "sexual" name (440) than a name that related to their race, ethnicity, religious beliefs, or cultural background (154).

Askew and Ross (1988) have argued that children's greater sensitivity to sexual name-calling arises from the fact that it is a direct attack upon the character of the individual rather than his or her racial, cultural, or religious backgrounds. In their study of sexism in an all-boys school, Askew and Ross noted that any physical interaction between two boys, other than an aggressive interaction, was likely to be construed as a sign of weakness on the part of one or both boys, and would, more often than not, result in them being called names such as "poof" and "queer" (p. 37). Yet, despite Kelly's (1988) findings demonstrating the effect such names have upon young people, Askew and Ross have argued that names of a sexual nature continue to be prevalent within the schoolyard or playground because they have become part of everyday banter, especially among men. This is a view supported by Mac an Ghaill (1994).

In his five-year qualitative study of the experiences of students attending an English secondary school, Mac an Ghaill (1994) considered the role of the educational establishment as a "masculinizing agent"—a vehicle for the promotion of one set of values and ideals (i.e., male) above all others (p. 1). In this study, the sociopolitical framework around which the students' narratives were explored presented the English secondary school as one where weakness was deemed as being anything that was not masculine or heterosexual.

Although Mac an Ghaill (1994) conceded that the school in which he conducted his study had recently gone through a process of reformation where education was being linked to the development of key vocational skills for all students, he argued that such a reformation had in fact resulted in the "remasculinization" of the curriculum and "the underrepresentation of female students" (p. 116).

Throughout his study, Mac an Ghaill (1994) suggested that the secondary school, by its very nature, has ignored or otherwise depreciated the intellectual and technological advancement of 50 percent of its students population. However, he did not imply that this had been a wilful act on the part of teachers, rather that it was endemic within an educational system geared towards a more traditional view of gender roles.

Mac an Ghaill (1994) has suggested that such traditional attitudes and beliefs are not only reinforced across genders, but are also being reinforced from within. For example, as previously mentioned, Askew and Ross (1988) noted in their study that a boy who portrayed behaviour that was anything other than aggressive when interacting with other boys would sometimes be given the label of "poof" or "queer" by his same-sex peers because he was not living up to his gender expectations (p. 37). As one girl commented, boys who were being "soft" in class would occasionally be ridiculed by teachers, who would draw attention to their perceived inappropriate behaviour by saying, "I'll get you two married off" (Mac an Ghaill, 1994, p. 126). According to Arnot (1994), within male-dominated societies, and, indeed, their microcosmic representations (e.g. schools), while femininity is ascribed, masculinity and ultimately manhood have to be earned through a process of "struggle and conformation" (p. 145). As Arnot argued:

> Not only do they have more at stake in such a system of
> classification (i.e., male power) but they have to try and
> achieve manhood through a process of distancing women
> and femininity from themselves and maintaining a hierarchy
> of social superiority of masculinity by devaluing the female world.
> (p. 145)

Mac an Ghaill (1994) also pointed out that this process, which actively disassociates women from the world of men, also repudiates those men who "love" other men, because they do not live up to the collective interpretation of manhood.

It is interesting to note that the negative attitudes expressed by the boys in Mac an Ghaill's (1994) study were as much the result of their fear of contamination (i.e., becoming "gay" themselves) as they were of their unease with the intimate aspects of gay male relationships.

Although many of Mac an Ghaill's (1994) observations are drawn from his own subjective study of one secondary school, they have been supported by other qualitative researchers and educational theorists both in the U.K. and overseas (see Anderson, 2008, 2009; Connell, 1992; Duncan, 1999; Epstein, 1994; Griffin, 1985; Rivers, Duncan, & Besag, 2007; Schneider, 1997; Unks, 1995). However, as the following discussion demonstrates, there have been a number of quantitative investigations illustrating how the anti-gay attitudes expressed by young men (attempting to achieve a heteromasculine ideal) affect the educational experiences of those students who identify or are identified by others as lesbian, gay, or bisexual.

Sexual Orientation and Homophobic Bullying

One of the first studies to address specifically the experiences of lesbian, gay, and bisexual youth in secondary school was conducted in the U.K. (see Warren, 1984). This study had four main objectives:

- To offer an insight into the pressures lesbian, gay, and bisexual teenagers faced in schools around the capital
- To identify the ways in which they were discriminated against in the classroom
- To demonstrate the positive contribution they could make to the school environment
- To offer recommendations on ways to challenge the traditionally held negative connotations of homosexuality prevalent within society

Warren's (1984) study was only one in a series of investigations into the lives of young lesbians, gay men, and bisexual men and women living in London. Over the course of a year, some 416 young lesbians and gay men completed detailed questionnaires about their experiences of growing up, which were published in three separate reports during 1984 (see Trenchard, 1984; Trenchard & Warren, 1984; Warren, 1984). Based upon the data provided by the young people he surveyed, Warren found that 39% of participants (164) had experienced "problems at school," which including bullying, or had faced pressure to conform because of the gender-atypical behaviour. When these results were analysed, of the 154 participants (115 gay and bisexual young men and 39 lesbian or bisexual young women) who had specified the nature of the "problems" they had encountered, 25% (28 young men and 10 young women) said they felt isolated at school and had nothing in common with their peers, 21% (29 young men and 2 young women) reported having been called names or otherwise verbally abused, 13% (15 young men and 5 young women) said they had been teased, 12% (18 young men and 1 young woman) said they had been physically assaulted, a further 7% (7 young men and 4 young women) recalled being ostracised (deliberately) by their peers, and another 7% (5 young men and 6 young women) said they had been pressured by peers to change their behaviour. A further 15% (13 young men and 10 young women) said that they had been bullied or pressured in "other" ways that were not specified in the report.

While all three reports provide a useful framework upon which to build a picture of the difficulties young lesbians, gay men, and bisexual men and women face as they come to terms with their sexual orientation, very little information is provided by the researchers relating to the methods they used to gather their data.

By comparison, in the U.S., several empirical investigations have been undertaken, often with the support of the state or national legislatures, investigating the experiences of young lesbians, gay men, and bisexual men and women at school. For example, in their study of anti-gay/lesbian abuse in schools across the state of Pennsylvania (which consisted of 461 gay men and 260 lesbians), Gross, Aurand, and Adessa (1988) noted that 50% of the gay men who were surveyed and 12% of the lesbians had experienced some form of victimisation in junior high school (12–14 years), rising to 59% for gay men and 21% for lesbians in high school (14–18 years). According to Berrill (1992), from the evidence collected by various state and national task forces and coalitions at the time, estimates of the prevalence of school-based victimisation for lesbian, gay, and bisexual youths in the U.S. ranged from 33% (N = 167; Aurand, Adessa, & Bush, 1985) to 49% (N = 721; Gross et al., 1988).

Much of the early data gathered by researchers working for state or national task forces has been criticised for its unrepresentativeness and its mode of publication (unreviewed reports rather than peer-reviewed journal articles; see Muehrer, 1995). In terms of representativeness, while many of the state reports have been based on small-scale localised studies (ranging from 133 to 1,363 participants), which were often reliant upon the participation of lesbian, gay, and bisexual youths who had already disclosed their sexual orientation to their family, teachers, and peers (a process commonly referred to as "coming out"), some of those reports that are based upon national surveys have used random samples with sizes that would normally be considered illustrative of population trends. For example, in 1984 in the U.S. the National Gay and Lesbian Task Force sampled 2,074 youth from eight cities in the United States, 37% of whom indicated that they had been victimised by peers in either junior high school or high school.

Pilkington and D'Augelli (1995), in their survey of 194 lesbian, gay, and bisexual youths (142 young men and 52 young women, aged 15–21 years) attending 14 community groups across the U.S., found that 30% of gay and bisexual young men and 35% of lesbian and bisexual young women had experienced some form of harassment or verbal abuse in school because of their sexual orientation. In terms of physical assault, 22% of young men and 29% of young women reported having been hurt by a peer: when these results were broken down further, Pilkington and D'Augelli found that White students were far more likely to be attacked (27%) than those from other cultural groups (19%). In terms of social support, the researchers found that 43% of the young men and 54% of the young women surveyed has lost at least one friend as a result of their actual or perceived sexual orientation, while a further 36% and 27% respectively feared they would lose their friends if they were "open" about their sexual orientation.

In a national postal survey of 4,216 lesbians, gay men, and bisexual men and women living in the U.K., Mason and Palmer (1996) found that, of those respondents under 18 years of age (N = 84), 40% of all violent attacks had taken place at school, with 50% of those being perpetrated by same- or similar-aged peers. Although this group was very small (primarily as a result of the survey being distributed via the lesbian and gay press), the results did show that approximately one quarter of those young lesbians and gay men who completed questionnaires had been physically assaulted by their peers, with just under half reporting having been harassed (44%) and well over three quarters (79%) having been called names because of their actual or perceived sexual orientation.

Similar results have been found in small-scale studies focusing upon the experiences of lesbian, gay, and bisexual adolescents growing up in the U.S. (see Remafedi, 1987). For example, Sears (1991) reported that, of the 36 young lesbians, gay men, and bisexual men and women he questioned, 35 recalled their classmates having negative attitudes towards homosexuality or bisexuality, and most feared being victimised or harassed if they "came out" in high school. This is a view shared by participants in Pilkington and D'Augelli's (1995) study: 28% of young men and 19% of young women indicated that their degree of openness about their sexual orientation was influenced by the fear of physical violence being directed against them. However, as Fricke (1981) pointed out in his autobiography, it is not just physical violence with which lesbian, gay, and bisexual students have to contend:

> One day while sitting in a science class, I happened to glance around the room and detect a fellow class-mate glaring at me. I overlooked it at first, but ten minutes later I noticed he was still staring. His name was Bill Quillar. He must have been a quiet student because I had hardly ever taken notice of him before. I never saw him fraternizing with anyone else. He was a small student, not intimidating in size, but the look in his eyes was petrifying. He stared at me with an uninterrupted gaze that could melt steel. It was a look of complete disgust. I ignored him. But the next day he was staring again. And the next . . . and the next . . . and the next. (pp. 28–29)

Although much of the research cited in this chapter has focused upon victimisation perpetrated by peers, Pilkington and D'Augelli (1995) also found that 7% of their sample reported being hurt by a teacher, especially the young women (11% for women and 7% for men). They also found that those students who were from cultural minority groups were more likely to report abusive behaviour by teachers than white students (10% and 6% respectively). In the U.K., both Warren (1984) and Mac an Ghaill (1994) have reported that although teachers did not actively engage in any form of physical, verbal, or emotional abuse, they had ridiculed pupils who exhibited gender-inappropriate behaviour and, on occasions, had been less than supportive when approached for help, as the following excerpts demonstrate:

> The Head of Sixth Form, who warned that I might get expelled, enquired if I had been dropped on my head as a baby. (Warren, 1984, p. 17)
>
> I went to a teacher and told him that I thought I might be gay. He said, no, I mustn't think like that, it was just a phase all boys went through. (Mac an Ghaill, 1994, p. 168)

Overall, Pilkington and D'Augelli's (1995) study, together with that of the National Gay and Lesbian Task Force, provided good constructive validation for Warren's (1984) findings: all three studies have suggested that approximately one third of young people who are lesbian, gay, or bisexual are victimised or bullied at school because of their sexual orientation. Having said that, Pilkington and D'Augelli acknowledged that their sample was largely haphazard, and this has raised questions about the applicability of their findings to the lesbian, gay, and bisexual population generally: they distributed 500 questionnaires to 14 metropolitan community groups (identified in a gay resources guide; Preston, 1991), of which 221 (44%) were returned, with 194 (39%) eventually being included in the survey results.

One of the strengths of Pilkington and D'Augelli's (1995) study was that it also explored the incidence of harassment outside the school gates, whereas other studies of peer victimisation have largely focused on the incidence of mobbing or bullying within. Although both Olweus (1991) and Whitney and Smith (1993) provide detailed information relating to the location of bullying at school, pupils were provided only with the optional response "other" if they had been bullied elsewhere. While Whitney and Smith reported that 10% of those pupils who reported being bullied by peers said that it occurred in locations other than school, little is known about the nature or frequency of such behaviour.

With respect to lesbian, gay, and bisexual young people, Pilkington and D'Augelli (1995) have provided data on victimisation and harassment for locations both within and outside school environs. For example, they found that of those young people with work experience (92%), 46% said they had felt it necessary to hide their sexual orientation at work, although only 3% of their sample had actually experienced abuse at the hands of their employers because of their sexual orientation. Concomitantly, 36% had either been insulted or otherwise degraded in the home by a member of their immediate family. When these results were analysed further, they found that 22% of young women and 14% of young men had been verbally abused, and that 18% and 8% respectively had been physically assaulted by a member of their family. When asked to identify the perpetrators of such behaviour, participants reported that mothers (22%) were more likely to be abusive to their children than fathers (14%), brothers (16%), or sisters (9%). It was also found that mothers were far more protective towards their lesbian, gay, or bisexual child (25%) than fathers (13%), brothers (11%), or sisters (10%).

In perhaps the largest online survey to date (The California Healthy Kids Survey), students in grades 7–11 (N = 237,544) responded to a series of questions about bullying because of their actual or perceived sexual orientation. Overall, 7.5% of those who participated reported having been bullied because of their actual or perceived sexual orientation, with two thirds of the students who identified as lesbian, gay, bisexual, or transgender reporting having been victimized (California Safe Schools Coalition & 4-H Center for Youth Development, University of California, Davis, 2004). These pupils were more likely to report a C-grade average or lower when compared to non-bullied students (24% vs. 17%), and they were more likely to report missing school in the past 30 days because they believed they would not be safe (27% vs. 7%). In addition, those students who were bullied because of their actual or perceived sexual orientation were also twice as likely to report having engaged in health risk behaviours (e.g., substance abuse, driving under the influence of alcohol, or being a passenger in a car where the driver had consumed alcohol). They were also six times more likely to report being threatened or hurt by someone wielding a weapon (28% vs. 5%) and were nearly four times more likely to carry a weapon to school (19% vs. 5%).

In contrast, in a U.K. survey of lesbian, gay, and bisexual youth in secondary and further education (N = 1,145), Hunt and Jensen (2007) reported that 65% of the students they surveyed had been bullied within the public school system, with the number rising to 75% for those attending faith schools (see Fig. 2.3). Finally, in their replication of

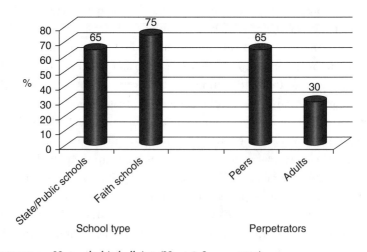

FIGURE 2.3   Homophobic bullying (Hunt & Jensen, 2007)

Warren's (1984) study, Ellis and High (2004) argued that their findings suggested that there had been significant increases in rates of bullying for lesbian, gay, and bisexual youth when compared to the data Warren had collected 20 years earlier. They found that the students surveyed in 2001 were four times more likely to feel isolated at school. They were five times more likely to be victims of name-calling, seven times more likely to be teased, three times more likely to be hit, kicked, or punched, five times more likely to be isolated by their classmates, and nearly nine times more likely to feel "pressured to conform."

Summary

Various researchers have demonstrated that when a young person is victimised because of his or her actual or perceived sexual orientation, the nature of the bullying he or she experiences ranges from incidents of hitting, kicking, and pushing to sexual assault and assault involving a lethal weapon. In addition, as Aaron Fricke's (1981) autobiographical account of "coming out" in high school demonstrated, indirect bullying can be as subtle as a look or stare (the existence and meaning of which may often go unrecognised by both peers and teachers).

Although the studies cited so far offer an overview of the diverse nature of bullying at school, there has yet to be a systematic investigation incorporating all of the behaviours identified by previous researchers. While large-scale surveys such as those conducted by Olweus and Smith and colleagues have provided information on the general incidence of bullying at secondary school, it is likely that such data have included the experiences of young people who were victimised because of their actual or perceived sexual orientation. However, analogous with my previous point, we do not, as yet, have a clear picture of the nature and form of such behaviour, though the California Health Kids Survey provided a great deal of information about the issues associated with bullying on the grounds of actual or perceived sexual orientation.

In the next chapter, I begin to unpack our understanding of bullying further and explore the theories and ideas that underpinned my research.

3

Theorising Bullying

Why does homophobic bullying, or indeed any type of bullying, exist? Does bullying, for example, represent a form of "power" that has its ori-   . gins in the competition for resources among individuals and groups? Is it dependent upon factors such as physical strength, size, ability, or force of personality among individuals, or are the hierarchical structures within societies the cause, where the numerical majority have the power to determine the conditions and limitations under which the numerical minority coexist? Furthermore, the question arises of how such "power" is socially and culturally defined. Who determines what is acceptable in terms of behaviour and, more particularly, what is not?

The significance a particular behaviour holds within a society or culture is in reality no more than that imposed upon it by those who wish to limit its prevalence or acceptance in some way. Some behaviours are prohibited because they deprive one or more others of freedom or life (e.g., slavery and murder). Others are prohibited because they challenge the accepted status quo (e.g., same-sex marriage). Finally, some are prohibited because of fear of the unknown or the different (e.g., gays in the military). Perhaps one of the most interesting issues to emerge as I wrote this book was the case of Constance McMillan, an 18-year-old woman from Mississippi who wished to take a girlfriend to her high school prom in 2010. The decision to close the prom by the school board was, to me, a knee-jerk reaction to the unknown rather than the "the distractions to the educational process" it would cause. However, in a world blighted by war, famine, and natural disasters, I wondered how significant this issue was and just how many young people's learning would be distracted by two young women attending a prom? For Constance McMillan it was an important issue, and certainly it was not a "new" issue for school boards to consider. Indeed, Aaron Fricke, in his autobiography *Confessions of a Rock Lobster,* had faced this very same issue some 30 years earlier. But once you strip away the fear and "hype" surrounding this issue, you are simply left with the fact that two young women wished to go to a school board-organised, adult-supervised, dance together. And what is wrong with that? Is it the fact that they might kiss on the dance floor, drink alcohol illicitly, or engage in heavy petting in some dark corner? Seemingly the fact that these things are also likely to occur more prevalently among the young heterosexuals attending the prom is not an issue that unduly worried the school board in Constance McMillan's case. However, every year teachers, parents, school governors, school boards, and administrators expect that "teenagers will be teenagers" on prom night, but seemingly they must only be heterosexual teenagers. So Constance became a scapegoat: she became the student who ruined the prom for her classmates. For many young lesbians, gay men, and bisexual men and women this will be a familiar story, and one that was used by those who hold power to maintain that power. In the remainder of this chapter I will review some of the classic and contemporary theories that seem to have relevance to our understanding of power within the context of bullying. I focus on the contributions of four disciplines—anthropology, ethology, psychology, and sociology—and demonstrate how the themes of power, hierarchy, and status are constants.

The Scapegoat

In the sixth century, the Greeks of Asia Minor, fearing the wrath of their gods during times of warfare or hardship, sought out a member of their community (the *pharmakos* or "scapegoat") to offer up as a sacrifice. The role of the scapegoat has been the subject of some interest within cultural anthropology for a number of years, due primarily to the fact that the person chosen to carry the burden of the community's sins was perceived as having little value within that society, and was thus considered expendable. Often this person was sickly or disabled (Frazer, 1923), but he or she could also be chosen from among those who had transgressed the community's laws or moral code. Intrinsic to the survival of the community was the belief that scapegoating would rid that society of its "evil," and that the person chosen to be the scapegoat deserved his or her punishment, torture, and ultimate death. For example, in classical antiquity, Frazer (1923) notes that the Athenians regularly maintained a number of "degraded and useless beings at the public expense," and when calamity befell the city-state, "they sacrificed two of these outcasts as scapegoats" (p. 579).

In his review of literature relating to scapegoating, Douglas (1995) determined that there were three essential elements relating to the role of the scapegoat: (i) by his or her death, the scapegoat reinstated members of the community to a position of favour by those they honoured (i.e., their gods); (ii) he or she would ensure the survival of that community; and (iii) his or her death would reinforce a particular belief system by way of example.

According to Douglas (1995) scapegoats have been known by various names across the centuries. These include "sin eaters," "whipping boys," and "fall guys." Interestingly, it is the term "whipping boy" that has become synonymous with bullying behaviour (see Olweus, 1978; Byrne, 1987, 1994; Hoover, Oliver, & Hazler, 1992). Historically, the whipping boy's role was to receive the punishment that otherwise should have been meted out upon his master. Depending on the nature of the transgression, the punishment the whipping boy received varied from flogging to the forfeiture of life.

Interestingly, the sociologist Erving Goffman (1969) argued that the process of transferring guilt or blame onto an innocent party has been employed by various societies and institutions in an attempt to retain identity, strength, and ideology. This can also been seen in Mac an Ghaill's (1994) exploration of the "masculinisation" of the secondary school. In his study, not only were gender identities reinforced, ensuring the predominance of those who sought to achieve the goals of "manhood" and "heterosexuality," but synonymous with the scapegoat of centuries past, the fear of contamination among those who sought to achieve such goals can be seen in their abject dislike of those whom they perceived to be "gay":

> If I was gay, I would try to change. I'm not against gays as long as they don't touch me. (p. 94)

Comparable with Goffman's (1969) assertion that society continues to utilise scapegoats in order to promote an institutional ideology, Aronson (1980) argued that the continued existence of scapegoats and whipping boys suggests that we still allow one person or a group of people to determine the comparative worth of another, and this is due essentially to the hierarchical nature of the way in which we structure our social relationships.

The concept of power is important in our understanding of the social framework within which scapegoating exists. Various researchers have commented upon the importance of certain types of power in peer relationships (see Björkqvist et al., 1982; Besag, 1989; Lagerspetz et al., 1982; Olweus, 1994). While some have argued that the degree of power that perpetrators of bullying have over their victims is a result of factors such as age (e.g., where older pupils are able to manipulate the social infrastructure more effectively), others have suggested that it may be the result of a much more fundamental imbalance, and that the so-called bully may be of greater size or physical strength than his or her victim (Olweus, 1973, 1993a). However, if one considers Mac an Ghaill's (1994) interpretation of the nature of secondary school education in the U.K., it can also be argued that a male-dominated hierarchy built upon the demonstration of "strength" and "power" by its apprentices will ulti- mately seek to make examples of those who do not live up to social or cultural expectations.

Scapegoating cannot explain all forms of bullying behaviour. The principle underlying the concept of a scapegoat is, as Douglas (1995) pointed out, about ensuring the survival of the community by sacrificing one of its members. While Frazer (1923) provides numerous examples of cultures that sacrificed the disabled, the infirm, or the treacherous, they did not sacrifice all who met those criteria. In some cultures the scape- goat was a willing sacrifice, a holy woman or man who gave up his or her life readily. Concomitantly, the act of choosing a scapegoat was accepted by all within the particular society or culture: it was not a prac- tise that was shunned or repudiated by certain groups or classes. Indeed, if one takes, as an example, the discrimination experienced by people of colour, it is clear that such behaviour is not universally condoned; rather, it is actively condemned. But racism has also remained a feature of the daily existence of many people of colour (Boulton, 1995; Fox & Stallworth, 2005; Kelly, 1988). Why should this be so? If a society and the institutions within it actively condemn such behaviour, then the institu- tional form of scapegoating (racist bullying) should not exist.

Valerie Besag, in her book *Bullies and Victims in Schools* (1989), provided an alternative context in which to consider institutional scapegoating. She discussed it from the perspective of the individual student
coexisting within a dual environment that consists of an official (school)
and unofficial (peer) hierarchy, both of which at different times of the
day govern social interaction. This view is supported by Rigby (1997),
who has demonstrated that within the official school setting, a subculture that involves both social stereotyping and prejudice can flourish.
But what is it that members of these unofficial hierarchies are seeking
to achieve by victimising an individual? From a psychoanalytic perspective, Klein (1946) has argued that the act of aggression is a "projective
process of transferring the unacceptable aspects of our own personality,
which are normally repressed, on to another who is more vulnerable
and who displays more overtly those very same characteristics" (Besag,
1989, p. 44). In contrast, Goffman (1968) has suggested that there exists
a subliminal "ideal" in every culture, and that those who do not live up
to it are deemed inadequate. Within a subculture (such as that of the
schoolyard or playground), that ideal (which may not be institutionally
avowed) continues to be reinforced by those who hold "power" over
others, but similar to Klein's observation, because so few in society
reflect that ideal, the authoritative figure mocks the individual who is
perceptibly different, and deflects attention away from his or her own
failings, retaining or augmenting his or her position in the social hierarchy. Rigby (1997) made the point explicitly when discussing the victimisation of young men and women who were perceived to be other
than heterosexual:

> Over the last ten years the fear of AIDS has, in some places in
> Australia, intensified prejudice against gays, resulting in the cruel
> harassment of people, including children, who are thought to be
> homosexual. Perceived grounds for discrimination and consequent
> harassment in a school can be almost limitless. In the Australian
> context sport may feature largely, for example—in one class of Year
> 12 students subgroups were identified by students according to
> whether they were Footballers or non-Footballers, and the latter
> group further divided into Fats (girls who were seen as overweight)
> and others who were dismissed as Faggots. (p. 79)

The inability of a person to play football relegated him or her to one of two social divisions, each of which provided that individual and those similarly classified with a social identity or label at school. While it can be argued that each child or young person has the potential to rid himself or herself of this label by being given the opportunity to demonstrate proficiency in one or more culturally valued activities, the unwillingness of peers to surrender a name once established often means that a cycle of abuse continues until the young person leaves school. Furthermore, once a name, label, or identity is applied to an individual, it is hard to get rid of it, as Lemert's (1967) seven stages of the labelling process show (Besag, 1989, p. 46):

1. Initially the target child displays factors perceived subjectively by others as being removed from the norm.
2. Having been identified, the factors are commented on unfavourably.
3. The subject is now more aware of these characteristics causing the adverse comments and, subsequently, tension and anxiety result in them becoming emphasized.
4. The subject is punished by the labellers for the unacceptable characteristics or behaviours.
5. The behaviours intensify and the punishment increases.
6. The subject accepts and begins to believe in the label, with a resulting lowering in self-confidence and self-esteem.
7. The subject is isolated and vulnerable and unable to call on support from others and fully accepts the role allocated to him or her.

Lemert's (1967) theory suggests that the scapegoat can never rid himself or herself of the mark of stigma. Yet, as both Frazer (1923) and Rigby (1997) have demonstrated, such stigma is often the result of fear: the fear of war or famine, or the fear of HIV infection. But how do such fears come about? As previously noted, Goffman (1968) suggested that the prejudice that underlies many of our fears is the result of the existence of a subliminal ideal—a perfect existence—that is threatened or undermined by the presence of those who do not achieve it. One way in which this ideal is "owned" is by alienating or ostracising others, thus creating groups, categories, or classes of people whose value is determined by their proximity to the ideal standard.

Social Categorisation and Social Identity Theory

The evolution of social categories is one that goes hand in hand with the evolution of power and powerlessness among certain groups that have certain characteristics in common. Thus, every individual is characterized by those social features that demonstrate his or her membership in or identity with a particular group or category. One of the earliest exponents of a theory of social identity based upon a principle of social categorisation was Henri Tajfel (1972), who described the definition of a group or category as a psychological process founded upon two bases: cognition and motivation.

One of the major effects of the process of social categorisation is that it simplifies the structure of the world in which we live and emphasises the differences between categories, and the similarities within them. Thus, each category is defined according to the number of common features shared by its constituent elements. This process remains constant whether dealing with inanimate objects or people: the process of social categorisation is, in fact, one of cognitive categorisation or stereotyping, where individuals are perceived to share one or more common features. At the social level, stereotyping may be defined as "the expression of the attribution of features shared by different members of a group without taking into account the inter-individual differences" (Deschamps & Devos, 1998, p. 4), but as Doise (1976) pointed out, this is not an unbiased or objective process, for social categorisation implies that the individual who categorises others has himself or herself been identified as a member of a social category, and holds one or more ideals or values common to that category.

To understand how discrimination arises from social categorisation, it is important to review the concepts underlying social identity theory, as determined by Tajfel (1972). According to Tajfel, social identity is connected to a person's knowledge and understanding of his or her belonging to a particular social group, and to the emotional and evaluative significance that membership entails. Thus, through membership in a group, the individual acquires a social identity that defines his or her specific position within the social order. Furthermore, membership has the potential for promoting the development of a positive social identity for the group, but only if it is evaluated favourably when compared to others. Thus, similar to Klein's (1946) and Goffman's (1968) commentary on scapegoating, Tajfel and Turner (1986) argued that an individual's perception of his or her own self-worth is intrinsically linked to the favourable way in which he or she is perceived relative to others. However, as noted above, at the macrosystemic level, Tajfel also argued that the maintenance of a positive self-image is reliant upon the individual's ability to identify with a group, and the way in which that group is itself evaluated relative to others. For example, Tajfel and Turner surmised that most societies were organised and stratified according to the identification of social traits that are desirable and those that are not: those individuals who portray desirable traits are allowed to join the "in-group," while those who portray undesirable traits are relegated to the "out-group."

According to social identity theory, an in-group may be defined as a collective wherein individuals hold similar belief systems or ideologies. By comparison, an out-group is a social group with which an individual compares his or her own in-group status. Out-groups act as points of reference, allowing individuals to consider how similar or different they are to their in-group peers. Similar to Goffman''s (1968) argument relating to the fear caused by the presence of those who are perceived to be different, Hamner (1992) has suggested that identification with an in-group confers a number of benefits upon the individual: not only does it assist in maintenance and promotion of self-esteem and social status, it also offers increased access to material resources while decreasing or denying access to those who constitute an out-group.

Social identity theory provides a useful framework for our understanding bullying behaviour at school. Both perpetrators of bullying and their victims have the potential to be members of an out-group in certain social situations. If perpetrators of bullying have moderate to low social status and are sometimes isolated among their same-age peers, they may gain heightened status and self-esteem outside their own peer group by drawing together an in-group consisting of younger or less able confederates who are willing to participate in the victimisation of others. Also, if victims have very low social status within their own peer group and, as a consequence, low self-esteem, they are also unlikely to be able to raise their self-esteem because their social networks are being continually eroded. However, Rigby and Slee (1993) argued that a child's tendency to be victimised or his or her tendency to bully others cannot be considered polar opposites. They have suggested that victims and perpetrators share a great deal of common ground: victims may be provocative as well as passive, while perpetrators in one situation may be victims in another (Besag, 1989; Olweus, 1984; Rivers, Poteat, Noret, & Ashurst, 2009). In their study of interpersonal relationships among 1,162 Australian secondary school children (604 boys and 558 girls), Rigby and Slee found that perpetrators of bullying behaviour were not necessarily antisocial or uncooperative; rather, they tended to show distinct social behaviour patterns and sought membership of a group (see also Sutton, Smith, & Swettenham, 1999). Furthermore, while Rigby and Slee found that the perpetrators of bullying in their study disliked school (possibly because they came into conflict with authority figures due to their aggressive behaviour, or as a result of their poor academic performance), they tended to have positive feelings about themselves, and this they ascribed to the fact that they had a network of confederates to bolster their self-esteem. Unsurprisingly, victims were generally found to be socially isolated and had lower levels of self-esteem, but, interestingly, they did not report being less happy at school. Rigby and Slee suggested that this outcome was a consequence of victims' pessimistic view of the world and their realisation that life outside school would not necessarily be any better than life within.

In terms of social identity theory, Rigby and Slee's (1993) results would seem, in part, to support Tajfel and Turner's (1986) hypothesis that an individual's self-esteem is intrinsically linked to group membership. Interestingly, their analysis of the perpetrator role is reminiscent of Douglas's (1995) description of the first essential element of the role of the scapegoat: the reinstatement of community members to a position of favour by those they honoured. Bullying provides the perpetrator with a method whereby he or she is able to deflect the criticism or ridicule of others by drawing attention away from himself or herself and by turning it towards the behaviour or demeanour of a third person (the victim or scapegoat), thus ensuring (i) the maintenance of his or her own positive self-image by remaining a member of the in-group, and (ii) that there is always another with whom he or she can be compared favourably.

In their study of the social behaviour of 164 children attending two Canadian schools, Craig and Pepler (1995) argued that those who engage in bullying may actually receive "reinforcement and encouragement from their peers" (p. 91), which then strengthens their social status. Their assertion that peers may actively encourage the perpetrator is based upon an analysis of the videotaped observations they made of peer victimisation in the playgrounds of both schools. Using observers who were blind to the social relationships of the children prior to coding the videotapes, they found that 85% of the incidents of bullying recorded involved peers either observing the behaviour or interacting with the perpetrator and victim. According to Craig and Pepler, such behaviour, whereby peers actively collude with the bully, shows not only disrespect for the victim and support for the perpetrator, but also their (the peers') assumption of higher social status, and even their belief in the deservedness of the victim's situation.

Craig and Pepler's (1995) findings can be explained with reference to both scapegoating and social identity theory. Similar to Rigby and Slee's (1993) observations of Australian schoolchildren, the perpetrator attains his or her social status by drawing peers into the bullying episode, and by receiving their attention. At the same time, peers ensure their own safety by urging the perpetrator on, thus deflecting attention away from themselves while, at the same time, safeguarding their own membership of the in-group (the *motivational* basis of social categorisation). In the case of the victim, comparable with the *pharmakos* of classical antiquity, peers actively collaborate in the process of goading, thus overestimating the difference between themselves and the victim; this, in turn, has the effect of legitimating such behaviour (the *cognitive* basis of social categorisation).

Craig and Pepler's (1995) findings suggest that bullying is a group process very similar in structure to that of mobbing, where the victim is harassed by multiple perpetrators. However, Whitney and Smith (1993) found that much of the bullying that took place within British schools was perpetrated by individuals rather than groups. Alternatively, as Olweus (1993a) pointed out, victims have, on occasions, outnumbered perpetrators, yet they continued to be victimised. Indeed, perpetrators take many forms, and there would seem to be a variety of ways in which membership of an in-group is determined.

To explore the process by which in-groups and out-groups are formed at school, three theories of social behaviour are presented below (deindividuation theory, social ranking theory, and status construct theory), each of which has drawn upon social categorisation and social identity theory as a foundation.

Deindividuation Theory

Deindividuation theory focuses on the collective action of members of a group. It is based upon Le Bon's (1895) classic crowd theory, in which the individual is "submerged in the crowd and loses self-control and becomes a mindless puppet capable of violating personal or social norms" (Postmes & Spears, 1998, p. 239).

Various researchers have used deindividuation theory to explain the aggressive behaviour of groups towards individuals or other groups (Diener, 1980; Festinger, Pepitone, & Newcomb, 1952; Prentice-Dunn & Rogers, 1982, 1989; Stott & Adang, 2004; Zimbardo, 1969). Festinger et al. (1952) proposed that the loss of individuality and submergence into a crowd was as much a defence mechanism on the part of an individual in a highly charged or volatile social situation as it was the result of him or her being overwhelmed by the sheer force of the collective will. By entering the group and being subsumed within it, Festinger et al. believed that the individual was released from the internalised moral constraints that would normally inhibit violent or aggressive acts. This release had the effect of reducing responsibility for individual behaviour and that of the crowd, thus giving licence for more extreme acts of aggression.

Building upon Festinger et al.'s (1952) hypothesis, Zimbardo (1969) argued that anonymity and contextual factors, such as a lack of overall responsibility, arousal, and a lack of structure, were important factors in understanding the psychology of anti-normative behaviour. However, what about individual aggression? Diener and colleagues (Diener, 1976, 1980; Diener, Westford, Dineen, & Fraser, 1973) found that anonymity did not have a significant impact upon levels of aggression. Indeed, in their study "Test the Pacifist," they found that when an individual acted alone, levels of aggression rose. Overall, their results showed that identified individuals tended to be more aggressive than anonymous individuals, and that "groups were less aggressive than individuals, with identified groups being least aggressive of all" (Postmes & Spears, 1998, p. 240).

Spears and Lea (1992, 1994) and Reicher, Spears, and Postmes (1995) have used social identity theory as a means of explaining deindividuation in certain social contexts. They have argued that the SIDE model (Social Identity Model of Deinidividuation Effects) predicts an individual's conformity to "norms associated with the specific social identity or group rather than conformity to any general norms" (Postmes & Spears, 1998, p. 241). Postmes and Spears (1998) suggested that, in line with classical deindividuation theory, SIDE suggests that factors affecting deindividuation such as anonymity, group cohesion, and a sense of group membership actively reinforce the salience of the group and promote conformity among its members. Thus, behaviours that would normally be inhibited at an individual level may be enacted at the group level if it constitutes the situational norm.

In terms of bullying behaviour, research on deindividuation theory has three contributions to make. First of all, where an individual is bullied by a group, classical deindividuation theory suggests that the nature of the behaviours to which he or she is exposed will be more aggressive and potentially more physically harmful than those perpetrated by a single individual due to a communal release from inhibition. Secondly, and somewhat contrary to the previous point, it can be argued that when a group is led by an identified individual, the aggressive behaviour of that person may be greater than that of the group, who may goad the victim and urge the perpetrator on but may not actively participate in the discriminatory behaviour. Thirdly, it can be argued that where an attitude, belief, or behaviour is perceived to be a situational norm, members of the in-group may identify with or participate in the perpetration of bullying to ensure that they will either retain or augment their social status within the schoolyard hierarchy.

There is evidence to support two of these three contributions. For example, in their study of the prevalence and correlates of youth gang affiliation among 11,000 secondary school students, Dukes, Martinez, and Stein (1997) noted that teenagers with a history of gang membership were involved in greater drug use and greater delinquency than non-gang members, and they were also in greater fear of being harmed and were more likely to carry a weapon at all times (see also Bjerregaard, 2002; Decker & Curry, 2000). Their results also showed that youth gang membership was correlated with lower self-esteem, perceived academic ability, and psychosocial health. Comparable with social identity theory, gang membership provided teenagers with a group identity and increased self-esteem (cf. Decker & Curry), but often this was at a cost: membership also required individuals to demonstrate their allegiance to the gang by engaging in delinquent and sometimes violent activity (for example, by participating in a drive-by shooting). Interestingly, Dukes et al. found that those who wished to join gangs had low levels of self-control and were, therefore, more prone to extremes of behaviour. Thus, these findings would seem to support the first argument: that the nature of the behaviour to which an individual is exposed by a group of bullies will be more aggressive and potentially more physically harmful than those perpetrated by a single bully because of the release from personal inhibition.

However, deindividuation theory also suggests that the behaviour of the group can be uncontrollable, erratic, and without purpose. In essence, deindividuation arises out of situational chaos, which various researchers have shown is not the case in bullying behaviour. There are a number of agreed points relating to what bullying entails: it is deliberate, it is repeated, and it takes place within a social context where there is an imbalance of power (be it in terms of physical or emotional strength, status, intellectual ability, or group membership). Bullying has order, structure, and intent: it is rarely spontaneous or disorganised.

If bullying is an orchestrated behaviour, then the question arises: who orchestrates it? It is at this point that Diener et al.'s (1973) findings would seem relevant. If, as I have suggested above, a group is led by an identified individual, it then follows that the aggressive behaviour of the identified individual has the potential to be more extreme than that of the group. To a certain degree this may be the correlate of the relationship of the perpetrator to his or her followers: the more distant or authoritative the leader, the more extreme his or her actions. But how might this proximity be determined? Interestingly, Salmivalli, Lagerspetz, Björkqvist, Österman, and Kaukiainen (1996) may provide the answer to this question. In their study of social status and bullying behaviour among a group of Finnish schoolchildren, they found that physical aggression was a common method of interacting among boys, and that it was used as a means to determine social order. Thus, they argued that, at least among boys, direct physical aggression played an important role in determining the hierarchical nature of peer relationships in the school-yard. Thus, if the divide (in terms of physical size or strength) between the leader, his second in command, and all his other followers is signifi-cant, then his behaviour may be more extreme and less open to challenge than if others were approximately the same build.

The third contribution that research on deindividuation theory makes arises from the work of Postmes and Spears (1998). If one defines a situational norm as an attitude, belief, or behaviour prevalent among the numerical majority (e.g., a society or culture) or among significant others (e.g., parents, teachers or peers), then it follows that acceptance of and identification with that attitude, belief, or behaviour will follow if the individual wishes to retain his or her in-group status. Where such an attitude, belief, or behaviour is prejudicial, as Allport (1954) pointed out, it is usually the result of the propagation of unwarranted stereotypes that seek to promote the assumption of higher social status by those in authority or those in the majority (Oldmeadow & Fiske, 2007).

For example, it has been suggested by various researchers that chil-dren can actively discriminate on the grounds of gender by the age of 3 (Duveen & Lloyd, 1986), and race by the age of 4 (Williams & Morland, 1976). Maras (1993) has shown that children are able not only to distin-guish differences in terms of gender or race, but can also use criteria linked to their understanding of cultural attitudes towards certain minor-ity groups. She asked a group of 9- and 10-year-olds to sort a series of photographs of children with and without disabilities into categories. One girl, she recalled, assembled three piles of photographs, saying, "They're boys, they're girls, they're handicaps" (p. 140).

Brown (1995) has suggested that when discrimination against minor-ity groups is embedded within the institutions that make up a society (e.g., schools), it has a resonating impact upon the expression of victimi-sation by its citizens. For example, Vollebergh (1991) found that discrim-ination against ethnic or cultural minority groups occurs irrespective of the social status of its perpetrators or their victims. Unlike school bully-ing, where perpetrators tend to have (or believe themselves to have) a higher social status than their victims, in cases where a person is victim-ised because of his or her colour or cultural background, perpetrators also come from alienated or lower social status groups. In Vollebergh's study, discrimination against Black middle-class citizens was often perpetrated by White citizens from poorer socioeconomic backgrounds who were, it is argued, "motivated in part by the desire to avoid identity-damaging comparisons" with those they considered less worthy (Brown, 1995, p. 181).

Findings such as those of Vollebergh (1991) suggest that discrimination serves a social purpose in maintaining not only individuals' self-esteem, but also that of the group or community. Indeed, Oldmeadow and Fiske (2007) have shown that status stereotypes are often used to provide moral and intellectual support for the maintenance of social inequalities. And while the authors claim that there are moderating effects, such as a belief in personal merit, status and competence are often highly correlated.

Within the school environment, incidents of discrimination on the grounds of disability or special educational needs have been found in a number of research studies, and it may be argued that such discrimination is directly related to children's lack of understanding about people they perceive as different and their unwillingness (often as a result of external pressure) to identify with those who may be from another culture, or those who may have a learning or motor disability. Similarly, for over 30 years, numerous studies have demonstrated that pupils have also been discriminated on the grounds of their gender and sexual orientation, often as a result of institutional bias or, as Allport (1954) intimated, by the propagation of stereotypes that feed people's fears relating to the disintegration of social order (see Gentry, 1992; Herdt & Boxer, 1996; Herek, 1984, 1986, 1992; Larsen, Reed, & Hoffman, 1980; Mac an Ghaill, 1994; Martin, 1982; Mondimore, 1996; Pilkington & D'Augelli, 1995; Poteat, 2007; Poteat, Espelage, & Koenig, 2009; Poteat & Rivers, 2010; Price, 1982; Ross, 1996; Sedgwick, 1990; Warren, 1984).

A recurrent theme within the discussion so far is that of social structure or social order underpinning individual and group behaviour. While classical deindividuation theory is not concerned primarily with the organisation of society, it is interesting to note that, historically, crowds have gathered and mob rule has occurred when there has been a social order to rebel against or to uphold. In the following sections I consider social ranking theory and status construction theory as means by which to understand how social order is determined and how groups are evaluated relative to others.

Social Ranking Theory

According to Hawker (1997), social ranking theory arises from the study of the aetiology of depression. It suggests that there are two aspects of social interaction that hold developmental significance in relation to the onset of depression: power and belonging. Gilbert (1992) argued that the onset of depression is causally related to the power differential found between individuals in a social situation. Based upon the ethological principle of involuntary subordination (a behaviour found in many species where the weaker animal automatically submits to the dominance of the stronger), Gilbert proposed that, among depressives, rather than the interaction between the weaker and stronger person ending when the dominance of the latter is established, involuntary subordination may not succeed in pacifying the winner or in eliciting appropriate behavioural signals from the loser. Where this occurs, Gilbert has suggested that it results in the "intense and prolonged" suffering of the loser, which manifests itself as a depressive illness (Hawker, 1997, p. 21).

In terms of peer victimisation, Gilbert (1992) argued that the process of ranking individuals or groups is a result of potential subordinates receiving "catathetic signals" from those who wish to dominate (p. 161). The purpose of these signals is to reduce the rank or status of the target by the issuing of threats or putdowns, or through a deliberate failure to recognise their achievements. Hawker (1997) suggested that there is a link between social ranking theory as defined by Gilbert (1992) and bullying at school. In his thesis, he cites a number of studies of dominance hierarchies among children in which observations of physical and verbal aggression equate with current definitions of overt bullying behaviour. However, as illustrated earlier in this chapter, it has also been shown that bullying has the potential to be covert, and may not take the form of acts of physical or verbal aggression where the dominance hierarchy is clear to the observer. As a result, theorists have argued that social order is based upon two modes of control: "agonic" and "hedonic." Agonic control refers to behaviours that are overt where the social order is determined by threat or acts of overt aggression. According to Gilbert (1989), in social groups where agonic strategies are used, the resource holding potential of the dominant male or female is determined by his or her "strength and fighting ability" (p. 44). Hawker (1997) has suggested that because weaker males or females will have lower resource holding potential, they will have subordinate status within the peer group and, as a correlate of their status, they are more likely to suffer from depression (this may be especially the case where their subordination is constantly reinforced over a long period).

In contrast, hedonic control is much more subtle and derives from the social nature of our existence (Gilbert, 1992, 1997). Unlike agonic control, hedonic control is not aggressive in intent; rather, it is exercised through the individual seeking reassurance or approval from significant others via verbal and nonverbal signals. It is primarily a mode by which the individual determines whether or not others find him or her attractive, and whether or not they are willing to invest both time and energy in maintaining a relationship: social attention holding power.

Both Gilbert (1997) and Hawker (1997) suggested that failure to attain the reassurance or approval of others also has the effect of diminishing the social status of the victim. However, unlike agonic methods of intimidation, which are overt and provide the victim with an opportunity to defend himself or herself, where the method is covert both resource holding potential and social attention holding power can be undermined without the knowledge of the individual or his or her ability to retaliate.

Both Gilbert's (1997) and Hawker's (1997) discussions of agonic and hedonic control suggested that the outcomes (i.e., depression) would be the same regardless of the mode. However, where an individual has the opportunity to defend himself or herself, regardless of the success of the venture, it could be argued that the very act of defence may guard against total loss of status and self-respect. This is supported in part by Sturman and Mongrain (2008), who found that, among university and college athletes, self-criticism together with neuroticism predict heightened perceptions of defeat. However, self-efficacy was associated with an adaptive response to defeat. Thus, a willingness to respond to a negative situation, even though it does not promise success in the future, may have protective value, especially in terms of mental health.

Gilbert (1992) has also argued that the issue of "belonging" is also central to social ranking theory. Essentially, he argued that it is important for every individual to have a sense of belonging, and that those who are victimised by others invariably do not belong and thus are isolated. However, as Hawker (1997) pointed out, while Gilbert was correct in his appraisal, some individuals may not be members of an in-group that holds both power and resources; they can be members of an out-group, but an out-group can also have cohesion.

As Tajfel and Turner (1986) pointed out, while in-groups and out-groups may be intrinsic to the way in which we cognitively structure society, out-group status does not necessarily result in a lack of group membership. Principally, an out-group is a group of individuals with whom a member of an in-group can compare himself or herself favourably, and determine whether his or her degree of affiliation to the in-group is greater than that to the out-group. Thus, if he or she feels a greater sense of identity with the group in which he or she is a member, then his or her in-group status will remain. But if he or she feels a greater sense of identity with an out-group, should the true nature of his or her feelings be discovered by other in-group members, the association with that group will be terminated. Yet those who constitute an out-group in one arena may constitute an in-group in another; therefore, social identity theory suggests that membership of an in-group is relative only to the out-groups to which an individual compares his or her own affiliation.

Theoretically, Gilbert's (1992) suggestion that belonging is intrinsic to the mental health of the individual is problematic. His argument rests upon the presumption that membership of a group conveys far more benefits than being an outsider. But it must be argued that, for some, the nature of the group to which they belong has a detrimental effect upon their mental health. This can be seen readily in many of the studies cited in Chapter 2 relating to the victimisation of young people with special educational needs, or those who constitute an ethnic minority, or, indeed, those who represent a sexual minority. Therefore, if social ranking theory is to be applied as a means to understand how the status of an individual is determined within a society or culture, it is also necessary to explore the way in which that society or culture perceives and organises its constituent groups, and this is where status construction theory has a useful contribution to make.

Status Construction Theory

Previously it was argued that where an attitude, belief, or behaviour is prejudicial, it is usually the result of the propagation of unwarranted stereotypes that seek to promote the assumption of higher social status by those who hold authority or those who constitute the majority. Thomashausen (1987) suggested that "apartheid" (the systematic segregation of communities on the basis of skin colour) is embedded within the cultural, political, legal, and religious histories of many countries, and the cultural advantage it provided the minority White South Africans was evident in the unequal treatment of Black South Africans, whose subjugation can be traced back to a period in world history where European traders and settlers were able to overwhelm the indigenous nations of Africa through force of arms, and sell them into slavery.

Since the conquest of the "New World" in the late fifteenth century, the justification underpinning the subjugation or enslavement of the indigenous peoples of North and South America, Africa, India, and southeast Asia has been one of Christian salvation: to bring a European god to idolatrous or polytheistic cultures. As the sixteenth-century theologian Juan Gines de Sepulveda wrote of the Spanish conquest of the Americas:

> How can we doubt that these people so uncivilized, so barbaric, so contaminated with so many sins and obscenities...have been justly conquered by such a humane nation which is excellent in every kind of virtue. (Williams, 1992, p. 138)

Such attitudes, which were by no means exclusive to the Spanish *conquistadors*, and which anthropologists have termed the "imperialist fantasy" (see Shapiro, 1998, p. 491), were not confined solely to the cultural and religious beliefs of conquered peoples: they were also intrinsic to the way in which Europeans viewed their own disabled, mentally ill, or, indeed, homosexual citizens (Williams, 1992; Rivers, 1998).

Ridgeway and Balkwell (1997) argued that the process by which a society or culture arrives at a series of consensual beliefs about its order or structure and the value of an individual's or group's behaviour can be understood in terms of a three-stage model of status construction. This model asserts that social structure is organised according to the distribution of resources, the distribution of the population on individual/difference variables, and the relationship between these distributions. They argued that the distribution of resources and the distribution of the population on individual/difference characteristics constrain face-to-face encounters between the various groups that make up a society or culture. As a result of such constraints, members of each group develop status beliefs about the individual/difference variables, determining a hierarchy of valued and unvalued traits. Eventually, through a lack of contact and the development of group-centred status beliefs, each group attempts to enforce its own beliefs about valued and unvalued traits through education, thus promulgating stereotypical representations that seek to denigrate the status of others.

Ridgeway and Balkwell (1997) suggested that where interaction occurs between groups with nominal characteristics (e.g., race or ethnicity) that are also found to correlate with resource characteristics (e.g., wealth or poverty), estimations of "situational esteem and perceived competence" follow (p. 14). Thus, access to resources is perceived as a competence, and those groups with access to resources (i.e., wealth) perceive themselves to be more competent than those without. Where access to resources (i.e., perceived competence) is found to correlate with race or ethnicity, the group with greater access to those resources evaluates itself more favourably than others, and promulgates stereotypes that portray those with fewer resources as less worthy (thus raising self-esteem). For example, Rogers and Frantz (1962) found that White immigrants to Zimbabwe (then Southern Rhodesia) acquired their anti-Black attitudes from other White immigrants, and that the longer they remained in the country the stronger their feelings became. Yet Rogers and Frantz (1962) also pointed out that the contact White immigrants had with Black Southern Rhodesians was so constrained that there was little opportunity for them to question the validity of the appraisals they heard (see also Henderson-King & Nisbett, 1996).

Within the context of children's social relationships, while Boulton's (1995) study showed that racial stereotypes are ever-present in the discourses of schoolchildren, they are not always applied when it comes to patterns of social interaction, particularly if a school's population is drawn from a number of ethnic and cultural groups. Thus, stereotypes and constructions of status can be challenged—and challenged effectively (Ridgeway & Correll, 2006).

And Homophobia?

So the question now arises: how do these theories link with the study of homophobia? Ultimately, understanding the social and cultural context in which human interaction takes place is vital to interpreting findings (Bronfenbrenner, 1977), and perhaps no more so than in studies of discrimination. For example, in their study of the antecedents of homophobia in adolescents, Morrison, McLeod, Morrison, Anderson, and O'Connor (1997) found a similar pattern of social interaction to that described by Ridgeway and Balkwell (1997). In their study, which focused on gender stereotyping, homophobia, and sexual coercion among 1,045 Canadian adolescents, Morrison et al. argued that participants' negative attitudes towards homosexuality were not only correlated with the propagation of gender stereotypes and the perceived social desirability of heterosexuality, but they were also correlated with popular misconceptions about the sexually coercive nature of lesbian and gay relationships. They argued that an inability to challenge such stereotypes and misconceptions is a result of the sociocultural pressures placed upon educators to adhere to an "idealised" standard, promoting a culture of "silence" wherein the individual is unable to speak with authority about that which he or she "knows, sees, or feels" (p. 367; cf. Goffman, 1968; Mac an Ghaill, 1994). This is an argument supported by McCann, Minichiello, and Plummer (2009) in their study of the forces that have constructed Australian masculinity. They have shown that, among heterosexual men, exposure to difference and "taking risks," often by meeting men who are gay or reading material about gay lives, does not challenge the salience of their existence or their masculinity. Rather, a world is revealed in which there are multiple legitimacies of existence, and multiple ways of living lives.

So, why does homophobia exist? From an ethological standpoint, Gordon Gallup (1995) argued that homophobia evolved as "a means of minimizing the likelihood that off-spring would become homosexual" (p. 54). In an early study (Gallup & Suarez, 1983), he suggested that parents have a reproductive investment in the sexual orientation of their offspring and, therefore, they promote anti-homosexual attitudes in an attempt to influence a child's emerging sexuality. While this theory

suggests that homosexuality may be social in origin rather than biological or genetic, it is framed within the context of Darwin's (1859) theory
of natural selection. Principally, comparable with Morrison et al.'s (1997)
findings, he found that many people hold beliefs about the sexually coercive nature of gay men and are afraid that homosexual teachers will
either abuse their children or lead them into homosexuality. To explore
this further, he undertook four surveys designed to explore the hypothesis that anti-homosexual attitudes may vary as a function of the contact
a lesbian or gay man has with children (Gallup, 1995). His results showed
that heterosexual participants were more likely to express discomfort
with lesbian or gay teachers, doctors, or school bus drivers than with any
other profession (lawyer, sales clerk, car mechanic). Furthermore, among
the medical profession, greatest discomfort was expressed by participants
for paediatricians and child psychiatrists, with the fear being primarily
situated around concerns relating to HIV/AIDS transmission. In terms
of fears of sexual coercion, Gallup's third survey showed that participants' concerns would be heightened if their child stayed at a friend's
house where the same-sex parent was lesbian or gay. Finally, in his fourth
survey he found that men were more homophobic than women, and
that those who reported being more religious, or reported being parents
already, were more likely to express anti-homosexual attitudes than their
counterparts.

Gallup (1995) argued that "homophobic reactions were shaped by
natural selection" and that they were likely to vary "as a function of the
perceived impact that a homosexual might have on a child's emerging
sexuality" (p. 65). However, he noted that the picture of anti-homosexual
attitudes he presented was based upon three assumptions relating to the
human condition: (i) that homosexuality has been a feature of human
evolution for a substantial period; (ii) that an individual's sexual orientation can be affected by "modeling and/or seduction effects" (p. 67); and
(iii) that there is a foundation to heterosexual concerns about the seduction of children by homosexuals.

Given that Morrison et al. (1997) argued that educators are often
forced into silence, which then results in the promulgation of the second
and third assumptions underpinning Gallup's (1995) model of homophobia, various researchers have attempted to demonstrate the fallacy of such
assumptions and have done so with a certain degree of success (see Bailey,

Bobrow, Wolfe, & Mikach, 1995; Biblarz & Stacey, 2010; Bigner & Bozett, 1990; Cramer, 1986; Dressler, 1978; Golombok & Tasker, 1996; Gottman, 1990; Miller, 1979; Patterson,1992; Stacey & Biblarz, 2001; Tasker & Bigner, 2007; Tasker & Patterson, 2007; Telingator & Patterson, 2008; Wainright & Patterson, 2008). Having said that, in those cultures where homosexuality has been actively condemned, such stereotypes are likely to have continued unabated, and as Hamner (1992) pointed out with reference to social identity theory, they will undoubtedly have had an impact upon social status and the provision of resources for lesbians, gay men, and bisexual men and women.

4

Psychosocial Correlates and Long-Term Effects

In the preceding chapters, I have presented data that suggest that victimisation in childhood and adolescence is positively correlated with psychosocial problems in later years. Although Olweus (1993b) found no indication of a systematic association between participants' experiences at school and being bullied in early adulthood, Hawker's (1997) study suggested that the subordinate role victims play within the peer group is likely to have an impact upon their susceptibility to depressive illnesses, especially where that subordination is constantly reinforced. In addition, unlike agonic methods of intimidation, which are overt and provide victims with an opportunity to defend themselves, where the method is covert a victim can be undermined without being given the opportunity to retaliate. However, both Gilbert's (1997) and Hawker's (1997) appraisal of agonic and hedonic control suggested that any long-term outcomes (e.g., depression) would be the same regardless of the nature of the bullying experienced by victims, and where they have the opportunity to defend themselves, the very act of defence may guard against total loss of status and self-respect. Consequently, those exposed to agonic (i.e., direct physical and verbal) methods of victimisation may fare better in the long term than those whose social status was eroded hedonically (i.e., indirectly). Thus, susceptibility to depression may vary as a function of the nature of the bullying they experienced at school.

In this chapter I review some of the clinical studies that underpinned the research in this book, focusing upon the psychosocial correlates and long-term effects of exposure to violence and trauma for both adults and children. I consider the effect of individual differences (i.e., personal resilience) in terms of levels of coping among victims of violence or abuse, and review some of the relevant theoretical debates currently surrounding the role of friendship and/or social support mechanisms in counteracting long-term negative outcomes. Following on from this,

I review studies relating to the long-term effects of bullying, and consider their ramifications for the present study. I then consider research focusing upon the correlates of psychological well-being among lesbian, gay, and bisexual youth. Finally, I provide a summary integrating both empirical and theoretical works, and identify those issues this book explores.

Long-term Effects of Exposure to Violence or Trauma

Researchers in the field of developmental psychopathology have long argued that traumatic events experienced in childhood and adolescence can have a long-term and debilitating effect upon the quality of adult life (Parker & Asher, 1987). For example, in their review of literature focusing upon internalising disorders in childhood, Kovacs and Devlin (1998) argued that many depressed adults can trace the onset of their affective disorder to an event occurring in childhood or early adolescence. Based upon an earlier study conducted by Newman, Moffitt, Caspi, Magdol, Silva, and Stanton (1996), Kovacs and Devlin suggested that the effects of a negative event occurring in childhood can remain in evidence for up to five decades and, perhaps, beyond. This is a view shared by Michael Rutter, a pioneer in the field of childhood psychopathology, who has argued that research in the field of lifespan development should take into account the continuities as well as the discontinuities that exist from childhood to adulthood (Rutter, 1989, 1996). In terms of the continuities, he maintained that links exist between "social isolation, peer rejection, odd unpredictable behaviour and attention deficits in childhood and schizophrenic psychosis in adult life" (Rutter, 1989, p. 27). Furthermore, he argued that adult vulnerability is a consequence of a failure to work through or come to terms with early negative experiences. Thus, those who cannot overcome the deprivations of childhood are unlikely to function successfully in the adult world. In terms of the discontinuities, has suggested that the physiological changes young people undergo during puberty and the new experiences they encounter as they grow older have a significant impact upon their psychological functioning in adulthood. However, he also provided a caveat to this argument, suggesting that despite such changes, it is impossible to remove entirely the effects of early experience from the psychological schema of the adult.

In terms of childhood experience, Rutter's (1989, 1996) observations suggest that there is a certain inevitability in the adult who was victimised in childhood becoming or remaining a victim in later life. For example, among children who are rejected by their peers, various researchers have found strong correlations with later delinquency (Farrington, 1995; Kupersmidt, 1983), low self-esteem, loneliness (Parkhurst & Asher, 1987; Williams & Asher, 1987), and depression (Achenbach & Edelbrock, 1981; Rubin, LeMare, & Lollis, 1990). While delinquency has been primarily associated with those children who are rejected because of their dishonesty, overt aggressiveness, or general antisocial demeanour (see Tolan & Guerra, 1994), issues such as low self-esteem, loneliness, and depression have been found primarily among those adults who, as adolescents, were considered "easy to push around" or "timid" (Parker & Asher, 1987, p. 382).

Some Clinical Studies

Comparable with Rutter's (1996) discussion of the link between childhood experiences and adult psychopathology, Ellason and Ross (1997) suggested that a linear relationship exists between experiences of physical or sexual trauma in childhood and adult psychosis (including schizophrenia). In their study of long-term clinical outcomes for a sample of 144 inpatients (131 women and 13 men; mean age 35 years) attending two treatment programmes for survivors of physical and sexual abuse, the authors reported finding particularly strong associations between factors such as the number of perpetrators of physical and/or sexual abuse and psychoticism. They also found significant relationships between both physical and sexual abuse experienced in childhood and symptoms indicative of dissociative, somatic, mood, anxiety, substance abuse, and borderline personality disorders. In terms of self-harming behaviour and suicidal ideation, they found significant relationships between reports of such behaviour and (1) the number of perpetrators of physical abuse and/or sexual abuse and (2) the number of types of sexual abuse experienced by participants in childhood.

Based upon their 2-year follow-up study of patients suffering dissociative disorders following trauma, Ellason and Ross (1997) argued that rather than viewing mental illness as "organic" in origin, researchers should also explore the possibility that clients may have suffered from some form of trauma that has increased their susceptibility to various disorders in adulthood. Hence, rather than using traditional methods of intervention (e.g., psychotropic drugs) to alleviate symptoms associated with various psychoses, they suggested that where trauma was the root cause of psychiatric disturbance, psychotherapy and counselling may be more effective in alleviating long-term symptoms.

Ellason and Ross's (1997) research does have pedigree and follows the findings of other researchers studying the psychiatric symptoms associated with physical and sexual abuse (see Cahill, Llewellyn, & Pearson, 1991). For example, in their study of the long-term effects of sexual abuse in childhood, Cahill et al. cited a number of clinical studies that suggested that survivors were likely to suffer from anxiety and depression, low levels of self-esteem, and high levels of dissociation (see Bagley & Ramsay, 1986; Briere & Runtz, 1987; Murphy, Kilpatrick, Amick-McMullan, Veronen, Paduhovich, Best, Villeponteaux, & Saunders, 1988). In addition, based upon research conducted by Herman and Hirschman (1981) with survivors of father–daughter incest, Cahill et al. reported associations between childhood experiences of sexual trauma and not only poor self-image in adulthood, but also difficulty forming and maintaining lasting intimate relationships.

According to Cahill et al. (1991), within relationships, adult survivors of child sexual abuse reported experiencing a number of problems in terms of communicating their concerns, fears, and insecurities to their spouses/partners. Such problems included the inability to "trust and to love, anxiety surrounding emotional and/or physical intimacy, fear of being abused, rejected, betrayed or abandoned, and feeling undeserving, misunderstood and overly dependent in relationships" (p. 122). Concomitant with problems in forming and maintaining relationships, they also noted that some researchers reported participants' experiencing difficulties in terms of defining their sexual orientation (see Browne & Finkelhor, 1986; Meiselman, 1978). In particular, Meiselman noted in her study of 23 former victims of father–daughter incest that 7 had experienced lesbian relationships, or had commented upon the confusion they had experienced in terms of coming to a decision about their own sexual identity.

Although there has been gradual recognition of the long-term emotional and behavioural impact sexual and physical abuse can have upon victims (see Bushnell, Wells, & Oakely-Browne, 2007; Herbert, 1998; Lansford, Dodge, Pettit, Bates, Crozier, & Kaplow, 2002), it is only recently that we have accepted the children can experience immediate and pervasive effects from exposure to violence and trauma. For example, in Yule and Williams' (1990) study, many of the children who had survived the capsizing of the ship "Herald of Free Enterprise" exhibited a number of classic symptoms associated with the onset of posttraumatic stress disorder (PTSD).

In Yule and Udwin's (1991) study, 24 girls (aged between 14 and 16 years) who had survived the sinking of the "Jupiter" in the Eastern Mediterranean were screened using three measures exploring the relationship between significant life events (i.e., the sinking), depression, and anxiety. The girls completed the battery of tests at two time points (10 days after the sinking, and subsequently 5 months later). The results indicated that 10 of the girls who scored highly in terms of depression and anxiety after 10 days also scored highly 5 months later, and reported "higher rates of intrusive thoughts, avoidant behaviour, anxiety and depression" compared to the remaining 14 girls (p. 137).

In contrast to the relative paucity of information that has been available relating to PTSD in childhood other than in sexual abuse cases, there have been a number of studies and clinical reports published over the past 20 years or so focusing upon the physical well-being and mental health of survivors of trauma occurring in adulthood. For example, studies have found that following Sept. 11, 2001, U.S. citizens exhibited symptoms of distress even though they had not been in New York City (Stein, Elliott, Jaycox, Collins, Berry, Klein, & Schuster, 2004). Similarly, research into the long-term effects of interpersonal violence has shown that victims have continued to be affected by their recollections of past events up to two decades later. In one study of the effects of rape upon victims, for example, Kilpatrick, Saunders, Veronen, Best, and Von (1987) found a 16.5% rate of PTSD among their sample up to 17 years after the incident.

Much of the research focusing upon the long-term impact of stressful life events has been conducted with war veterans, particularly those from the Vietnam conflict of 1965–1975. In one study conducted by King, King, Fairbank, Keane, and Adams (1998), the researchers explored the relationships between experiences of extremes of violence (e.g., war), threats to personal safety, and long-term resilience/recovery patterns. Their study, which was primarily retrospective, was conducted with 1,632 Vietnam veterans (1,208 men and 424 women) who were contacted via the Veterans Affairs Medical School in Boston, Massachusetts. King et al. (1998) proposed that post-war well-being was related to three particular factors: personal hardiness, social support, and the number of additional stressful life events veterans faced on their return home. In line with Kobasa's (1979) earlier enquiry into stressful life events, coping strategies, and personality types, personal hardiness was described in terms of three primary components: (1) the sense of having control over one's life; (2) a sense of commitment and meaning underpinning one's existence; and (3) an ability to view life changes as challenges. It was hypothesised that veterans who were deemed more hardy would be able to use coping strategies better than those who were deemed less hardy, and, therefore, were less likely to suffer from stress-related illness affecting both physical and mental health (e.g., PTSD).

The second factor in King et al.'s (1998) study was an exploration of the level of social support veterans received on return home in terms of continued social interaction, instrumental assistance, and emotional aid provided by Vietnam veteran networks and organisations. They argued that veterans who had been exposed to high levels of war zone stress but received a high level of functional social support were likely to exhibit fewer symptoms associated with PTSD than their counterparts who received little in terms of functional social support after the war.

The third factor in King et al.'s (1998) study focused upon the additional stressful life events that were likely to occur in the lives of veterans. Earlier studies of PTSD among rape victims had found that the long-term effects of sexual aggression were compounded by factors or events occurring elsewhere in the personal history of the individual: although an individual may have successfully adjusted following a traumatic episode in his or her life, he or she may remain sensitised to respond to any additional life stressors in a dysfunctional way. Thus, King et al. argued that veterans who were exposed to additional life stressors after the war were more likely to exhibit symptoms associated with PTSD than those with fewer stressors following their return home.

Added to the above three factors, King et al. (1998) also built into their study a consideration of other potential influences upon recovery rates among veterans. These included the nature of the combat to which veterans were exposed; exposure to atrocities or extraordinary episodes of violence; experiencing one or more episodes in which there was a perceived threat to personal safety; and discomfort resulting from exposure to a malevolent environment (i.e., war zone).

Among male veterans, King et al. (1998) found that PTSD was directly and positively associated with perceived threats to personal safety, exposure to atrocities or extraordinary episodes of violence, and, on return home, exposure to stressful life events. Among female veterans, they found that PTSD was also directly associated with exposure to atrocities or extraordinary episodes of violence and threats to personal safety, and, concomitantly, on return home, exposure to stressful life events.

King et al. (1998) argued that their findings illustrated that personal hardiness and social support had a significant effect upon susceptibility to PTSD. They particularly noted the fact that the indirect effect of hardiness upon PTSD through the variable "functional social support" accounted for 80% of the variance in men and 67% of the variance in women. Consequently, exposure to negative life events would have a direct effect upon the likelihood of veterans' suffering from PTSD because of their inability to expend additional personal energy in combating unforeseen stressful experiences.

Social Networks and Personal Resilience

In their model of social networking, Marsella and Snyder (1981) proposed that the efficiency of a social network in providing support for an individual is related to its effectiveness on four interconnected dimensions: structure, interaction, quality, and function. In terms of structure, Marsella and Snyder (1981) argued that the size of the network is an important factor, as is its stability (longevity), and the density or connectedness of its members (the extent to which members develop or maintain relationships independent of the network). They also suggested that networks that do not provide regular support from a collective of like-minded people are unlikely to assist the individual in coping with lifetime transitions. In terms of interaction, they argued that it is important for the individual to have a multidimensional relationship within the network, taking on more than just one role. This is especially important in ensuring that the network is, itself, self-supporting so that members engage in a reciprocal relationship where they are able to support other members of the network in addition to receiving support themselves. In addition, they suggested that this multidimensional relationship should include an appreciation of the level of support (intensity) members require to ensure their well-being. Additional features related to the interaction dimension include the homogeneity of members (do they all have similar backgrounds or experiences?), their geographic location (can they meet up easily?), and the duration or frequency of contact with members (can they meet up regularly over a number of months and/or years?).

In terms of quality, Marsella and Snyder (1981) suggested that the nature of the relationships members of the network have with each other is of considerable importance, as is the degree of intimacy they share. They proposed that the level of affiliation individuals feel towards other members of the social network will have an impact upon the efficacy of the support they receive. Thus, those who do not share a common outlook or experiential base will not gain as much from being a member of the social network as those whose experiences or backgrounds are closely connected. Finally, the fourth dimension—function—applies to the specific purpose of the network in providing support (i.e., who are its client group?), and whether or not the network is effective in providing such support.

Although King et al.'s (1998) research demonstrated that social networks can play a significant role in promoting recovery from violence or trauma, Frable, Platt, and Hoey (1998) showed that in terms of supporting marginalised groups within society, the ability of a network to assist in an individual's recovery depends on a certain degree of visibility and confidence for both network members and those who require their assistance. Where a client group is hidden or concealed, social support networks do not materialise, and thus individuals are left to cope with their difficulties alone. However, where the client group has a visible presence within society, lines of communication are established and resources are made available to those who require them.

In Frable et al.'s (1998) landmark study, they considered the potential impact social support mechanisms could have for those who had a concealable stigma (being lesbian, gay, bulimic, or coming from a family earning less than $20,000 per annum) compared to those with a non-concealable stigma (being black, overweight, or physically disabled). They hypothesised that those who had concealable stigmas were more likely to suffer from negative self-perceptions because they were unable to seek similar others.

According to Goffman (1968) and Mar (1995), individuals with concealed stigmas locate others who are similar to themselves only by attending particular venues (e.g., gay bars/clubs, clinics, and discount stores) on certain dates, or at certain times, or by wearing insignia or clothing identifying their affiliation to a particular group (e.g., a red ribbon). However, both Goffman's and Mar's hypotheses also suggest that the very act of seeking out similar others in various venues at particular times constitutes a personal statement on the part of the individual about his or her affiliation to similarly stigmatised others. Although this inconsistency in theory has been in existence for over three decades, it has never been explored fully, and, thus, it remains unclear whether or not those who seek out similar others at certain times and in certain venues are truly hidden from public scrutiny.

To explain the relationship between concealable stigmas, self-perception, and social support, Frable et al. (1998) asked 978 Harvard undergraduates to complete a 200-item personality and lifestyle questionnaire, together with a measure of depression, anxiety, and hostility, two measures of self-esteem, and a measure focusing upon participants' memberships of social networks. Their results showed that participants with concealable stigmas were found to be more anxious and more depressed than four comparison groups. They also scored negatively in terms of self-perception, self-esteem, social confidence, self-worth, and physical appearance and in their estimates of physical abilities. Those with concealable stigmas were found to spend a great deal more time in class or study than comparison groups, and tended to be alone more often. However, they were more likely to feel better about themselves and less anxious when they attended venues for similar others.

Frable et al. (1998) argued that because those with concealable stigmas are not easily identified in society and, consequently, are more likely to lack support, they may also lack expert knowledge about their social group, resulting in negative appraisals of themselves and their stigma (which may be reinforced by the mores of the society or culture in which they live). In addition, the researchers also suggested that because of the limited and biased knowledge individuals hold about their concealed stigma, they may react in a more extreme manner when they meet similar others: unlike those with positive perceptions of themselves, those with biased or negative perceptions are more likely to deny or criticise those with whom they share a common bond.

Friendship

In addition to those formal networks that seek to assist or support traumatised or marginalised groups within society, the majority of individuals can also rely upon an informal network of friends who are able to provide emotional sustenance and guidance based upon mutual attraction. According to Klinger (1977), the emotional support we receive from our friends includes such things as "loyalty, trust, intimacy and fun" (Hartup & Stevens, 1997, p. 355). Although some individuals are unsuccessful in forming or maintaining friendships, in most societies friendship is valued and sought after by the majority, and the process of seeking or maintaining friendships tends to be life-long, beginning in early childhood and continuing throughout adulthood and on into old age.

In their review of research focusing upon friendship and adaptation across the life course, Hartup and Stevens (1997) identified a number of studies showing that adolescents and young adults bereft of friendships during the early part of their development are more likely to suffer from low self-esteem, and are less likely than their more popular peers to have coped successfully with upheavals such as changing schools.

Additionally, Haugaard and Tilly (1988) suggested that, for heterosexual young people, the absence of friends during middle childhood may be a precursor of later difficulties in forming and maintaining romantic relationships in adolescence. However, in reply Hartup and Stevens (1997) have argued that such difficulties in forming or maintaining romantic relationships may not be causally related to the absence of friendships at school; rather, they may reflect individual differences in self-esteem and social confidence, which in turn may be linked to the absence of friends in middle childhood. For example, longitudinal data gathered over 12 years by Bagwell, Newcomb, and Bukowski (1996) found that sociometric status in childhood (i.e., being popular versus rejected) was a predictor of school performance, career success, personal aspirations, and sociability in adulthood, whereas simply having friends was not. However, they also found that childhood friendships not only predicted positive attitudes towards family members and feelings of self-worth, but, surprisingly, they also predicted depressive symptoms, implying that friendship may not always act as a buffer against the impact of violence or trauma.

Notwithstanding, Hartup and Stevens (1997) have suggested that friendships serve two social purposes: they facilitate the individual's well-being through the reciprocal (i.e., giving and receiving) nature of the relationship, and they provide a supportive arm in times of need. Furthermore, they argued that friendship is not a one-dimensional social interaction; it, like all human behaviour, can vary by degrees. For example, Hartup (1996) has argued that friendships vary as a function of those with whom an individual is friendly, and the level of intimacy he or she shares with each person. Thus, Hartup maintained that friendship is multidimensional, and in order to assess the efficacy of friendships as buffers against adversity it is necessary to assess their strength in terms of their content (e.g., what friends do together), constructiveness (e.g., how disputes between friends are resolved), closeness (e.g., willingness to disclose), symmetry (i.e., whether friends exert the same amount of influence on each other in terms of "social power"; p. 357), and affective character or attachment style (i.e., secure or insecure attachment).

The significance an individual attaches to friendship across the life course can be seen in the various investigations researchers have conducted relating to the number of friends we have across the lifespan. Within nursery school, correlations between teachers', nurses', and parents' reports of children's social behaviour have suggested that about 75% of preschoolers are involved in reciprocal relationships with peers (Hinde, Titmus, Easton, & Tamplin, 1985; Howes, 1989). During adolescence, this figure rises to between 80% and 90%, it remains high (approximately 90%)

until middle age, and then it tends to decline slowly (Van der Linden & Dijkman, 1989; Wright, 1989).

Various researchers have suggested that not having any friends, particularly in adolescence, has developmental significance in that it predicts outcomes such as delinquency, low self-esteem, loneliness, and depression (Vitaro, Tremblay, Kerr, Pagani, & Bukowski, 1997). However, as Parker and Asher (1987) pointed out, this prediction varies according to the reasons underpinning the individual's rejected status: those who were aggressive as children are more likely to have a record of delinquency in adolescence than those who were shy or withdrawn (Kohlberg, LaCross, & Ricks, 1972).

In their review of literature focusing upon the impact of peer relations upon later adjustment, Parker and Asher (1987) presented an alternative perspective for understanding the dynamics of children's social relationships, and their impact upon the development of the individual. Unlike many of the studies cited above, which have tended to focus upon friendships formed within an institutional setting (e.g., school), Parker and Asher suggested that researchers should take a more dynamic approach in order to understand the nature of social interaction by "stepping out of the classroom" (p. 381). They argued that in addition to comparing the behavioural characteristics of *popular* and *rejected* children, researchers should focus upon the differences between *rejected* (disliked) and *neglected* (neither liked nor disliked) children. Indeed, in Kupersmidt's (1983) study, comparison of *rejected* and *neglected* children indicated that *rejected* children were more at risk of academic failure, dropping out, and delinquency than those who were characterised as *neglected* children. In addition, Parker and Asher also argued that there is a qualitative difference between *acceptance* (getting along with one's peers) and *friendship* (forming an emotional bond to another), and that the two may not share common ground.

Beyond the school grounds, Parker and Asher (1987) also highlighted the importance of friendships with peers who are not classmates. Those who are unable to function effectively at school as a result of their social rejection may be able to function more effectively in alternative environments where they are valued and accepted. A corollary of this hypothesis is that those children who are popular outside school but not within it may not exhibit many of the long-term sequelae of peer rejection

I identified earlier in this chapter. Finally, they argued that a rejected child's non-peer social relationships with siblings, parents, grandparents, and extended family members (aunts, uncles, and cousins) may militate against factors such as delinquency, loneliness, and social maladaptation by providing not only emotional support, but also a forum whereby those social skills usually associated with peer interaction can be learnt effectively.

Personal Resilience

As I noted above, among Vietnam veterans, coping strategies and personality types played a significant role in determining the likelihood of recovery following exposure to violence and trauma. King et al. (1998) used the construct "personal hardiness" to explain why some veterans more than others were able to cope with post-war stresses, and they described this construct in terms of three primary components. Firstly, those who were described as being "hardy" had a sense of having control over their lives and believed themselves to be active rather than passive in the shaping of future experience. Secondly, they had a sense of commitment and meaning underpinning their existence and had a number of goals to strive towards. Thirdly, they showed an ability to view life changes as challenges, rather than as barriers to success. As King et al. (1998) argued, veterans who were deemed more hardy would be able to use coping strategies better than those who were deemed less hardy, and, therefore, were less likely to suffer from stress-related illness affecting both physical and mental health.

For example, in their review of the literature surrounding resilience across the lifespan, Fonagy, Steele, Steele, Higgit, and Target (1994) argued that there are a number of defining attributes of resilient children compared to their vulnerable counterparts. Such attributes include higher socioeconomic status; gender (female before puberty; male subsequently); the absence of organic deficits; easy temperament; being young at the time of the trauma; and an absence of early separations or losses. Combined with these attributes, they also argued that there are a number of social circumstances that also provide a cushion against adversity; these include competent parenting; a good relationship with at least one primary caregiver; the availability in adulthood of social support from partner, family, or other figures; a good network of informal relationships and formal social support via better educational experiences; and an involvement in organized religious activity and faith.

At a personal level, Fonagy et al. (1994) also argued that psychological functioning was an important attribute that appeared to protect young people from stress. They described such functions as a high intelligence quotient (IQ) and good problem-solving skills; superior coping styles; task-related self-efficacy; an internal locus of control; a high sense of self-worth; interpersonal awareness and empathy; a willingness or capacity to plan; and a sense of humour.

While Fonagy et al.'s (1994) summary of the defining attributes that make a resilient child are very closely associated with those factors identified by King et al. (1998) as having an impact upon resilience/recovery among Vietnam war veterans (personal hardiness, social support, and the ability to cope with stressful life events), they also identified a number of other attributes that cannot always be measured empirically (e.g., religiosity, educational experience, empathy, sense of self-worth, the ability to plan, a sense of humour, and coping style).

Fonagy et al. (1994) argued that individuals who are allowed to reflect upon their experiences (the so-called reflective self) are better able to "think of their own and other's actions in terms of mental states" and are better able to recall "'feelings, beliefs, intentions, conflicts and other psychological states in their account of past and current attachment experience" (p. 241).

Bullying and its Long-term Effects

As I described earlier, adolescents and young adults who were bereft of friendships during the early part of their development were more likely to suffer from low self-esteem, and were less likely than their more popular peers to have coped successfully with upheavals such as changing schools. In addition, the absence of friends during middle childhood may be a precursor of later difficulties in forming and maintaining romantic relationships in adolescence. However, such difficulties in forming or maintaining romantic relationships may not be causally related to the absence of friendships at school; rather, they may reflect individual differences in self-esteem and social confidence, which, in turn, may be linked to the absence of friends in middle childhood.

Researchers interested in identifying the long-term effects of bullying behaviour have also attempted to establish links between difficulties in forming romantic attachments in adulthood and peer victimisation in childhood. For example, in a study conducted in the United States, Gilmartin (1987) compared two groups of heterosexual men (one older $N = 100$; one younger $N = 200$) whom he described as "love-shy" (unable to form a lasting intimate relationship with a member of the opposite sex) to a sample of young men ($N = 200$) whom he described as being "socially successful with women and who engage in a great deal of informal heterosexual interaction including dating, partying, and lovemaking" (p. 475). Gilmartin presupposed that "love-shyness" in men was the result of an inborn temperament factor (see, for example, Eysenck, 1976), and that those with an "inhibition gene" were more likely to experience chronic bullying at school and had learnt to associate feelings of "painful, anticipatory anxiety with the thought of informal, sociable interaction with male peers" (p. 471). Based upon this presumption, Gilmartin argued that both samples of love-shy men would compare less favourably than "non-love-shys" on various measures, including the number of friends they reported, their participation and enjoyment of contact sports, and the number of intimate relationships they had enjoyed. In addition, he hypothesised that love-shys would recall a great deal more peer victimisation at school than non-love-shys, and that they were more likely to agree with the statement, "Throughout most of my life I never had any friends" (p. 473). His results showed that not only had the love-shys experienced a great deal more victimisation at school than the non-love-shys, but that they had disliked contact sports and "rough-and-tumble" play, and scored low on the Eysenck Personality Questionnaire (EPQ) scale for extroversion (Eysenck & Eysenck, 1975). Additionally, in terms of friendship, 73% of the older love-shy group (aged 35–50 years) reported never having had a friend, compared to 53% of the younger love-shy group (19–24 years). (No one from the non-love-shy group reported similarly.) Related to this finding, while 57% of the non-love-shys recalled having three or more close friends as children, this was true in no one individual from the older love-shy group and only 11%

from the younger love-shy group. In terms of sexual relationships, neither of the two love-shy groups reported having had meaningful relationships with a member of the opposite sex.

In contrast, in their study of the long-term outcomes of early victimisation among 134 Japanese male university students, Matsui, Tsuzuki, Kakuyama, and Louonglatco (1996) found that current self-esteem and affective state were linked to both experiences of victimisation in junior high school and recollections of self-esteem and affective state in elementary school.

Gladstone et al. (2006) acknowledged that there remains little empirical research on the historical and clinical correlates of bullying at school among adults. In their study, they explored the relationship between bullying and depression among outpatients attending a depression clinic. They found that bullying in childhood was strongly correlated with high levels of anxiety. Furthermore, exposure to bullying predicted higher levels of state anxiety and a tendency to exhibit anxious arousal when stressed. The authors argued that their results were compatible with the findings from other studies and highlighted the significant role bullying at school plays in adult depression and anxiety.

A decade earlier, Olweus (1993b) charted the effects of repeated victimisation in school (occurring over a period of 3 years) for a sample of 71 young men whom he followed up until the age of 23. Using teachers' and peers' nominations collected 7 years prior to the follow-up study, Olweus assessed the men on a number of measures of negative affect and social functioning to determine whether or not there was a relationship between current affective state and socialisation skills, and teachers' and peers' estimates of the victimisation.

When he compared the data gathered from the bullied participants to a comparable group of non-bullied peers, he found no indication of a systematic association between their experiences at school and being bullied in early adulthood. Nevertheless, he did find that on two related dimensions—depression and self-esteem—former victims of bullying behaviour differed significantly from their non-bullied peers, an outcome he related specifically to their experiences of school. Yet in terms of internalising characteristics such as social anxiety, introversion, non-assertiveness, and levels of stress, he found that former victims of bullying did not exhibit any of the symptoms or traits usually associated with such affect or behaviour, and thus he argued that because the young men who participated in his study were no more likely than their non-bullied peers to experience harassment at work, childhood bullying was a situational phenomenon, and not one grounded in the personality or individual characteristics of the victim. However, in the United Kingdom, Smith (1991) presented anecdotal evidence that did not support Olweus' (1993b) claim. In his article, Smith recounted the story of one 28-year-old woman who had been bullied throughout her middle school years, and as an adult she continued to experience feelings of self-doubt, anxiety, and fear when she came into contact with children. Indeed, her fear of children was such that she expressed discomfort at the thought of her forthcoming marriage and her fiancé's desire to start a family.

While studies such as those by Gilmartin (1987), Matsui et al. (1996), and Gladstone et al. (2006) have identified negative outcomes associated with school bullying, Olweus' (1993b) longitudinal study suggested that, other than an increased likelihood of suffering from depression and low self-esteem, the impact of school bullying upon adulthood is minimal, with little evidence suggesting that participants experienced harassment in later years. Yet, studies of the psychological trauma caused by work-based bullying have shown that exposure to long-term harassment, either by coworkers or line managers, can have a debilitating effect upon the individual.

Bullying at Work

According to Randall (1997), in the United Kingdom incidents of adult and workplace bullying have been so poorly recorded that only in the past few years have we been able to gauge just how serious a problem it has become. Although Adams (1992) presented a number of anecdotal reports and case studies demonstrating the various ways in which victims have been bullied at work, it has been suggested that current estimates of the number of employees who are bullied in their working environments remain speculative, as it continues to go underreported.

According to Einarsen, Raknes, and Matthiesen (1994), as with older victims of school bullying, adult samples tend to report very little overt physical aggression within the workplace (Einarsen, 2000). Verbal behaviours such as name-calling and threatening are much more frequent, as are indirect behaviours such as rumour-mongering and social isolation.

Rayner and Hoel (1997) proposed that workplace bullying should be divided into the following five behaviours: threats to professional status (e.g., belittling remarks, public humiliation, criticism relating to lack of effort); threats to personal standing (e.g., name-calling, labelling, hurling insults, intimidation, and devaluative comments relating to a person's age); isolation (e.g., withholding information or preventing access to opportunities, information, or social events); overwork (e.g., the setting of inappropriate deadlines, the exertion of undue pressure, or continued disruption of the working environment); and destabilisation (e.g., non-recognition of input, removal of responsibility, setting of menial tasks, or repeated reminders of past errors)

In her study of the incidence of workplace bullying in the United Kingdom, Rayner (1997) explored the nature of employee harassment and victimization with a sample of 1,137 part-time students enrolled at Staffordshire University. Overall, she found that 53% of her sample reported having been bullied within the working environment and that 77% had witnessed similar incidents. Although gender-wise comparisons found no significant differences in the number of men and women who said they were bullied at work, more women said they had been bullied by men as well as by women versus the number of men who said they were bullied by members of the opposite sex. In terms of the perpetrators of bullying behaviour, Rayner (1997) noted that the majority of bullying was committed by line and senior line managers (71%). Very little (15%) was perpetrated by coworkers or subordinates. In terms of the antecedents of bullying behaviour, 82% of participants said that their experiences of being bullied followed either a change of job or a change of manager, and given the relatively young age of the sample (87% were under 40 years of age), perpetrators tended to be considerably older than their victims.

In one small-scale study ($N = 30$) conducted in the United Kingdom, primarily among retail employees, Ellis (1997) found that victims of workplace bullying regularly reported a series of medical disorders, which, he argued, affected the number of days they took as sick leave. In addition to general feelings of unhappiness and lethargy, participants reported suffering from depression, migraine headaches, hypertension, skin disorders such as eczema and rashes, chest pains, muscular tension and pain, vomiting, diarrhoea, coughs and asthma, and abdominal pains. Similarly, Earnshaw and Cooper (1996) argued that issues such as work overload, hostility/persecution, and bullying/pressure management have not only resulted in employees' seeking medical assistance for occupational stress, but have also been causally attributed to serious somatic disorders, including high blood pressure and thrombosis. Furthermore, the past few years have seen a rise in the number of reported cases of PTSD associated with workplace bullying.

In Denmark, Mikkelsen and Einarsen (2008) investigated the associations between workplace bullying and psychological and psychosomatic health among 224 workers. They found that reports of bullying at work were associated with increases in psychological health complaints, psychosomatic complaints, and elevated levels of negative affect. While the studies cited above provide some evidence of somatic and psychological trauma associated with bullying in the workplace, their data suggest that the arguments supporting a link between bullying and mental health problems have some foundation.

Long-term Effects of Homophobia

In their study of 194 lesbian, gay, and bisexual American youths, Hershberger and D'Augelli (1995) found that 42% of those they surveyed had attempted suicide on at least one occasion as a result of being victimised or otherwise alienated by peers, family, or community members. In contrast, in the United Kingdom, Warren (1984) found that 20% of the teenagers he surveyed had contemplated or attempted suicide because of their sexual orientation. According to Bagley and Tremblay (1997), suicidal ideation is considerably higher among sexual minority groups than within the general population. Based upon a random sample of 750 men (identified via census data) ages 18 to 27 years living in Calgary, Canada, they found that gay and bisexual men ($N = 115$) accounted for no less than 62.5% of all attempted suicides and self-harming behaviours found among participants. Based upon these results, Bagley and Tremblay estimated that gay and bisexual men are nearly 14 times more likely to attempt suicide than heterosexual men, a conclusion that mirrors the findings of a number of previous investigators.

While Bagley and Tremblay's (1997) study did not focus particularly upon the correlates of suicidal ideation among gay and bisexual males, as previously stated, their results are drawn from a random sample and, thus, unlike the studies identified above, provided much more robust data relating to the effect that being gay or bisexual can have upon a young person.

Although in their study Hershberger and D'Augelli (1995) were cautious about linking the number of attempted suicides (42%) with peer, family, and community intolerance directly, they found that the best predictor of mental health among the young lesbians, gay men, and bisexual men and women they surveyed was self-acceptance. However, they also found that self-acceptance was intrinsically associated with the receipt of family support, but only for those who had experienced low levels of victimisation. For those who had experienced high levels of victimisation, support from family members did not mediate against the onset of mental health problems or, indeed, thoughts of suicide.

In an earlier survey of 500 young lesbians, gay men, and bisexual men and women who sought the support of the Hetrick–Martin Institute in New York (an educational and support facility for sexual minority youth), Joyce Hunter (1990) found that nearly half the youth questioned (46%) had experienced a violent assault perpetrated against them because of their sexual orientation; of that number, 61% said that it had occurred within the home. According to Pilkington and D'Augelli (1995), of the 194 youths who took part in their survey, 36% had been insulted or otherwise degraded by a member of their immediate family. When these results were analysed further, the authors found that 22% of young women and 14% of young men had been verbally abused and 18% and 8% respectively had been physically assaulted by a member of their family. The authors then asked participants to identify the perpetrators of such behavior: mothers (22%) were more likely to be abusive to their children than fathers (14%), brothers (16%), or sisters (9%). However, mothers tended to be far more protective towards their lesbian, gay, or bisexual child (25%) than fathers (13%), brothers (11%), or sisters (10%).

Parental reactions to a child's homosexuality have been found to vary considerably. While some parents are entirely accepting of their child's sexual orientation, others, as mentioned previously, have reacted with verbal taunts and physical violence. In the United Kingdom, it has been suggested that one of the reasons why mothers in particular are more likely to be abusive towards their lesbian, gay, or bisexual children arises from the fact that they may face a great deal more social condemnation than fathers or siblings because they are viewed as having been responsible for their child's upbringing. Any perceived variation in their child's development is likely to be attributed to poor parenting skills rather than any genetic, biological, or social-developmental factor outside parental control. In addition, it has also been suggested that parents use more covert and insidious forms of rejection when they find out that their child is lesbian, gay, or bisexual. For example, parents may distance themselves from their children by withdrawing affection or by excluding the child from recreational activities such as family meals, outings, and holidays. Voluntary agencies have also reported that while parents may react positively when their child "comes out," in the face of mounting criticism from others, such reactions can turn sour (Rivers, 1997a).

Evans and D'Augelli (1996) noted that the lesbian, gay, and bisexual undergraduates they interviewed reported also having to negotiate their sexual identities at college or university. Not only did they have to decide whether or not to "come out"—particularly if they share accommodation or decide to join a fraternity/sorority—but, as the murder of Matthew Shepard exemplified, they also had to decide how they were going to manage their lives on and off campus in order to avoid life-threatening situations. In one particular study conducted at a large state university in the United States, D'Augelli (1992) demonstrated the difficulties 121 lesbian, gay, and bisexual students faced living day to day on campus. D'Augelli found that most students had hidden their sexual orientation from their roommates (70%) and fellow students (80%), and 57% had also made specific changes to their lives to avoid harassment on campus. Such changes included avoiding gay clubs and venues or other well-known lesbians and gay men on campus, or pretending to have a boyfriend or girlfriend of the opposite sex.

More recently, research conducted by Savin-Williams (2005) in the United States and Taulke-Johnson (2008) in the United Kingdom suggests that there has been a general shift in societies' attitudes towards lesbian, gay, and bisexual students. Savin-Williams argued that for many young people sexual orientation is not an issue that they either hide or are particularly concerned about. Indeed, he has described such young people as "banal," suggesting that they differ little in their development from heterosexual young people. Taulke-Johnson suggested that while there remains an element of negotiation in identity management, universities provide lesbian, gay, and bisexual students with an environment where prejudice and discrimination on the grounds of sexual orientation are becoming less and less apparent. He argued that the students in his study were able to make "positive sense of their experiences, and how through careful negotiation they were able to address, explore and engage with their (homo)sexual identities and orientation" (p. 121).

Studies such as these, together with those focusing on the experiences of young lesbians, gay men, and bisexual men and women in the workforce, show that unlike many of the findings from research on school bullying, where the discriminatory factor is one of sexual orientation, victimisation is not localised, nor does it necessarily end when a young person leaves statutory education. Yet in his longitudinal study of 71 former victims of bullying (all male) whom he followed up at 23 years of age, Olweus (1993b) found no indication of a systematic association between participants' experiences at school and being bullied in early adulthood (e.g., at work, college/university). However, on two related dimensions—depression and self-esteem—he found that former victims of bullying behaviour differed significantly from their non-bullied peers, an outcome that he related specifically to their experiences at school. Yet, as previously noted, in terms of internalizing characteristics such as social anxiety, introversion, non-assertiveness, and levels of stress, he found that former victims of bullying did not exhibit any of the symptoms or traits usually associated with such affect or behaviour. Thus, he argued that because the young men who participated in his study were no more likely than their non-bullied peers to experience harassment at work, childhood bullying was a situational phenomenon, and not based upon in the personality or individual characteristics of the victim.

Nevertheless, Olweus (1993b) did not specify why his sample of 71 young men had been bullied at school, despite the fact that his earlier research had identified a number of behavioural and emotional traits that he linked to victim status (Olweus, 1973; 1993a). Furthermore, if, as Rigby (1997) has argued, young people are victimised because of their inability to participate in activities traditionally associated with their sex, then it would seem highly likely that where gender stereotypes are reinforced within the workplace, similar levels of victimisation will ensue.

In the United Kingdom, while isolated references have been made to anti-gay/lesbian/bisexual victimisation in the workplace by some researchers (Randall, 1997, for example), there have been few empirical investigations into its nature and frequency. While anecdotal evidence suggests that statements such as, "Backs to the wall, lads, here comes Gary" are a common occurrence within the work environment, there is also evidence to suggest that little action is taken by line managers or those in authority when this form of teasing becomes more direct: "I don't have to work with you, you pervert" (Moriarty, 1997, p. 19).

It has also been suggested elsewhere that the fact that a person is known to be lesbian, gay, or bisexual, can, in some environments, be taken as licence for sexual harassment. As the following extract from Cathy, a 17-year-old lesbian, demonstrates, if the perpetrator is also the employer, any attempt to fight back may result in dismissal:

> My male boss continually pestered me to have sex with him. When I told him no, he grabbed me and began to put his hand up my shirt. I told him to stop but he didn't pay any attention… He [the boss] threw me to the floor saying that he wasn't going to have some fucking homosexual working for him. (Rivers, 1997b, p. 38)

Pilkington and D'Augelli (1995) found that of the youths with work experience who took part in their survey (92%), 46% said they had felt it necessary to hide their sexual orientation at work. In a more recent study, researchers from the University of California at Davis found that less than half of their sample of 2,300 were open about their sexual orientation either at work or at school (see Rivers, 1997b). Although Pilkington and D'Augelli found that only 3% of their sample had actually experienced abuse at the hands of their employers because of their sexual orientation, 27% said that they ascribed their lack of openness about being lesbian, gay, or bisexual to a fear of losing their jobs. Similar concerns have been expressed anecdotally by researchers and theorists working with lesbians, gay men, and bisexual men and women who are employed in the military and in schools and among lesbian, gay, and bisexual academic staff in institutions of higher education (see Tierney, 1997).

Summary

Researchers in the field of developmental psychopathology have argued that traumatic events experienced in childhood and adolescence can have a long-term and debilitating effect upon the quality of adult life. While Michael Rutter (1989, 1996) provided a caveat to this argument, suggesting that the process of growing up will have an influence on the severity of the long-term outcomes associated with trauma, he also pointed out that it is impossible to eliminate the impact of early experience from the psychological schema of the adult.

The fact that homophobia has been found within most of the institutions that make up our societies means that for most lesbians, gay men, and bisexual men and women, re-victimisation and co-victimisation remain real concerns. Consequently, it is important for us to understand the resilience found among lesbians, gay men, and bisexual men and women, and explore ways in which recovery takes place and the coping styles and strategies used in later years. Therefore, to assess the psychosocial correlates of school-based bullying (in all its forms), it is necessary to consider not only the relative impact of factors such as suicidal ideation, bullying in adulthood, social support, and relationship status upon affective state, self-acceptance, and susceptibility to PTSD in adulthood, but also the personal accounts of participants. We must use their narratives to explore the ways in which they have interpreted and coped with their experiences of victimisation.

Bagley and Tremblay (1997) noted, in their study of suicidal ideation and parasuicidal behaviour among a random sample of 750 young men living in Calgary, that gay and bisexual young men were estimated as being 14 times more likely to engage in self-destructive behaviours than heterosexual young men. The authors attributed this to "family and community reactions to an emerging homosexual identity" (p. 32). Although Hershberger and D'Augelli (1995) were cautious about making a link between suicidal ideation and peer, family, and community intolerance, much of the research focusing upon self-harming behaviours among sexual minority youth (lesbian, gay, bisexual, and transgender) suggests that both personal and societal negative appraisals of homosexuality and bisexuality affect a young person's mental health and his or her susceptibility to self-harming and suicidal behaviours.

In line with Bagley and Tremblay's (1997) findings, in developing my own programme of research, it seemed likely that rates of self-harming behaviour and suicidal ideation would be affected by participants' experiences of homophobic bullying at school. Taking the reported level of suicidal ideation (20%) found by Warren (1984) in the United Kingdom as a baseline for comparison, it was expected that participants' reports of self-destructive behaviours would be higher than those reported in early studies conducted in the United Kingdom and the United States.

In the following chapters I explore the experiences of lesbians, gay men, and bisexual men and women at school and consider the ramifications of their experiences for education, policy, and practice. I also consider how education can be improved and some of the issues that the parents of young lesbians and gay men faced when they found out that their child was being bullied at school. Ultimately, my aim in presenting these data is to inform but also to explore and understand this phenomenon and its long-term effects as fully as possible.

5

The School Experience

In this chapter, I introduce three research studies I have conducted that relate to homophobic bullying. My central aim in this chapter is to illustrate the experiences that lesbians, gay men, and bisexual men and women have faced in U.K. schools. Some of the data I discuss are prospective and some are retrospective. However, unlike many other studies of homophobic bullying, my aim here is not necessarily to indicate prevalence rates (although they are important) but to provide a rich account of the lives of young people bullied in school because of their actual or perceived sexual orientation, and to provide a context in which such behaviour can be explained. Much of the work cited in this chapter has been conducted with co-authors, whom I duly acknowledge throughout, and I provide references to our articles and chapters that provide further accounts of our research.

To tell the story of my research on homophobic bullying, I have opted to provide not a chronological account but a thematic one, moving from a brief review of prevalence to individual experiences. I offer in this chapter a mixed-methods approach, combining quantitative data drawn from several cross-sectional and longitudinal studies with qualitative accounts drawn from 16 in-depth interviews and, at the end, link these back to the theories and ideas I used to inform these studies. Ultimately, I hope to provide the reader with a holistic view of the phenomenon of homophobic bullying.

Being Bullied Because You are Called "Lesbian" or "Gay"

Between 2002 and 2006, my colleague Nathalie Noret and I engaged in a series of studies on behalf of two local education authorities to

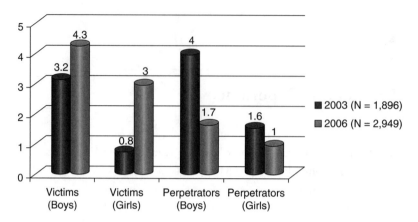

FIGURE 5.1   Prevalence of homophobic bullying in U.K. secondary schools, 2003–2006

understand the nature and correlates of bullying in secondary schools (high schools) in the North of England. Part of our survey asked students whether or not they had been bullied "Because I am called lesbian/gay," and this provided a rich source of information on the extent of homophobic bullying not only for young people who perhaps were beginning to identify with a lesbian, gay, or bisexual identity, but also those other young people who were perceived to be different and were simply labelled "gay" because it represented the ultimate insult.

As our data show in Figure 5.1, rates of homophobic bullying rose for boys and girls between 2003 and 2006, although fewer students reported being perpetrators of such behaviour. In particular, rates of homophobic bullying among girls were three times higher in 2006 than in 2003. When we looked at the data from the 2003 study in particular, we found that while rates of homophobic bullying were highest for boys (particularly in terms of name-calling, and being hit or kicked), girls were more likely to engage in rumour-mongering and social isolation. Comparing this data with Ellis and High's (2004) study, which replicated Warren's (1984) survey, *Something to Tell You*, it is clear that homophobic bullying has been on an upward trajectory since the early 1980s (Table 5.1).

In an earlier study (see Rivers, 2001a) former victims of bullying behaviour recalled the ways in which they had attempted to evade their bullies: some recalled wanting to disappear while others tried to physically

TABLE 5.1   Something more to tell you (Ellis & High, 2004)

Experience	1984 (N = 416)		2001 (N = 384)		% Difference
	n	%	n	%	
Isolation	38	9.1	137	35.9	+26.8
Verbal abuse	32	7.7	140	36.6	+28.9
Teasing	20	4.8	118	30.9	+26.1
Physical assault	19	4.8	59	15.4	+10.8
Ostracised	11	2.6	54	14.1	+11.5
Pressured to conform	11	2.6	88	23.0	+20.4
Other	23	5.5	29	7.6	+ 2.1

hide themselves away during breaks or recess, or tried not to draw attention to themselves in class:

> I kept trying to hide I think all of the time. (Alex, aged 19)
> For almost a year of my school life I spent every break and every dinner break sitting in the back of the...of the toilet area reading because I knew I was safe there, that I was isolated, and no one would give me any hassle. (Paul, aged 27)
> I think my aim in life was to keep as low a profile as possible...so, wanting to...to merge with the background. I suppose I had a few friendships, but they weren't particularly close. That's how it went on. There were flashes where, you know, merging into the background didn't actually work. So, that's how the five years passed I suppose. (James, aged 30)

James' recollection that he spent five years in secondary/high school trying to hide away was not unusual. Indeed, most participants in my first study of homophobic bullying (detailed below) recalled being bullied persistently for the same length of time.

Former victims of homophobic bullying recalled a myriad of feelings that they associated with being bullied at school. These ranged from anger and fear about being bullied to a sense of helplessness, vulnerability, and humiliation because they were unable to escape their tormentors. Significantly, the focus of their anger was not so much upon their aggressors, but on their own inaction and lack of power.

> I just get angry because I'm pointed at and people will say things about me in the classroom. (Tessa, aged 16)

I think [I felt] partly frustrated because I couldn't do anything about it…Angry as well I think. Annoyed at the fact I was being shouted at. Getting all the attention. I didn't like that. (Liam, aged 16)

I think it made me feel angry, but I wasn't in a position to have done anything about it. (Michael, aged 26)

In their interviews former victims also recalled being frightened about going to school because they knew they would not receive support from their teachers. These fears were not simply linked to unsupervised times in the school day such as break or recess; some recalled being fearful in classrooms even when teachers were present.

I can identify the emotions that I was feeling at the time because the things you experience—the emotions—that you have quite readily, and other things, and it was a real feeling of absolute panic…that things would suddenly get out of hand somehow. (Tom, aged 32)

I spent the first…I would say…two or three years in secondary school frightened on most days to go in. I was frightened of certain groups of girls. (Susan, aged 30)

I was usually chatting to the person next to me, maybe just reading or writing or something…trying not to look as if I were affected… [I felt] terrible really…very fearful I think of being attacked. (Marcus, aged 31)

As noted earlier, in addition to feelings of anger and fear, recollections of an overriding sense of helplessness were common.

I tried fighting back, but it was useless. (Nathan, aged 19)

I was a good fighter, I learnt to be a good fighter, but it meant nothing. It meant nothing. The next day I was right back to square one. (Paul, aged 27)

I suppose I should have fought back in some way, but when you have a sort of hierarchical structure in a school where it…it's boys who are in a position of power…when it's them who is [sic] doing it to you…you feel you can't fight back really. (Michael, aged 26)

Related to this helplessness, they also described feeling a sense of total vulnerability. In the absence of support from family members, teachers, or friends, some former victims remembered how they had been forced to rely upon their own counsel in order to continue through school, and the isolation they felt as a result.

> I didn't feel very secure there and that…as a consequence I kept myself to myself. (Tom, aged 32)

> [I was] even more reserved than I should have been…felt even more threatened by what was going on around me…even stronger senses of wanting to withdraw from anybody basically. (Steve, aged 30)

> I don't think I've ever reached a point [as an adult] where I've felt so vulnerable and isolated. (Matthew, aged 36)

Finally, as a result of the constant bullying they experienced, interviewees recalled experiencing a profound sense of humiliation coupled with self-criticism and self-loathing when they were at school.

> I was unclean, I was very dirty, and all I wanted to do was just wash and just get clean. (Steve, aged 30)

> I don't think anyone who isn't gay can ever understand the complete 100% humiliation you feel because all you know is you are yourself. You have no other way of expressing yourself because it's simply you. (Paul, aged 27)

> I blame myself that it went on so long because I didn't do anything to fight back. (Susan, aged 30)

So what exactly did these men and women endure at school that made them angry, fearful, helpless, or vulnerable? What were their daily lives at school like? Who supported them? Who victimised them? In the following sections of this chapter, I review the data I gathered from my first study of homophobic bullying, and comment upon the implications of these findings in terms of their relevance to the theories and ideas I outlined earlier.

The School Day: Experiences of Homophobic Bullying

When I began researching homophobic bullying, one of the first questions I wanted to answer was: *What was it like to be the victim of homophobic bullying at school?* I also wanted to know what stereotypes underpinned that behaviour. As Allport (1954) argued, where an attitude, belief, or behaviour is prejudicial, it is usually the result of the emergence of unwarranted stereotypes that seek to promote the assumption of higher social status by those who hold authority or those who constitute the majority. In my first study, which I conducted between 1993 and 1997, I explored the phenomenon, asking 190 lesbian, gay men, and bisexual men and women to recount their experiences at school (see Rivers, 2001a).

Briefly, my research was made up of three related investigations of the nature and correlates of exposure to homophobic bullying at school conducted between 1993 and 1997, following a pilot investigation. The three studies consisted of a survey of 190 self-selecting former victims of homophobic bullying (all of whom were asked to provide evidence of the names they were called at school, or evidence that the bullying they experienced was motivated by homophobia), a follow-up investigation with 119 former victims, and subsequently 16 in-depth interviews (some of the extracts have already been presented in this chapter). As the first study was retrospective, a reliability study was conducted with a sample of 60 participants completing the survey twice 12 to 14 months apart (see Rivers, 2001b).

The survey instrument I used was an extended version of the Olweus Bully/Victim Questionnaire (Olweus, 1991; Whitney & Smith, 1993). Overall, 464 questionnaires were distributed following advertisements in community newspapers and magazines and through direct approaches by the researcher to lesbian and gay organisations and support groups. Of the questionnaires distributed, 216 were returned by post (47%) and 190 complete submissions were eventually included in the study from 150 gay and bisexual men, 39 lesbian and bisexual women, and one male-to-female transgender person. The majority (97%) were Caucasian, and most attended state/public schools (84%).

The Nature of Homophobic Bullying

Overall, participants recalled being bullied because of their actual or per-ceived sexual orientation for five years on average (see Rivers, 2001b). Name-calling was found to be the most frequent form of homophobic

TABLE 5.2   Types of bullying experienced at school

Types of bullying behaviour	Men (N = 151)		Women (N = 39)		Total	
	n	(%)	n	(%)	n	(%)
I was called names	129	(85)	27	(69)	156	(82)
I was teased	88	(58)	22	(56)	110	(58)
I was hit or kicked	102	(68)	12	(31)	114	(60)
I became frightened when a particular person looked in my direction	82	(54)	17	(44)	99	(52)
No one would speak to me	36	(24)	16	(41)	52	(27)
Rumours were spread about me	86	(57)	26	(67)	112	(59)
I was ridiculed in front of others	113	(75)	21	(54)	134	(71)
I was sexually assaulted	19	(13)	2	(5)	21	(11)
They took my belongings	71	(47)	12	(31)	93	(49)
Other	53	(35)	10	(26)	63	(33)

bullying experienced by the men and women in this study, followed by being ridiculed in front of others (Table 5.2). Teasing was also reported by a large number of participants, with 60% also reporting being hit or kicked by bullies. Just under half said that their belongings were taken from them and two thirds recalled that rumours were often used to intimidate them. Just like Aaron Fricke's (1981) recollections, just over half of those who responded said that they were often frightened by the way in which a particular person looked or stared at them. One quarter recalled being isolated by their peers and 11% said that they had been sexually assaulted at school.

Contingency table analysis (χ^2) with post hoc Cramer's V test of association (φ_c; denoting the strength of the association) indicated that there were significant associations between gender and specific types of bullying behaviour experienced by participants at school. Being hit or kicked was found to be most strongly associated with gender, with the men in this study recalling such behaviour much more frequently than women, $\chi^2_{(1)} = 17.47, p \leq .0001, \varphi_c = .30$. Men were also much more likely to recall being ridiculed publicly, $\chi^2_{(1)} = 6.57, p \leq .01; \varphi_c = .19$, or being called names at school, $\chi^2_{(1)} = 5.53, p \leq .02, \varphi_c = .17$.

However, women were much more likely to recall that no one would speak to them than men, $\chi^2_{(1)} = 4.61, p \leq .03, \varphi_c = .16$.

Stereotypical Representations of Homosexuality

Former victims remember being called names that related specifically to their actual or perceived sexual orientation, together with a number of other names that related to behavioural characteristics, features, or attributions identified by perpetrators. It should be noted here that those names that are reported as not being homophobic were recalled by participants who had also been called names about their sexual orientation, or had recalled one or more homophobic experiences at school (Table 5.3).

The most common names or labels gay, bisexual, and transgendered men were exposed to at school included "poof/poofter/puff" (45) and "queer/queer boy" (33). Several names related to perceived homosexual sexual practices ("arse licker," "bummer/bum boy/bum bandit," "cock sucker," "shirt lifter," and "shit stabber"), while others emphasised gender atypicality ("fag/faggot," "girly," "mary," "queen," "sissy/sissy boy," and "woman"). For some participants, the names they received related to the various negative stereotypes recounted by Gallup (1995): these included names such as "AIDS victim," "perv/pervert/pervy," and "rapist."

In marked contrast to the names men were called, those names used to describe women in this study were few in number (4). As Table 5.4 demonstrates, the most common name women remembered being called at school was "lesbian/lesbo/lessie" (15) followed by "dyke" (6). In addition, they were also called "lemon" (a derivative of "lesbian") or "queer."

The Context of Homophobic Bullying

Homophobic bullying was reported to occur most frequently in the schoolyard (81%), followed by the classroom (68%) and the corridors (66%). A significant number of participants also recalled being bullied in the changing rooms before or after sports lessons (52%), and on the way home (62%). In addition to these locations, participants also recalled being bullied in numerous other places outside the school grounds (e.g., on the school bus, in the park, out shopping, or on school trips).

TABLE 5.3   Names and labels used by the bullies of gay and bisexual men

Homophobic name	n	Other/Uncertain origin	n
AIDS victim	1	Bastard/dirty bastard	2
Arse licker	1	Big bum	1
Batty boy	2	Big nose	1
Bender/bent	11	Brown shit	1
Blossom	1	Creep	1
Bummer/bum boy/bum bandit	5	Fat boy	1
Cock sucker	1	Four eyes	4
Fag/faggot	10	Freak	1
Fruit	2	It	1
Gay/gay boy/gay lord	7	Mange	1
Girly	2	Mo	1
Him-she-geezerbird	1	Mister dandruff	1
Homo	6	Mummy's pet	1
Mary	1	Posh git	1
Nancy/Nancy boy	3	Scabby	1
Pansy	5	Shit head	1
Perv/pervert/pervy	1	Sick	1
Ponce	1	Sieve head	1
Poof/poofter/puff	45	Smelly	1
Queen	1	Snob	1
Queer/queer boy	33	Spotty	1
Quentin (Crisp)	1	Square	1
Rapist	1	Stain on toast	1
Sailor	1	Swot	1
Shirt lifter	1	Thing	1
Shit stabber	1	Weed	1
Sissy/sissy boy	2		
Twat	1		
Wanker	2		
Wanky piss	1		
Woman	1		
Total	152	Total	30

Taken from: Rivers (2001a).

Contingency tables analysis (χ^2) indicated that the men in this study recalled being bullied in the classrooms, $\chi^2_{(1)} = 4.44, p \leq .04, \varphi_c = .16$, and on the way home much more than women, $\chi^2_{(1)} = 3.73, p \leq .05, \varphi_c = .14$. All other comparisons were not found to be significant at $p = .05$.

In terms of the frequency of being bullied, 69% of the sample reported that it occurred on a regular basis (once a week or more), with

TABLE 5.4   Names and labels used by the bullies of lesbian and bisexual women

Homophobic name	n	Other/Uncertain origin	N
Dyke	6	Hippo	1
Lemon	2	Smelly	1
Lesbian/lesbo/lessie	15	Slag	1
Queer	4	Tart	1
Total	27	Total	4

Taken from: Rivers (2001a).

the majority (56%) reporting being bullied several times a week. Participants recalled being bullied by members of their own class or year group (82%) as opposed to pupils from upper and lower years (14% and 3% respectively). A strong association was found between gender and the number of perpetrators reported by participants, $\chi^2_{(4)} = 74.5, p \leq .0001$, $\varphi_c = .63$. Men recalled being bullied most frequently by several other young men (60%), while the women in this study recalled being bullied most frequently by either groups of young men *and* women (49%) or several young women (33%). Very few men and women recalled being bullied by single members of the same sex (10% and 8% respectively) or opposite sex (0 and 3% respectively).

Very few participants (22%) reported telling their teachers about being bullied at school and even fewer (16%) said that they told a teacher the reason why they were being bullied. Significantly more women (28%) felt able to approach their teachers for support than men (20%), $\chi^2_{(1)} = 15.48, p \leq .01$ (although not all who approached their teachers disclosed why they were being bullied). One of the reasons why teachers were rarely approached related to the fact they were unsure of what to do, or worse were sometimes complicit in the bullying.

> I went to go and see the headmaster about it. He said that…well, basically…he basically said, "There is nothing I can do about it because it's such a large group. If it was 2 or 3 boys then I could sort it out, and I could have them in the office." And then he sent me to the counsellor who didn't know what to do. (Liam, aged 16)
>
> I do remember one time with him [PE teacher]. It was in the hall, we were doing gym and he asked me the time and I

responded like…I don't know…quarter to ten, or something and I heard the other kids laugh…and I was in another room because I wasn't taking PE so I was just calling. I didn't hear what he said but I just heard the other kids laugh and then he asked me again, and then he made me come out to say the time and every time I said the time, he repeated it but did a kind of John Inman act. I just used…I just had to stand there and keep repeating it while he did "puffy" interpretations and the class fell about…and it affects me more now as an adult to think that that man was in authority and he did this and the school did nothing about it. (Paul, aged 27)

Significantly more participants (39%) felt able to tell someone at home they were being bullied rather than their teacher (22%; $\chi^2_{(1)}$ = 11.28, $p \leq$ .001) and, of that number, slightly more women (49%) than men (36%) said that they had talked to someone at home (e.g., parent, guardian, or sibling). However, only 15% (7 men and 4 women) of those who had told someone at home said that they had given the reason why they were being bullied. In some instances the ways in which participants' families reacted or could react demonstrated the emotional pressure placed upon a young people to remain in hiding.

I felt so…I just hated myself so much because I didn't know what to do to make myself appear better so that people wouldn't pick on me so much, so my family wouldn't feel ashamed. Even my brothers and sisters were ashamed because I was such a puff. (Paul, aged 27)

She [mother] wants me to dress more feminine too so I don't get as much hassle at school. (Tessa, aged 16)

My dad would probably be…well, I'd expect both my parents would be shattered. Disappointed slightly as well…well disappointed. I think my mum would possibly be able to deal with it better than my dad. I think that's purely because me and my mother have always been close. (Suresh, aged 22)

Finally, 50% of those surveyed (49% of men and 54% of women) recalled that teachers never intervened on their behalf to stop bullying. Of the remainder, 34% (38% of men and 28% of women) recalled teachers intervening occasionally and 17% (13% of men and 18% of women) recalled them intervening sometimes.

Interestingly, more peers than teachers were said to intervene on the behalf of participants when they saw bullying taking place, $\chi^2_{(1)} = 8.80$, $p \leq .03$. Although 31% of the sample reported that peers never came to their assistance, 41% (45% of men and 23% of women; $\chi^2_{(1)} = 6.20$, $p \leq .01$) said peers intervened occasionally and 27% (25% of men and 27% of women) reported that they intervened sometimes. Only two men (1%) reported that peers intervened regularly on their behalf.

Avoidance of School

Of the participants who admitted to missing school, 50% reported feigning illness, 42% said that they played truant, and 5% said they avoided school in other ways. By comparison, when they were asked how often they avoided school, no significant differences were found between the sexes in terms of the frequency of such behaviour, with 81% reporting avoiding school sometimes or more often, including 22% (15) who admitted missing school at least once a week, with 16% (11) who admitted avoiding school several times a week.

Friendships and Social Isolation at School

The majority of participants in this study (59%) recalled having at least two or three good friends or more when they were being bullied. 24% reported having one good friend and only 18% recalled have no good friends at the time they were being bullied. When these results were compared according to gender, this pattern was not found to differ significantly. However, when asked how often they were left alone in the schoolyard, 67% of participants reported being left alone "sometimes" or more often, with 50% reporting being left alone at least once a week and 10% recalling being left on their own several times a week. Only 18% recalled never being on their own in the schoolyard. Once again, this pattern was not found to vary significantly according to gender, $\chi^2_{(4)} = 2.83$, ns. Indeed, for some the friendships they had were not close, or existed entirely outside school.

> I can't call them "mates" because I didn't really have any friends at school. There was one or two that I tended to hang around. (Marcus, aged 31)

I suppose I had a few friendships, but they weren't particularly close…I am basically quite shy and…and not confident and maybe even though other people have these traits, I had them a lot more than other people. (James, aged 30)

It was a bit odd actually because I didn't have any friends at school. All my friends were not associated with school at all, they were all people I grew up with when I was younger. (Tom, aged 32)

In-depth Analysis

A series of correlational analyses were undertaken to provide a better understanding of the context in which homophobic bullying takes place. One of the first analyses explored the relationships between reports of the types of bullying behaviour that participants had experienced at school and. The second set of analyses (Tables 5.5 & 5.6) focused on the correlates of the location of bullying: specifically, I was interested to see if there were associations between recollections of being bullied in various locations both within and without the school and (1) frequency and (2) Number of perpetrators. The third and final set of analyses consisted of a series of gender-wise comparisons where reports of the frequency and type of bullying behaviour experienced by participants at school were correlated according to sex; I hoped they would identify whether

TABLE 5.5   Location of bullying by frequency: Phi (φ) coefficients and significance levels

| | Frequency of bullying at school | | | |
	Once or twice	Sometimes	Once a week	Several times a week
Location				
Corridors	-.30***	-.12	-.02	.24**
Classroom	-.26***	-.14	-.01	.23**
Schoolyard	-.14*	-.13	.02	.17*
Changing rooms	-.11	-.14	.03	.15*
On the way home	-.27***	-.10	-.12	.25***
Other	-.08	-.09	.04	.08

Note: *$p < 0.05$, **$p < 0.01$, ***$p < 0.001$ (Pearson's χ^2 probability)

TABLE 5.6   Location of bullying by gender/number of perpetrators: Phi (φ) coefficients and significance levels

	Gender/number of perpetrators				
	Mainly one man	Several young men	Mainly one young woman	Several young women	Both
Location					
Corridors	-.31***	.02	.00	-.04	.18*
Classroom	-.12	.01	-.09	-.09	.16*
Schoolyard	-.20**	-.02	-.05	-.06	.19**
Changing rooms	-.09	.03	-.05	-.11	.10
On the way home	-.12	-.01	-.16	.02	.10
Other	.08	.03	-.06	-.05	.02

Note: *p < 0.05, **p < 0.01, ***p < 0.001 (Pearson's χ^2 probability)

or not there were associations between the types of bullying behaviours being perpetrated against young men and women, and the frequency with which such behaviours occurred.

Types of Homophobic Bullying by Location

Direct physical behaviours such as hitting or kicking were significantly associated with outdoor locations such as the schoolyard (φ = .25, $p \leq .01$) or on the way home (φ = .23, $p \leq .01$). By comparison, sexual assaults were associated with bullying taking place in the changing rooms of the school, most likely before or after sports lessons (φ = .20, $p \leq .05$). Reports of personal belongings being taken were related to recollections of bullying either in the schoolyard (φ = .20, $p \leq .05$) or in the changing rooms (φ = .16, $p \leq .05$).

Generally, direct verbal behaviours were found to correlate most significantly with locations within the school building. Name-calling and labelling was significantly associated with locations such as the classrooms (φ = .32, $p \leq .001$), corridors (φ = .23, $p \leq .001$), changing rooms (φ = .16, $p \leq .05$), and "other" places (φ = .19, $p \leq .05$). Teasing was more likely to occur in the changing rooms (φ = .16, $p \leq .05$). Having said that, participants' reports of being ridiculed in front of others suggested that such incidents occurred both within and without the school building;

the most significant associations were recorded in the classrooms (φ = .34, $p \leq$ .001) and corridors of the school (φ = .26, $p \leq$ .01).

Indirect or relational bullying was found to be associated with the majority of locations identified by the questionnaire. Being frightened by a look or stare was found to correlate significantly with various locations, including the classroom (φ = .19, $p \leq$ .01), corridors (φ = .15, $p \leq$ .05), changing rooms (φ = .26, $p \leq$ .01), on the way home (φ = .25, $p \leq$ .01), and "other" places (φ = .18, $p \leq$ .05). Interestingly, no significant associations were found between location and being socially isolated ("No one would speak to me") at school (all: $p >$ .05). However, rumour-mongering was significantly associated with reports of bullying taking place in the corridors (φ = .26, $p \leq$ .01) and changing rooms (φ = .27, $p \leq$ .01) at school.

Location and Frequency of Homophobic Bullying

As the results in Table 5.5 illustrate, significant positive associations were found between reports of bullying occurring several times a week with all locations excluding "other." As expected, significant negative associations were also found between very occasional bullying ("once or twice") and locations such as the corridors (φ = -.30, $p \leq$ .001), classrooms (φ = -.26, $p \leq$ .001), schoolyard (φ = -.14, $p \leq$ .05), and on the way home (φ = -.27, $p \leq$ .001).

Homophobic Bullying by Gender/Number of Perpetrators

Significant positive associations were found between reports of bullying occurring in locations such as the corridors (φ = .18, $p \leq$ .01), the classrooms (φ = .16, $p \leq$ .05), and the schoolyard (φ = .19, $p \leq$ .01) and recollections of being bullied by multiple perpetrators of both sexes.

Types of Homophobic Bullying by Frequency and Gender

Generally, direct physical behaviours such as hitting and kicking or having personal belongings stolen were associated with reports of bullying behaviour occurring several times a week ($p \leq$ .01), particularly for gay, bisexual, and transgendered men ($p \leq$ .001).

In terms of direct verbal bullying, significant negative correlations were found for both men and women in terms of reporting being called names and occasional bullying (-.26 and -.46 respectively; $p \leq .01$); however, a significant association was found between male participants' reports of name-calling and being bullied "once a week" ($\varphi = .17$, $p \leq .05$). Teasing was also found to be significantly associated with recollections of frequent bullying ("several times a week") for all the participants ($\varphi = .17, p \leq .05$), but more especially for the men in this study ($\varphi = .18, p \leq .05$). Being ridiculed in front of others was also significantly associated with recollections of frequent bullying for male participants ($\varphi = .29, p \leq .001$).

In terms of indirect or relational bullying, significant positive associations were found for male participants in this study rather than female ($\varphi = .34, p \leq .001$). Concomitantly, significant positive associations were found between reports of social isolation ("No one would speak to me") and frequent bullying: once again, these were significant for men rather than for women ($\varphi = .21, p \leq .01$).

Overall, these analyses provided me with a framework to better understand the experience of victims, but not the motivation of the perpetrator. However, in 2004, I was offered an opportunity to undertake a study that looked not only at the experiences of victims but also the motivations of those who bullied others.

Why do Bullies Bully?

Earlier in this book, I described some theories that explored the possible roots of homophobia as a group phenomenon. In the study I conducted with Nathalie Noret, supported by Nigel Ashurst, a psychiatrist, I was able to explore the world of the bully more closely. In this study, we sampled a range of students attending 13 co-educational schools (rural and urban) and one residential all-boys' school providing extended services for students with special educational needs, including those with emotional and behavioural difficulties. Supported by teachers, we asked our sample of students (N = 2,002; average age 13.6 years) to complete a battery of instruments, including an extended version of the Olweus Bully/Victim Questionnaire, which included questions for victims and perpetrators on why they were bullied or bullied others. Students also completed the adolescent version of the Brief Symptom Inventory (Derogatis, 1993), which provided mean scores on nine dimensions of psychopathology or psychological distress: somatisation (7 items; e.g., faintness, heart/chest pains), obsessive-compulsiveness (6 items; e.g., checking and double-checking things, difficulties concentrating), inter-personal sensitivity (4 items; e.g., feelings hurt, feelings of inferiority), depression (6 items; e.g., suicidal ideation, hopelessness), anxiety (6 items; e.g., nervousness, restlessness), hostility (5 items; e.g., annoyance/irritation, urges to inflict harm on another), phobic anxiety (5 items; e.g., afraid of open spaces, uneasiness in crowds), paranoid ideation (5 items; e.g., blaming others for own misfortunes, distrust of others), and psychoticism (5 items; e.g., beliefs of being punished for sins, others controlling thoughts).

We identified 188 students who were perpetrators of bullying behaviour, and found that, in comparison to those students not involved in bullying, perpetrators were more to live in family formations other than with two parents (cf. Olweus, 1993a) and were more likely to be exposed to alcohol, tobacco, and other drugs. Most significantly, we found that hostility or anger towards others was associated with victims' poor athletic or academic performance, perceived sexual orientation' and personal possessions. Furthermore, perpetrators reported most frequently bullying others whom they perceived to be gay or lesbian.

Our results added weight to the belief that perceived sexual orientation was not only used as a frequent reason for bullying other students, but together with other marks of "outsiderness" (i.e., poor athletic and academic performance) reinforced the in-group and out-group divide within schoolyard peer relationships.

Understanding Homophobia at School: Applying Theory

Allport (1954) argued that where an attitude, belief, or behaviour is prejudicial, it is usually the result of the propagation of unwarranted stereotypes that seek to promote the assumption of higher social status by those who hold authority or those who constitute the majority. To explore the nature of the prejudice participants were exposed to at school, not only were they asked to complete a revised version of the bullying questionnaire used by Smith and his colleagues in the U.K., but using a methodology similar to that employed by Kelly (1988) in Manchester, participants were also asked to list the "names" they were called, thus providing an index of the stereotypical representations that young people have been exposed to concerning homosexuality.

As I noted in Chapter 1, various studies have documented both age and gender differences in the types of bullying behaviour experienced at school by young people. However, while Warren's (1984) study made general references to the experiences of young lesbian and bisexual women, very little information was offered relating to gender differences in the types of victimisation they experienced at school. In contrast, while Pilkington and D'Augelli (1995) did compare the experiences of the male and female youths who participated in their survey, their results showed that lesbian and bisexual young women were more likely to report being victimised (35%) than gay or bisexual young men (30%), a result that does not fit the mould of previous reports of female bullying.

Name-calling and being ridiculed in front of others were the most frequently cited forms of bullying experienced by participants (82% and 71% respectively). In line with both Allport's (1954) and Gallup's (1995) stereotyping hypotheses, lesbian, gay, bisexual, and transgendered participants were, for the most part, called names that related specifically to their sexual orientation, and among gay, bisexual, and transgender (1) men, such names tended to focus upon perceived homosexual practices (e.g., "arse licker"), gender atypicality (e.g., "sissy/sissy boy"), and presumptions of illness/abnormality (e.g., "AIDS victim"). According to Gallup (see also Gallup & Suarez, 1983), homophobia arises from a general belief in Western cultures that gay men are sexually coercive and are more likely to abuse children or lead them into homosexuality. This view was supported by Mac an Ghaill (1994), who found that the young men in his study believed that being in close proximity to a gay man would not only have an effect upon their own sexuality, but might also have a more sexually invasive connotation:

> I'm not against gays as long as they don't touch me. (p. 94)
> They must be looking at you, undressing you in their minds.
> They're just sick. (p. 95)

The types of names the men in my study were called were much more varied, and much more focused towards conceptions of illness/abnormality, gender atypicality, and homosexual sexual practises, than those applied to women. Similarly, these names reinforced Mac an Ghaill's (1994) suggestion that the schools these men attended were masculinising agents that required boys and young men to earn their masculinity through a process of conformity. Where such conformity was not in evidence, those who were perceived to be different were ridiculed and provided with an alternative status within the group. As Rigby (1997) suggested in his brief discussion of the impact of HIV/AIDS on bullying behaviour, the purpose of such names or labels is also to deflect criticism away from the perpetrator by drawing attention to the actions, behaviours, or demeanour of others who are less able to defend themselves. Thus, calling another boy "gay" not only became a method by which other boys identified those who do not conform, it was also a means by which they highlighted their own conformity. This view of name-calling is reminiscent of both Klein's (1946) theory of projection, where the individual transfers unacceptable aspects of his or her own personality that are normally repressed onto others, and Goffman's (1968) theory of the existence of a subliminal "ideal" within society that all must accentuate or seek to attain or face ridicule and criticism. Indeed, as Rigby pointed out, following the advent of HIV/AIDS during the early 1980s, names that were associated with homosexuality became much more potent in terms of their impact upon victims of bullying, and thus those who did not accentuate the heterosexual "ideal" were relegated to the group labelled "faggots," identifying them to others as individuals from whom they should stay clear.

For the majority of former victims, bullying was a frequent occurrence ("several times a week"), but very few of the associations from the in-depth analysis were significant; thus, they did not offer a clear indication of who the perpetrators were likely to be (in terms of their gender and number). Having said that, being socially isolated was significantly associated with being bullied by groups of young men *and* young women, and, based upon Craig and Pepler's (1995) observation of Canadian schoolchildren, this suggests that once a pejorative name or label was associated with a particular individual, peers would either collaborate with the perpetrator(s) or would keep their distance. Indeed, analysis of the data provided by participants relating to friendships at school indicated that being alone in the schoolyard was not only related inversely with the number of friends they had when they were being bullied, it was also related (but positively this time) with frequency of being bullied. This is very reminiscent of the seventh stage of Lemert's (1967) model of labelling wherein the victim is "isolated and vulnerable and unable to call on support from others" (Besag, 1989, p. 46). However, Lemert also argued that once a name or label is ascribed, the victim "fully accepts the role which has been allocated to him/her" (p. 46). The idea that a student "fully accepts" the role he or she has been allocated by peers is problematic. It suggests that where a name or label relates to a person's sexual orientation he or she may actually take on a homosexual identity and, perhaps, act out those behaviours popularly associated with being "gay." This would seem to be an oversimplification of the effect of name-calling and labelling upon a young person, and, as I show below, may be interpreted differently.

Olweus' (1978) assertion that 75% of those children he identified as victims of bullying behaviour were "clumsy children" was potentially flawed because he had inadvertently "bought into" a self-fulfilling prophecy. He drew heavily upon the fact that male victims were physically weaker than their aggressors, which, together with "a certain sensitivity and anxiousness, lack of assertiveness and self-esteem" (p. 140), he believed contributed to their social rejection at school. However, such a profile does not necessarily equate with motor deficiency. It could also be argued that children, especially boys, who are physically weaker than their peers, and are anxious in social situations, are more likely to fail or, at the very least, are likely to be perceived as being unable to compete effectively with their peers in activities such as sports where good eye–hand coordination is required. Thus, such a negative appraisal by peers and, correspondingly, by teachers could result in a boy being relegated or otherwise passed over in sporting activities which would not only promote further the popular perception of his poor coordination skills, but also deny him the opportunity to practice those skills and thus improve upon them. This argument can also be employed when considering Rigby's (1997) observation relating to those children who were labelled "fats" (if girls) and "faggots" (if boys) by their peers because they were unable to contribute to sporting activities. While it has been argued that each child or young person has the potential to rid himself or herself of his or her label by being given the opportunity to demonstrate his or her proficiency in one or another culturally valued activity, it is clear that the unwillingness of peers to surrender a name once established often means that the cycle of abuse can continue until a young person leaves school. Therefore, rather than children or young people accepting a name or label as part of their social identity (as Lemert, 1967, suggested), they may not be given the opportunity to effectively challenge such a name or label, and thus it becomes part of their social identity for others.

Much of the bullying that participants were exposed to was localised within their own class or year group. This suggests that homophobic bullying may not have been school-wide, but concentrated specifically to those classes in which victims sat. If this were found to be the case more generally, it suggests that, where homophobia is found, intervention strategies implemented on a class-by-class basis may be more effective than whole-school strategies, ensuring that the appropriate level of intercession is exercised without drawing undue attention to the issue—especially where parents are concerned about the welfare of younger pupils. Secondly, as the data illustrated, homophobic bullying was rarely carried out by individuals of either sex (10% among men and 8% among women); it was generally a group activity where the perpetrators, their cohorts, and bystanders forcibly ostracised individuals who did not conform to the institutionally avowed standard. If, as Mac an Ghaill (1994) suggests, it is true that among young men "masculinity" is a prize that has to be earned, then the inherent competition within the traditional educational philosophy would, by design, seek to separate out or otherwise identify those who accentuate "masculinity" and those who do not. As the results show, the victimisation experienced by gay, bisexual, and transgendered men in this study was primarily perpetrated by groups of young men who, it is suggested, were ensuring that they would not be associated with an individual who did not conform in order to promote their chances of achieving the prize of "masculinity."

If one follows the logic underpinning Mac an Ghaill's (1994) sociological analysis of statutory education, it then becomes apparent that, to facilitate a change in behaviour, there must be a concomitant change in the philosophy or ethos of the educational system. I discuss this further in Chapter 8.

Although verbal abuse was found to be the most common form of victimisation reported by former victims, both physical and indirect methods of aggression were also very much in evidence. Of considerable interest was the fact that a small but not insignificant group of participants (19 men and 2 women) recalled being sexually assaulted at school, an issue rarely mentioned in the educational literature. Furthermore, where this occurred, there was little evidence from participants' responses to indicate that the school and/or teachers were aware of it and able to take action. A significant association was found between reports of sexual assault at school and bullying taking place in the changing/locker rooms, suggesting that this was the most likely venue for such behaviour. Indeed, the changing/locker rooms were associated with most types of bullying behaviour identified in the survey instrument, which again reinforces Rigby's (1997) earlier comments about the central role that sports play in the definition of those who are members of the in-group, and those who are relegated to out-group status—particularly among men.

According to Griffin (1995), the intense homophobia often found among athletes in the U.S. is a result of the fact that the sports field has been culturally conceptualised as "a training ground where young boys learn masculine skills" (p. 55). She argues further that, unlike many other public venues, the sports field allows men to openly demonstrate their emotional closeness to each other without fear of chastisement or ridicule. In addition, concomitant with the emotional intimacy she describes comes physical closeness, where the admiration of "physicality" is central to athletic prowess.

Changing/locker rooms therefore represent a situation where there is an opportunity for physical contact between men and, by implication, between women who are in a state of undress. Consequently, it suggests that the fact that an athlete is lesbian, gay, bisexual, or transgendered will result in some form of sexual interaction or coercion (re: Gallup 1995) or, at the very least, sexual gratification for the individual observing his or her teammates (Klein, 1989).

Peer Collusion

Craig and Pepler (1995) argued that peer collusion in bullying shows not only disrespect for the victim and support for the perpetrator, but also their (the peers') assumption of higher social status in the unofficial hierarchy of the playground or schoolyard. They suggested that bullying is a

group process very similar in nature to that of mobbing (English definition) where the victim is harassed by multiple perpetrators. In addition,
Festinger et al. (1952) argued that an individual who is a member of a
group will be released from certain internalised moral constraints that
would normally inhibit violent or aggressive acts, thus reducing his or
her personal responsibility for his or her own behaviour and, by implication, that of others. However, in the U.K., Whitney and Smith (1993)
found that much of the bullying that took place within primary and
secondary schools was perpetrated by individuals rather than groups,
suggesting that deindividuation theory is not a perspective that has overly
concerned researchers working in the field. Yet, where the issue underlying bullying behaviour is one of sexual orientation, it would seem fea-
sible to assume that deindividuation theory has a role in explaining this
form of aggression.

Significant associations were found between participants' recollections of being bullied in the corridors, classrooms, and schoolyard, and
being bullied by groups of young men and young women, rather than by
individuals or groups of same-sex peers. Similarly, in terms of the nature
of the bullying experienced, significant positive associations were also
found between participants' recollections of rumour-mongering, being
called names, being socially isolated, and having belongings taken, and
being bullied by groups of peers (same-sex and mixed). In terms of frequency, the results show that in terms of both the nature and location of
bullying behaviour, positive and significant associations were found with
reports of being bullied "several times a week," especially for those who
were hit or kicked, who were frightened by a person's look or stare, who
were socially isolated, who were ridiculed before others, or who had
their belongings taken.

According to Olweus (1994), the term "bullying" is used only when
there is an imbalance of strength between perpetrator and victim: "the
student who is exposed to the negative actions has difficulty in defending
him/herself and is somewhat helpless against the student or students who
harass" (p. 1173). As previous researchers have demonstrated, this imbalance of strength may be the result of factors such as age, or it may be the
result of the number and/or physical strength of the perpetrator. Early
research on bullying behaviour suggested that perpetrators sought popularity and status by demonstrating the "power" or control they had over

others. For some, this acquisition of "power" over other children was necessary to counter increasingly poor academic performance; for others, it was necessary to counter their average-to-low popularity among their same-age peer group, which may also explain why they choose victims who are themselves failing, or not reinforcing a particular stereotype.

Where bullying takes place because of a child's or young person's cultural or ethnic background, it tends to be perpetrated by peers in the same class or year group as the victim, rather than by those in upper or lower years. Why should this be so? According to Boulton, young people tend to gravitate towards those from their own ethnic or cultural group, rather than exploring relationships with young people from different backgrounds (see also Boulton & Smith, 1992). Similarly, until relatively late in their school career both boys and girls tend to remain within same-sex, same-age peer groups, preferring the company of those who are both physically and emotionally similar to themselves. As a result, social interaction among children and adolescents is founded upon the categorisation of people on a same/different basis, and such categorisations are influenced by the cultural stereotypes children are exposed to from an early age. Thus, those who are considered "different," for whatever reason, may find themselves isolated by members of their same-age peer group who are themselves attempting to demonstrate their similarity to others (the in-group). In terms of the experiences of the former victims of bullying behaviour I surveyed, bullying not only acted as an affirmation of heterosexuality for perpetrators, it was also a demonstration to others (both at school and further afield) of their dissimilarity to those who were perceived to be culturally and/or socially undesirable.

Peers would have faced a great deal of pressure not to intervene when participants were being bullied by groups of young men and/or young women. As Salmivalli et al. (1996) argued, other pupils may intervene only where such action has little cost to themselves (e.g., where they are older than the victims, the perpetrators, and their supporters). Furthermore, since most of the bullying reported by former victims was localised within the same class or year group, the potential for intervention by older pupils was theoretically limited (such limitations resulting not only from the indirect nature of much of the bullying that occurred, but also as a consequence of the reasons underpinning it). Indeed, as Mac an Ghaill's (1994) study illustrated, pupils are cautious when interacting with other pupils or teachers who have come to the aid of young lesbians, gay men, bisexual, and transgendered men and women, and perceive them as having being contaminated or, at the very least, "affected" by their intervention:

> It's like you look after the weak ones, so you've probably been affected by it and you see things different. (p. 95)

Teachers

In Pilkington and D'Augelli's study (1995), 7% of their sample reported being hurt by a teacher when they were at school, especially the young women (11% for women and 7% for men). While very little continues to be known about the rate of bullying perpetrated by teachers who appraise homosexuality negatively, or, indeed, the level of support lesbian, gay, and bisexual students receive from members of staff at school, anecdotal evidence has suggested that some teachers may actively collude with students in victimising or harassing another student who is perceived to be lesbian, gay, or bisexual.

Very few former victims in my study recalled having told a teacher about being bullied at school. While significantly more women said that they had felt able to tell a teacher compared to men, only a small minority disclosed the reason for their bullying (16%). In addition, when one considers the data gathered from other studies of school bullying, the data imply that when bullying is related to an individual's sexual orientation, fewer participants may be willing to tell a teacher. Given that just over one quarter of former victims of homophobic bullying said that they believed they had been bullied by a teacher because of their actual or perceived sexual orientation, approaching a member of staff for help may have been seen as an unquantifiable risk—especially in schools where sex or religious education presented homosexuality as sinful or aberrant, or, as previously mentioned, where teachers did not actively sanction homophobic language or abuse.

Alternative Sources of Support: Family and Friends

Overall, the results from the survey of former victims of homophobic bullying indicated that significantly more had told someone at home when compared to the number who had told a teacher. However, very few (6% of the total sample) said that they had felt able to disclose why they were being bullied. Interestingly, of the 169 participants who had "come out" at the time they were surveyed, just over one quarter said that they had been relatively open about their sexual orientation while they were of school age, indicating that the majority had kept and continued to keep their experiences of bullying a secret from family members. Consequently, few families were given the option or opportunity to offer support because of the stigma participants associated with being bullied at school.

Contrary to expectations, two thirds of former victims recalled peers intervening on at least one occasion, with just under a half recalling intervention occasionally and one quarter receiving assistance "sometimes" or more often when they were being bullied. Notwithstanding, two thirds also reported being left alone in the schoolyard during breaks and recess "sometimes" or more often. Furthermore, of those who were asked about the number of times they avoided school, just under three quarters indicated that they had either feigned illness or played truant "occasionally" or "sometimes" to escape being bullied. Thus, school was a solitary experience with little social interaction or involvement in recreational group activities for many.

Case Study: David

On the first day at my new high school I was full of a kind of optimistic trepidation. I was very pleased that I had come this far and I was happy to be surrounded by potential new friends. I did not know that it would be the start of something terrible, and that I would soon be playing truant and taking Valium because I was the subject of violence and ridicule.

It all started one morning after registration. A boy from the same year group yelled "poofter" and, like everyone else, I turned around to see who he was shouting at. It was me. From that day I was subjected to beatings and verbal abuse. Many, many, many times things were stolen, not just by my bullies, but also by classmates. I was branded "a gay" and was punished for being gay. There was one particular boy, who though he never touched me, always stared at me. One day I asked him why and he said, "I'm not sure if you are a boy or a girl."

The injuries I received during my time at school are too many to recall. I had my left arm broken by bullies and all they said to me was that I was lucky it wasn't my right arm. Cigarettes were stubbed out on the back of my neck as I was held down by the bully's drones. I was kicked repeatedly even when a teacher was nearby. One teacher told me that my problems were my own fault because I refused to say that I was straight. My days at school were frightening, and in the end I stopped going. I found refuge in a local café, and there I met other school kids who were bullied. Away from school, I could be me, but eventually I had to return. Prescribed Valium to help calm the fear, I failed my exams. After five years of high school I left, hooked on Valium, with little in the way of a future.

6

Practical Issues for Parents and Teachers

In this chapter I present data from some of the qualitative studies I have conducted with parents of lesbians, gay men, and bisexual men and women who have been bullied or harassed at school. I review some of the legal cases and human interest stories that have brought homophobic bullying and harassment to the attention of the courts. I also present some of the resources I have written or edited on behalf of the U.K.'s Health Development Agency (HDA; now the National Institute of Health and Clinical Excellence) on tackling homophobic bullying. I am grateful to the institute's legal department for allowing me to reproduce the materials in this chapter. My aims in this chapter are to provide an overview of the lived experiences of parents whose children have been victims of homophobia at school, and to provide guidance to educators and administrators in schools on how to address the issue of homophobia and homophobic bullying in particular.

Parents and Homophobia

Building upon my early research with former victims of homophobic bullying, between 2002 and 2005 I gathered stories and reminiscences from the parents of women and men who had been bullied or otherwise harassed because of their sexual orientation at school. It is not my intention in this chapter to present all of the data I have collected, but rather to demonstrate the profound effect that bullying has upon a family. I also hope to illustrate how parents are often the last to know, not only about their child's sexuality, but also about the child's experiences at school.

Perhaps one of the most profound stories I heard was that recounted by a senior academic with a strong track record in equalities research. In her story she describes how her daughter's experiences of homophobia were ignored and she was left without personal and professional resources to take on an uncaring system:

> I am angry that I was so "disabled" by an uncaring schools system. I was also unaware of any source of support for me or for her [my daughter]. My ex-husband was not comfortable dealing with issues of sexual orientation—or with "authority." I am shocked now by my own ineptitude and that of the school.

As she reflects on a missed opportunity to help her bisexual daughter, the word this mother used to describe herself—"disabled"— epitomises the power schools are perceived to have in deciding whether or not to tackle abusive behaviour perpetrated by students or by staff. It was clear in this case that the school system did not take seriously the issue of homophobic bullying or her daughter's complaint that, at age 14, she was being sexually harassed by a male teacher. This is not uncommon in the stories I was told. For example, another mother told me how powerless she felt when her son came home complaining that he had been bullied by a senior member of the teaching staff.

> I spoke to other teachers about it and was told that he [the teacher] was like that in the staff room. The teacher who was homophobic was the assistant head and that week he married the head teacher of the school, so I was unable to talk to either of them personally. I wish that I had complained at a higher level. I suppose that I was scared that my son wouldn't be able to cope because the teacher was in a senior position and there may have been repercussions. I wanted to go to the person and explain about the pain they had caused.

Such powerlessness was a common feature in many of the stories that I heard from parents and from former victims of homophobic bullying. However, not all parents know that this type of abuse goes on. For some the revelation that their child has been the subject of constant harassment comes as a blow to their perceptions of their abilities as mothers and fathers. As the following extract taken from a letter I received from an educational psychologist with a gay son illustrates, even the most vigilant parent does not always see the challenges that his or her child faces at school:

> I'm ashamed to say that I was not really aware of what he had to contend with at school, neither from the perspective of being gay

and struggling with his sexuality, nor from the bullying he daily put up with. He demonstrated all the classic signs of a youngster in crisis. The irony is that I was a psychologist for the secondary school my son attended, and I managed to miss what was happening. Was I deaf and blind?

As Frable et al. (1998) pointed out, one of the difficulties faced by children or young people who have a hidden stigma is the fact that they often try to compensate or adapt their behaviour to fit in with others. For example, Martin, the son of the educational psychologist mentioned above, wrote that he did everything in his power to hide the difficulties he faced at a new school in a different part of the country.

MARTIN'S STORY

I was always an outgoing boy but not in the real "boyish" sense. I got by on wit; I could always raise a laugh and was probably perceived as been a bit different, even extrovert. Right from day one I had problems. The girls rallied around me, they loved the way I pronounced their names in my English accent, "Go on, say Sharon again." The boys hated me for the attention I got. As I have said, I didn't like regular boyish things. I just hated P.E. (Physical Education) and sports of any kind. I am diabetic and so I could muster up endless sick notes. I annoyed Mr. ****, the P.E. teacher, no end; I was pathetic when forced to participate in any team games. In desperation one day he shouted, "Away and join the knitting group."

My absolute lowest point in school was age 15. I was totally confused, not so much about my sexuality, I knew I was gay, but about what I should do or not do about it. I was making up stories about having girlfriends to put my parents off the scent. At the same time I felt totally isolated, the only gay boy in the school-town-world. I was smoking, drinking, not eating, not controlling my diabetes at all well, which was literally life-threatening.

I was really bad at maths, and I found myself in the special help group at school. Each session was like entering some kind of black hole.

I never quite knew what I would meet in there, but for certain it would be a bad experience. A new student, a girl, from another school entered the class. She managed to make life even more of a hell than I thought possible. She punched me, spat at me, stuck chewing gum on my clothes and in my hair. I just couldn't tolerate any more. Physical fighting broke out between us. Still teachers did nothing. At the same time, within the same class was a boy called Simon. Simon would chose always to sit next to me, calling me names, "poofter," "shirt lifter," etc., in an alliance with the girl. Again, nothing was said or done by school staff.

I was really good at English. I wrote an essay about a gay boy who was being bullied at school. I got a really top grade. No one seemed to make any connection between the fictional character and my plight. If they did, there was no one on hand to support me. If they had offered me support, I am not sure what I would have done.

Martin eventually "came out" to his parents; he described this not only as "a relief," but also as a turning point where it ceased to matter who knew, and he felt he could get on with his life. His parents were supportive and subsequently took part in many annual gay pride events, but it was only long after he had "come out" to them that he told them about his school experiences.

For some parents, a child's decision to "come out" can be an isolating experience. Who can they tell? Where do they go to seek advice? The following extract demonstrates the isolation and soul-searching that some parents face as they come to terms with their child's sexual orientation. It may be particularly difficult for those with a strong faith or belief, or those who fear the repercussions of disclosure in their local communities.

CHRISTINE'S AND NEVILLE'S STORY

Our relationship with our son has always been close and we felt guilty that we had not sensed any underlying tension. We grieved that he would lack much in his life that we have taken for granted in ours. We felt as confused and isolated as he must have done when he was "in the closet." It was difficult to accept that our son could experience prejudice, inequality, and injustice, not for anything that he had chosen or done, but because society disapproves of homosexuality.

It was more than two years before we felt confident enough to tell anyone, and yet we wanted and needed to talk as others do about their families and their relationships. We questioned God. We worked through the seven or so texts in scripture quoted as proof that God too disapproves of homosexuality. They did not support our belief in a God of Love. But in the Gospels we found no mention of homosexuality, only Christ's command that we love one another and His warning that we are not to judge.

The paradox of our experience is that is that it has strengthened us as a family. It has increased our belief in the power of love—God's love, family love, the love of friends, Christian and non-Christian, to whom we have "come out" as parents of a gay son. Amongst such family and friends, our son has found love and acceptance as a gay person in ways that he never thought possible, nor would have known, if he had not been given the courage and the strength to face the risks involved in leaving "the closet."

It is four years since we learned that we have a gay son. By God's grace our family has survived. Others are less fortunate.

The "paradox" that homosexuality brought this family to understand both God's love and the meaning of love among themselves and friends demonstrates that faith, in reality, does not require us to discriminate against lesbians, gay men, and bisexual men and women. The strength in this story lies in the fact that this family found their own God through scripture, and not through the church. Yet they too had to deal with the knowledge that school had not been a safe space for their son, and while he had not endured many of the torments described in earlier chapters, it was only when he left to go to university that he felt he was finally entering an educational environment that was "safe and non-threatening."

Neville and Christine demonstrated that a young person's homosexuality, or indeed bisexuality, does not provide those who promote intolerance or perpetrate acts of aggression with the excuse that they have right on their side. The condemnation of homosexuality, particularly condemnation by those in positions of power or authority, can never provide a moral defence for acts of discrimination or harassment. While many religious communities have made supportive statements about the inclusion of lesbian, gay, and bisexual people in their congregations, it would also be true to say that there is often a perception that all faiths condemn homosexuality. So what exactly do the various faiths say about homosexuality and, more particularly, homophobia?

Homophobia, Faith, and Belief

The role that faith plays in the maintenance of negative attitudes towards lesbians, gay men, and bisexual men and women is one that continues to be a source of anxiety for those who wish to build schools that embrace diversity and support parents and young people who identify as lesbian, gay, or bisexual. Within Judaeo-Christian traditions, the Book of Leviticus (18:22) clearly states that men cannot lie with other men.

Thou shalt not lie with mankind as with womankind: it is abomination.

Yet some scholars argue that such rules and ordinances, which form part of the Torah's *Holiness Code,* apply only to members of the Jewish faith, as the following excerpt suggests (Angell, 2003, p. 9):

> Orthodox Judaism has always perceived the Torah to be the record of God's revelation to the embryonic Jewish nation. Only Jews are expected to abide by all 613 precepts. According to ancient rabbinic sources, non-Jews to be considered righteous need only adhere to a much smaller number of rules, none of which relate to homosexuality.

By the time of the Protestant Reformation in the fifteenth century, the majority of laws and ordinances found within the *Holiness Code* had long been abandoned by Christian denominations; however, the laws relating to homosexuality were retained. Nevertheless, between the thirteenth and eighteenth centuries same-sex marriages were sometimes allowed by the Roman Catholic Church, even taking place before the altar, as the following extract from Michel de Montaigne's diaries of his travel through Italy between 1580 and 1581 illustrates (see Boswell, 1996, pp. 264–265):

> Two males married each other at mass, with the same ceremonies we use for our marriage, take Communion together, using the same nuptial Scripture, after which they slept and ate together.

In 1991, the Church of England's House of Bishops published a document entitled *Issues on Human Sexuality*, in which they concluded that committed same-sex relationships are acceptable among the laity, but not among clergy, and that Christians should reject all forms of hatred against lesbians and gay men, and protect those who are victimised.

Indeed, in his capacity as Prefect of the Congregation for the Doctrine of the Faith, Cardinal Joseph Ratzinger (later Pope Benedict XVI) wrote to bishops in 1986 stating the Roman Catholic Church's opposition to homophobia and its requirement that priests condemn it:

> It is deplorable that homosexual persons have been and are the object of violent malice in speech or in action. Such treatment deserves condemnation from the Church's pastors wherever it occurs.

While many Muslims today condemn homosexual acts as sinful and unlawful, the Qur'an describes male sexual intercourse as deviant and excessive. Some of the Hadith (a collection of sayings attributed to the Prophet Muhammad and other early religious leaders) condemn it in far stronger terms. Punishment today varies according to the ways in which religious laws in a particular country draw upon the Hadith. While some states impose the death penalty on those who engage in homosexual acts, others require no physical punishments at all.

For the majority of Buddhists, personal relationships are exactly that—personal. Loving relationships should not be condemned as sexual misconduct. In his text *Beyond Dogma*, the Dalai Lama pointed out that homosexual sexual behaviour is not in itself improper, but any sexual act (heterosexual or homosexual) that involves parts of the body other than the genitals is sexual misconduct. However, in 1997, the Dalai Lama's spokesperson made it clear that he opposed all forms of discrimination, including that experienced by lesbians and gay men:

> His Holiness was greatly concerned by reports made available to him regarding violence and discrimination against gay and

lesbian people. His Holiness opposes violence and discrimination based on sexual orientation. He urges respect, tolerance, compassion, and the full recognition of human rights for all.

Clearly, with the exception of more conservative Muslim states, many faiths today condemn acts of violence perpetrated against lesbian, gay, and bisexual people, and where homosexuality remains illegal the way in which nations choose to deal with this issue varies dramatically. In the end, faith is not a barrier to promoting the safety of all young people in schools, and as I show below, a failure to ensure the safety of lesbian, gay, and bisexual students can be costly.

The Risks of not Addressing Homophobic Bullying at School

While personal beliefs about the acceptability or unacceptability of homosexuality and the right to express those beliefs are guaranteed under the First Amendment to the Constitution in the U.S., we should also remember that the Fourteenth Amendment ensures that all citizens receive equal protection under the law. In the U.K., the Human Rights Act guarantees freedom of speech as long as it does not inhibit the human rights of any other group within society. Thus, victims of bullying do have the right to seek legal redress, and that right has been exercised successfully.

Ultimately, the risks of not addressing homophobic bullying within the school can be seen in the gradual increase in legal cases being brought before the courts by students and their parents. For example, in 1996, a Wisconsin school district was forced to pay damages of $900,000 after the 7th U.S. Circuit Court of Appeals ruled that the school district had violated a student's right to equal protection under the Fourteenth Amendment. Subsequently, in 2004, a school district in California was forced to settle out of court (which included legal fees estimated at $1.1 million) following a case that involved a group of students who were taunted with sexual slurs and pornography, and, in one case, was physically assaulted by peers. The school district's case was based on the understanding that as public servants they were immune from legal action because their obligation to protect students against homophobic attacks was unclear. Lawyers acting on behalf of the school district also argued that the efforts that it made to tackle the issues absolved the district of liability. The 9th U.S. Court of Appeals disagreed; the judges determined that inaction on the part of school administrators to address the harassment experienced by the students constitutes intentional discrimination. Several states (Alaska, California, Connecticut, Florida, Massachusetts, Pennsylvania, Rhode Island, Utah, Vermont, and Wisconsin) have now adopted specific legislation or introduced regulations that prohibit discrimination on the grounds of sexual orientation in elementary and secondary education.

DONOVAN *ET AL.*, V. POWAY UNIFIED SCHOOL DISTRICT *ET AL.* (2008)

Megan Donovan and Joseph Ramelli entered Poway High School in California as freshmen in 2000. They endured what was described as "severe, pervasive and offensive" peer sexual orientation harassment while attending high school. They experienced death threats; being spit on; physical violence and threats of physical violence; damage to personal property; and name-calling such as "fag," "faggot," "fudge packer," "dyke," and "fucking dyke."

Megan, Joseph, and their respective parents had met with the school principal, Scott Fisher, to complain about the harassment these young people had experienced and witnessed at the school. They had also complained to the superintendent of the district, Donald Phillips, and to the assistant principal, Ed Giles, about the harassment.

In court, lawyers acting on behalf of the district claimed that it had "adequately" responded to the harassment by Megan and Joseph, and that Megan and Joseph had not provided them enough information about the perpetrators for the school or district to take action.

After a trial of six weeks, the jury found for Megan and Joseph. The district was found to have violated Section 220 of the California Education Code, which prohibits discrimination on the grounds of sexual orientation (as well as other protected characteristics) in any activity that is conducted in a publicly funded educational institution. The school's principal and assistant principal violated Joseph's rights of equal protection, and the principal alone had violated Megan's rights of equal protection. The superintendent was not found liable. The jury awarded Megan Donovan $125,000 in damages and Joseph Ramelli $175,000.

At the appeal, the District argued, among other things, that the jury had been erroneously directed by the judge. The appeals court ruled that, as principal, Fisher was the "appropriate person" to act on behalf of the District to "address the alleged discrimination and to institute corrective measures" to end the discrimination experienced by Megan and Joseph. Therefore, the jury's verdict stood in relation to Section 220 of the California Education Code, and the district was liable for "its own wrongdoing based upon its legally insufficient response to harassment."

For parents and educators in the U.S. this particular case is significant because it demonstrates that a school's failure to take appropriate and demonstrable action resulted in a lawsuit. While there are few similar cases elsewhere in the world, in the U.K. the case of Laura Rhodes demonstrates how systemic failures in dealing with issues of homophobic bullying can result in the death of a young person.

LAURA'S STORY

Laura Rhodes died of an overdose at the age of 13 in September 2004 in Wales. She died as part of the suicide pact she had made with a 14-year-old friend whom she met on the Internet and with whom she had developed an extremely close relationship. Laura's mother blamed the school for much of Laura's unhappiness as a teenager. She had been the subject of a number of homophobic taunts and jibes as well as hurtful comments about her weight. These taunts had become more frequent after Laura had told a friend that she may be gay. Although the school maintained that it did everything to support Laura, the head teacher acknowledged that all the strategies available to the school had been exhausted in an attempt to ensure Laura's safety.

However, Laura's education had suffered as a result of her unhappiness at the school. She refused to attend school and complained that she was fearful of what would happen when she went into the class-room. Eventually she was removed to a separate education unit, where reports suggest that many of the problems she encountered in her school dissipated. There had been suggestions that Laura was clinically depressed or had a chemical imbalance that resulted in her difficulties at school. However, assessment by a community psychiatric nurse indicated that there was no organic basis to her unhappiness, so attention once again turned to the actions of the school.

Following Laura's death, at the coroner's inquest a child psychiatrist stated that whilst Laura's problems were not caused by the school, her decision to form a suicide pact with a 14-year-old girl was motivated by their fears of separation from each other and the fear of homophobia. In returning a verdict of suicide the coroner said that it was indisputable that Laura was unhappy at school; however, the situation at school was not at the root of the suicide pact. Laura's parents did not accept the fact that the school did all it could to deal with the bullying that Laura faced on a daily basis and decided to pursue the case further through the courts. Subsequently, in an article in *The Times* (4th April, 2005), reporter Lewis Smith received documents that showed that Laura was regarded by the school and by employees of the local authority as the author of her own misfortune, and that the most appropriate solution was to remove her from the school. Furthermore, it was reported that the psychiatric assessment was done at the behest of the school three weeks after Laura had complained about being bullied. In the end Laura's parents dropped their case, but questions remain. Did the school and its head teacher do enough to support Laura? And was it easier to remove the victim than to tackle the problem of homophobic bullying?

Laura's parents published the following letter, which she wrote shortly before her death.

There we were, outside the school, people looking at this fat lump which is myself but oh well. "Bye Dad, see you tonight." I did not want to leave the car, I wanted to die. I walked to the doors, down the corridor, here are boys standing just before the stairs, legs out, waiting to trip me up, how wonderful.

I hated it so much. I used to talk to myself in my head, only thing that kept me OK to live. Why were they doing this? Why me? I was fat. Still a person. It had gone on for six months now, same thing every day. I saw some boys laughing at the fact I was fat and possibly a "dyke." I wanted to cry so much but I couldn't. I had on Friday, I can't again. At last! Here Mrs. Stephens comes: "Morning 7c, nice weekend?" I felt like saying "Oh yes, it was wonderful. I cried all the time. How was yours?" But no one cared anyway, so what was the point? Yes, I have told my parents. They thought I just didn't like going to school. Anyone else heard that one? So great, no one believed me while I got fatter and fatter and sadder and sadder. Everyone got meaner and meaner.

I was standing clutching my bag, holding myself together as if to let go of this bag would be to let go of any pride, or anything I had left. I wasn't too stubborn to ask for help. I did ask, but they did not pay any attention.

AT LAST! The final run, HOME. I rush down the road, holding the tears back. "Hiya, how was school?" "Fine," I replied. Didn't seem any point in saying anything else, did there? They didn't listen. "I'm going to the loo." I didn't enter the bathroom. I went into the box room, I took out scissors, I knew what I was doing. Maybe this would show them what they are doing.

I dragged it over my wrists a few times, the next few times pressing harder, it felt really good. It hurt, but I pressed harder. S***, there was a mark, a deep red one, what can I do?

However, intransigence is not the only reason why schools fail to tackle homophobia. In their study of educators' beliefs about raising lesbian, gay, bisexual, and transgender issues in schools, Schneider and Dimito (2008) found that 68% of teachers did not feel that enough resources were available in schools to deal with issues of sexual orientation or gender identity. Furthermore, 60% felt that they had not had appropriate training or sufficient opportunity to attend workshops on these issues, and 56% believed that parents would protest if sexual orientation or gender identity were raised in school.

The Responsibilities of Educators

In the U.K. and in many states in the U.S., policy statements about good behaviour that include references to sexual orientation are becoming common, and thus now require educators to take responsibility for their enforcement. A school that is determined to challenge homophobic bullying should have a nondiscrimination policy that includes clear and unambiguous statements about actual or perceived sexual orientation. The New Jersey Department of Education (NJDOE, 2006) provides an excellent model of good practice in which schools are required to have a definition of harassment, intimidation, and bullying that is *no less inclusive* than the following:

> Harassment, intimidation and bullying means any gesture or written, verbal or physical act that is reasonably perceived as being motivated either by any actual or perceived characteristic, such as race, color, ancestry, national origin, gender, sexual orientation, gender identity and expression, or a mental, physical or sensory handicap, or by any other distinguishing characteristic, that take place on school property, at any school-sponsored function or on a school bus and that:
>
> a. a reasonable person should know, under the circumstances, will have the effect of harming a student or damaging a student's property, or placing a student in reasonable fear of harm to his person or damage to his property; or
>
> b. has the effect of insulting or demeaning any students or group of students in such a way as to cause substantial disruption in, or substantial interference with, the orderly operation of the school.

School administrators in New Jersey are required to develop and implement procedures that ensure that perpetrators of bullying (students or members of staff) face appropriate consequences and also that all such behaviour should take into account personal (life skills deficiencies, social relationships, talents, traits, hobbies, strengths and weaknesses) and environmental factors (school culture, staff ability to prevent and manage inflammatory situations, community connectedness, neighbourhood and family circumstances). Table 6.1 provides an eight-point guide to help schools ensure that they are prepared and able to tackle homophobic bullying. Each point has been phrased as a question, and requires schools

TABLE 6.1   Challenging homophobic bullying in your school: Eight points for demonstrating good practice

Question	Where can you locate this evidence?	Is this an action point for your school?
School administration		
1 Can you demonstrate that you challenge and respond to homophobic bullying as part of a school behaviour policy?	• School Non-Discrimination Policy?	☐ No (If not, why not?) ☐ Yes
	• School Handbook?	☐ No (If not, why not?) ☐ Yes
	• Student Handbook?	☐ No (If not, why not?) ☐ Yes
2 Can you provide evidence of commitment to promoting inclusion and challenging homophobic bullying when it occurs?	• Is homophobic bullying on the agendas of teachers' meetings?	☐ No (If not, why not?) ☐ Yes
	• Is homophobic bullying on the agenda of PTA/PTSA meetings?	☐ No (If not, why not?) ☐ Yes
	• Is it an item on the agenda of school council meetings?	☐ No (If not, why not?) ☐ Yes
3 Can you demonstrate how homophobic bullying is monitored and addressed through surveys/audits and through student disciplinary procedures?	• Do you record incidents of homophobic bullying?	☐ No (If not, why not?) ☐ Yes
	• Do you conduct student surveys or hold student consultations on this issue?	☐ No (If not, why not?) ☐ Yes
	• Do you report back to students and parents on your activities to challenge all forms of bullying?	☐ No (If not, why not?) ☐ Yes
Curriculum and resources		
4 Do you have an opportunity to address homophobia and homophobic bullying within the curriculum?	• Do you promote debates on social issues among students?	☐ No (If not, why not?) ☐ Yes
	• Do you plan classes that deal with different forms of discrimination, including homophobia?	☐ No (If not, why not?) ☐ Yes
5 Do you make resources available to teachers, parents and students about homophobic bullying?	• Are those resources available in the library?	☐ No (If not, why not?) ☐ Yes
	• Are those resources online and easily accessible?	☐ No (If not, why not?) ☐ Yes
	• Are those resources permitted by the School Board?	☐ No (If not, why not?) ☐ Yes
	• Have staff been trained to use resources?	☐ No (If not, why not?) ☐ Yes

TABLE 6.1   Challenging homophobic bullying in your school: eight points for demonstrating good practice (*continued*)

Question	Where can you locate this evidence?	Is this an action point for your school?
Supporting students and parents		
6 Do you provide an environment that supports students who are distressed as a result of homophobic bullying?	• Do you guarantee confidentiality on issues of sexual orientation?	☐ No (If not, why not?) ☐ Yes
	• Have teachers, school counsellors, and administrators received training on homophobic bullying and the appropriate way to support students (recognising any legal limitations)?	☐ No (If not, why not?) ☐ Yes
	• Does the school celebrate diversity and demonstrate its commitment to equality (e.g., posters)?	☐ No (If not, why not?) ☐ Yes
	• Are procedures for reporting bullying clear, and how do you ensure students understand them?	☐ No (If not, why not?) ☐ Yes
7 Do you provide parents with a means of raising concerns about all forms of bullying, including homophobic bullying?	• Does it appear in the School Handbook?	☐ No (If not, why not?) ☐ Yes
	• Does the PTA/PTSA have a role in supporting parents concerned about bullying?	☐ No (If not, why not?) ☐ Yes
8 Do you ensure that letters/communications to parents are non-discriminatory (i.e., do not always assume that a student has two parents, or that her/his parents are heterosexual)?	*Have you checked:* • School Handbook?	☐ No (If not, why not?) ☐ Yes
	• Student Handbook?	☐ No (If not, why not?) ☐ Yes
	• Student Record System?	☐ No (If not, why not?) ☐ Yes

to evidence their activities to ending homophobic bullying (see Rivers et al., 2007).

Addressing Homophobia at School: Suggested Activities

So how can parents and teachers ensure that homophobia is addressed in school effectively? The following pages provide examples of some classroom activities that may help teachers address the issue of homophobia with students of different ages. The activities were developed for use in U.K. schools but have resonance in other educational contexts. These activities were developed following a review of Sex and Relationship Education in English schools by the Office for Standards in Education (OfSTED, 2002).

In the U.K. education is divided into four key stages, with each key stage relating to an age group. At key stage 1 (5- to 7-year-olds; equivalent to U.S. kindergarten and first grade), students should be able to demonstrate the following:

- Awareness of their feelings towards others and that their actions have consequences for others
- An understanding of friendship and love and be able to talk about the differences between them

At key stage 2 (7 to 11 years; equivalent to U.S. elementary school, second to sixth grade), students should be able to:

- Understand the concept of relationships
- Understand the different "types" of relationship they may have
- Understand that families come in many shapes and sizes
- Form opinions and articulate arguments about the meaning of difference, their own understanding of difference, and society's views of difference
- Feel good about themselves and others, and have a positive view of their own and others' self-worth
- Understand the emotional impact bullying and homophobic bullying in particular can have upon an individual, a school, and a community
- Consider how a person who is bullied feels, and discuss ways in which it can be challenged

At key stage 3 (11 to 14 years; equivalent to U.S. middle school, sixth to eighth grade), students should be able to:

- Understand the emotional nature of opposite-sex and same-sex relationships
- Develop an awareness of the different types of families that exist today

- Understand the impact society, religion, and culture have upon the way in which lesbian, gay, and bisexual people live, thus gaining insights into why some people feel it necessary to hide
- Recognise that relationships come in different forms, and that all relationships based upon love and commitment are worthwhile
- Develop an empathic understanding of the experiences of those who have experienced homophobic bullying through case-study material

Finally, at key stage 4 (14 to 16 years; equivalent to U.S. high school, ninth and tenth grades), students should be able to:

- Develop an understanding of alternative life-styles/sexualities and others' views of those life-styles/sexualities
- Offer a considered view of the ways in which lesbians, gay men and bisexual men and women are discriminated against, the reasons underpinning their discrimination and how such discrimination can be tackled
- Challenge offending behaviour and contextualise such challenges through an appreciation of the ways in which discrimination on the grounds of sexual orientation is legislated against
- Appreciate the contributions lesbians, gay men and bisexual men and women make to society and consider how each would feel if they worked with someone who is lesbian, gay or bisexual

The activities presented here are designed to be "light touch" and flexible, integrating current practices and developing connections between children's and young people's experiences and their abilities and backgrounds. I have provided a minimum of two activities for each key stage.

The key stage 1 activities address specific issues dealing with respect for people who come from different family formations and the meaning of "family." The "Whose Baby" activity is not about colour, but about acknowledging that children and young people should be treated equally and respectfully whether they have two parents (same-sex or opposite-sex) or one parent, or come from families where they live with adoptive or foster parents. While the images are presented here in grey, originally the baby was green and the parental combinations were made up of blue, yellow, and green.

The key stage 2 activities consider the different ways various groups were persecuted during the Holocaust. The aim here is to offer students the opportunity to consider how multiple groups can be discriminated against, and to reflect upon the ways in which we discriminate today. Finally, the activities ask students to consider how they can challenge discrimination and bullying behaviour in their own schools.

At key stage 3 students are asked to consider why homophobia exists and in what ways lesbians, gay men, and bisexual men and women differ from heterosexual men and women. Students are also asked to consider why homophobia exists, and to review their own school's anti-bullying policies and practices. Discussion and debate are essential elements of the activities at this stage.

Finally, at key stage 4 students are asked to consider why students hide away, and are presented with a number of case studies that provide them with discussion points. In particular, they are asked to focus on their own school's policies and practices and to construct a letter in which they tell a young gay man why he would feel safe in their school.

As I noted earlier, these examples are provided with the permission of the HDA. Should they be used, it is requested that the following acknowledgement is given, "edited and containing material developed by Ian Rivers and commissioned by the Health Development Agency."

Key Stage 1 (Activity 1): Who is in My Family?

Introductory activity

Question:

1. What is a family?

Guidance:

A family does not always live together.

A family is where we feel safe.

In a family we look after each other.

Main activity

While students are constructing their imaginary families, ask them to do the following:

1. Label each member of their family (e.g., mother, father, sister, brother, etc.).

2. Explain to the person sitting next to you the relationship each family member has with each other.

Reflection

Question:

1. Why do you think there are so many families?

Teacher Guidance

Purpose:

The purpose of this activity is to consider the different forms families take.

Time:

50–60 minutes

Material required:

Paper, magazines, scissors, glue

Introductory activity (5 minutes)

Ask students to explain what they understand by the word 'family'? Point out that families come in different shapes and sizes.

Main activity (30 minutes)

Students should work in pairs and make an imaginary family from cuttings and images provided. Point out that no every family includes natural parents, and that some people come from foster or adopted families, and that these are just as important as natural families.

Reflection (5 minutes)

The purpose of this task is to bring the class together so that each pair can describe the families they have created. At the end ask why students think some people's families are different from others.

Key Stage 1 (Activity 2): Whose Baby?

Introductory activity

Questions:

1. Are all families the same?
2. How many people are in your family?

Main activity

While students are constructing their imaginary families, ask them to consider the following:

1. Explain whose baby it is.
2. How many different combinations can you find using the key?
3. How many couples have a baby?
4. How many single people have a baby?

Reflection

Question:

1. Why do you think there are so many families?

Teacher Guidance

Purpose:
The purpose of this activity is to develop students' awareness and understanding of the fact that we come from different sorts of families, and no one family unit is better than the other

Time:
30 minutes

Material required:
Transparencies or powerpoint

Introductory activity (5 minutes)
Refer back to the last activity in which students made collages of families. Recap on the different families the class created.

Main activity (15–20 minutes)
Using the images provides (which can be enhanced by the use of colour), ask students to identify the different combinations of families the baby can have. Use Whose Baby Image 1 as the guide for students. Whose Baby Images 2 and 3 provide some answers for students based upon single parent and couple families (same-sex and opposite sex).

Reflection (5 minutes)
This task is about respecting different families. Suggest to students no one family type is better than the other.

Whose Baby? Image 1

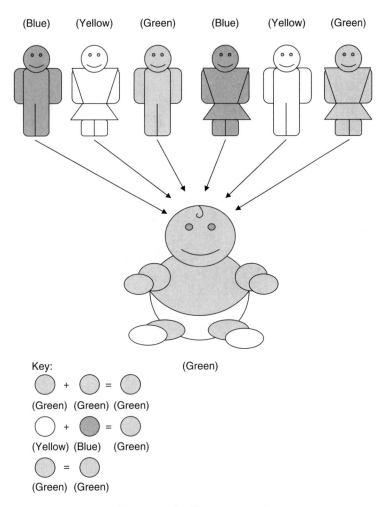

How many families can you see?

Whose Baby? Image 2

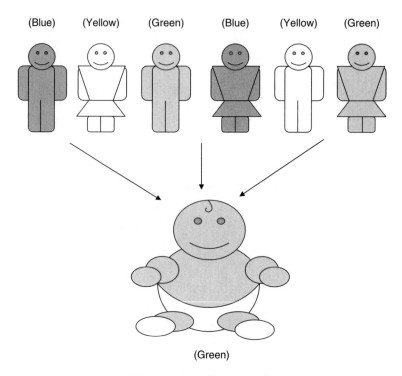

How many families are there?

Whose Baby? Image 3

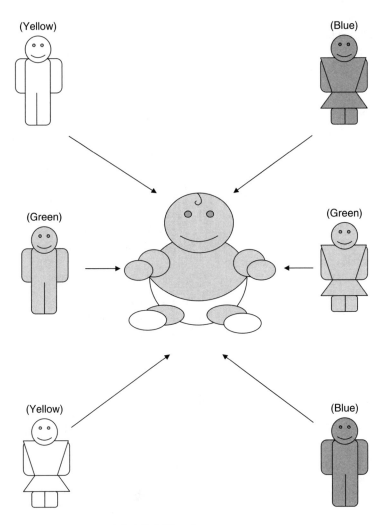

(Yellow)

(Blue)

(Green)

(Green)

(Yellow)

(Blue)

Not all children have two parents

Key Stage 2 (Activity 1): Homophobia, What is It?

Introductory activity

Question:

1. What is homophobia?

Main activity

Part 1

Question:

1. Do you know the significance of the pink triangle?

Part 2

Yellow Star—Jews

Yellow Triangle—one Jewish parent

Black Triangle—Communists, Socialists, Gypsies, prostitutes

Red Triangle—political prisoners

Blue Triangle—emigrants

Green Triangle—criminals, murderers

Lilac Triangle—religious prisoners, priests

Note: Those who wore a green triangle were often put in charge of the others.

Reflection

Question:

1. What do we use today to identify people as being different?

Teacher Guidance

Purpose:

The purpose of this lesson is to explore the meaning of 'homophobia'.

Time:

40-50 minutes

Material required:

None

Introductory activity (10 –15 minutes)

Ask the question, what is homophobia?

Main activity (20 minutes)

Part 1 (10 minutes)

Ask students to speculate on the meaning of the pink triangle. Explain to them the significant of the colour pink and its association with homosexuality.

Part 2 (10 minutes)

In this part talk about the Second World War and the significance of the stars and triangles in the concentration camps. The significance of the other triangles should be explained.

Reflection (10-15 minutes)

Ask students to consider why such symbols were used? Explore with students the ways in which we identify people who are different today e.g. social isolation, name-calling, bullying.

Key Stage 2 (Activity 2): Homophobia, Who Does it Affect?

Introductory activity

Question:

1. Why did people wear stars and triangles in prison during the Second World War?
2. Can you remember what the colours mean?
3. Do you think the people who imprisoned these people were afraid of them? Why?

Main activity

Begin by making a list of all the different types of bullying students have seen. Ask the following questions:

1. What do you think you would do if you heard someone being called "lesbian" or "gay"?
2. Why do you think some people are called "lesbian" and "gay" at school, and others are called different names?
3. Do you know what the school's anti-bullying policy says?
4. Is homophobic bullying included? If not, should it be?

Reflection

Question:

1. Why do you think homophobic bullying was/was not included in the school's anti-bullying policy?

Teacher Guidance

Purpose:

The purpose of this lesson is to explore 'homophobia' in detail.

Time:

35–40 minutes

Material required:

School's anti-bullying policy

Introductory activity (10 minutes)

Reflect upon the previous lesson and the fact that although prisoners were sent to concentration camps for different reasons they were treated the same. Stress that people are treated unfairly for lots of different reasons, and some people find it easy to use one name or one symbol for all people they dislike.

Main activity (20 minutes)

Ask students to describe the different ways in which they have seen people being bullied at school. Write them down so they can be seen. Then ask students to think about what they would do if someone else was bullied because of their sexual orientation. Go on to explore the school's anti-bullying policy.

Reflection (10–15 minutes)

Take a vote: should homophobic bullying should be kept/included in the school's anti-bullying policy?

Key Stage 2 (Activity 3): Not In This School!

Introductory activity

Question:

1. What is homophobia?

Main activity

Provide groups of students with a large sheet of paper to design a poster entitled, "Not In This School."

Not In This School

Reflection

Allow each group 2 minutes to describe how their poster addresses all forms of bullying.

Extension

A natural extension of this activity is to allow students to finish their posts and display them on school notice boards next to copies of the school's anti-bullying policy.

Teacher Guidance

Purpose:

The purpose of this activity is to develop students' awareness of all forms of bullying.

Time:

60 minutes

Material required:

Large sheets of paper, paints, coloured pencils/pens

Introductory activity (10 minutes)

In this activity ask students to explain all the different types of bullying that occur in schools.

Main activity (40 minutes)

In groups of 304 ask students to design an anti-bullying poster which includes all forms of bullying entitled, 'Not In This School'.

Reflection (10 minutes)

Ask students to describe their design to the class. Close by commenting on the different ways the posters address all forms of bullying

Key Stage 3 (Activity 1): Homophobia

Introductory activity

Questions:

1. What is homophobia?
2. What does it mean to be homophobic?
3. Why do you think people are homophobic?

Main activity—group Task (3 or 4 students)

Questions:

Part 1

How many different ways do you think people express homophobia?

Part 2

In what ways are lesbians, gay men, and bisexual men and women different from heterosexuals?

Part 3

What would a class statement about valuing difference say?

Reflection

Question:

If <u>applicable</u>:

1. Should we include lesbians, gay men, and bisexual men and women in this statement?

Teacher's Task:

Draft a statement and put it to a vote.

Teacher Guidance

Purpose:

The purpose of this activity is to get pupils to think about homophobia in terms of their own behaviour.

Time:

60–80 minutes

Materials:

None

Introductory Activity (10 minutes)

To begin the class ask a series of questions about homophobia and why people are homophobic. Record their answers

Main Activity (30–40 minutes)

Part 1 (10 minutes)

Groups should list all the different ways in which they think that homophobia can be expressed.

Part 2 (10 minutes)

Groups should list all the ways in which they think Lesbians, gay men and bisexuals are different to heterosexuals.

Part 3 (10 minutes)

Develop a class statement about valuing difference

Reflection (15–20 minutes)

Ask the class to vote on adopting the statement. Consider under what circumstances such a statement might be considered problematic and why.

Key Stage 3 (Activity 2): Homophobia

Introductory activity

Questions:

1. What is homophobia?
2. Do you think homophobic bullying is an issue for this school?
3. Do you think we challenge homophobia enough in this school?

Main activity—group Task (2–4 students)

Ask each group in turn to write a short statement about homophobia at school.

Consensus statement:

'This group believes...."
A spokesperson for each group should read out the statement.

Reflection

Class Statement:

The statement should begin with:

"This class has voted on and adopted the following amendment to the School's Anti-Bullying Policy."

Teacher Guidance

Purpose:
The purpose of this activity is to consider whether homophobic bullying is an issue the school should address.

Time:
40 minutes

Materials:
School's anti-bullying policy

Introductory Activity (15 minutes)
To begin, ask students to reflect upon what they have learnt about homophobia and how it might affect their school. In this activity students should debate and reach a consensus on whether or not homophobia is wrong. Stress that all views are respected, all views are valid, and there are no wrong answers.

Main Activity (20 minutes)
In groups, students should devise a statement about homophobia. Each group should then read out their statement

Reflection (15–20 minutes)
Students should vote on the statement they wish to adopt as an amendment to the anti-bullying policy. This amendment should then be reproduced and recommended for inclusion in the school's policy.

Key Stage 4 (Activity 1): Feeling Different

Introductory activity

Questions:

1. Why do people hide?
2. What sorts of feelings do you think are associated with hiding away?

Main activity—group task

Questions:

1. How would you feel if this happened to you?
2. Do you think the person in the story has any other options other than hiding?
3. How would you advise her/him?

Reflection

Question:

1. Do you think the reasons why Paul, David, and Justine tried to hide are the same?

Possible extension

This lesson could be extended by using interactive drama methods. If the class group is used to demonstrate and explore issues through drama, the scenes could be processed by role-play.

Teacher Guidance

Purpose:

The purpose of this task is to consider why people feel they need to hide away from others

Time:

30–40 minutes

Materials:

Extracts from the resource sheet provided for each group

Introductory Activity (10 minutes)

Students should consider why people want to hide away from others. They should consider the ways in which people 'hide' from others at school, and the feelings associated with hiding.

Main Activity (20 minutes)

Give each group one story to consider and ask them to answer the questions provided

Reflection (15-20 minutes)

Each extract should be read out in turn with pupils feeding back their answers to the three questions. End with the last question.

Feeling Different: Resource Materials

Extract 1: Paul is a young gay man

For almost a year of my school life, I spent every break and every dinner break sitting in the back of the toilet reading because I knew I was safe there, that I was isolated, and no one would give me any hassle.

Extract 2: David is a young man with special needs

It was easy for me not to go to school. Mum and Dad worked and I often left the house after them and got back before them. They didn't know I was not going to school. I didn't do homework, the boys would take my bag off me when I got to school and throw the books about. When I didn't have my homework I couldn't tell the teacher it had been thrown away so I got into more trouble. It was better to stay at home.

Extract 3: Justine is a young woman of colour

I liked my old school, but not my new school. In my old school I had lots of friends who were also of colour; in this school, I'm the only girl of colour. In class it's OK, but I hate break and dinner time. I get called all sorts of names because of the colour of my skin and because of the beads in my hair. This is supposed to be a better school, but I don't like it and I want to go back to my old school.

Key Stage 4 (Activity 2): Feeling Different, Being Gay

Introductory activity

Questions:

1. How did the experiences of Paul, Susan, and Justine differ?
2. How do you think society views people who are lesbian, gay, or bisexual?

Main activity

Part 1: Individual Task

Questions:

1. How does Aaron describe being "gay"?
2. Why has he not told all of his friends?
3. How important do you think it is for Aaron to know there are other people in the world like him?

Part 2: Class Letter to Aaron

Questions:

1. If Aaron were at our school would he feel safe?
2. Would other lesbian, gay, or bisexual people feel safe?
3. Would Paul or Susan be welcome?

Reflection

Questions:

1. Is our school a safe place for Aaron?
2. If not, how can we change it?

Teacher Guidance

Purpose:

The purpose of this ___ is to consider what it is lik___ being lesbian, gay and bisexual, a___ d how difficult it can be to go to sch___ ol.

Time:

60 minutes

Materials:

Aaron's letter

Introductory Activity

(15 minutes)

Ask students to consider what they learned in Activity 1 and answer the two questions posed.

Main Activity (30 minutes)

Part 1 (15 minutes)

Student should read Aaron's letter. Ask them to identify how Aaron feels about being gay. Provide students with an opportunity to feedback on the questions asked.

Part 2 (15 minutes)

As a class draft a letter to Aaron telling him how supportive school is. Outline any changes you have made to the anti-bullying policy. If no changes have been made, pupils should focus on the questions provided

Reflection (15 minutes)

Ask students to reflect upon all they have learned about their school, guide questions are provided.

Feeling Different, Being Gay: Resource Materials

Letter from Aaron—aged 16

I experience homophobia indirectly every day of my life. I have the pleasure of being gay (although only out to my three best friends) at the most homophobic school ever! No one is out at my school, and so it is impossible to see how people really would react around a gay boy or lesbian, but that doesn't stop verbal abuse and comments. A couple of examples (toned down): "He's gay? Someone needs to hang…" and "F**king homo freaks, scum of the earth." It is no wonder then why no one would want to come out.

This in turn causes its own problems, aside from the obviously abusive things said. Firstly, it makes it almost impossible to find anyone else who is gay to talk to or form a relationship with, leading to feelings of isolation and loneliness. It's only through the Internet that I have been able to talk to other gay people and establish a sense of self-worth. Secondly, when you are coming to terms with your sexuality it can be extremely depressing and as your only experiences of people's opinions are these, you can become very lonely. I was coming to terms with being gay two years ago when I was 14, and during that time I came to view myself as disgusting and unnatural. I could only see a lifetime of fear and rejection ahead of me and it got to a point where I took some pills out of the medicine cabinet and seriously contemplated suicide. I decided in the end, though, that I shouldn't be made to feel bad if some ignorant, narrow-minded, Nazi people had a problem, and cheered up.

After that I started talking to people on the Internet and about 6 months later told my best friend (girl) who turned out to be bi. Since then my other two best friends found out through a combination of me telling them and bad secret keeping on my bi-friend's behalf. I am constantly thankful that rather than being "ok with it" they are actively supportive, encouraging me to go out and get a boyfriend and to talk about it.

I still wouldn't come out at my school, people there don't seem to mature as they age, but now I am completely comfortable with being gay and would strongly urge anyone feeling as bad as I did to talk with some people who are gay/bi/lesbian first and not just accept the opinions of those immediately surrounding them.

Gay in both senses of the word

Reproduced with permission of Gay Youth UK (www.gayyouthuk.org).

Summary

In this chapter, I have introduced the issue of homophobic bullying from the perspective of parents and teachers. In particular I have been keen to emphasise the fact that homophobic bullying affects families and schools in different ways. For parents, the knowledge that their child has been bullied because of his or her actual or perceived sexual orientation can be a terrible revelation: not because their child is lesbian, gay, or bisexual, but because they were oblivious to the daily taunts that he or she experienced at school. As the parents in this chapter attest, being alone and not knowing where to turn is a common experience. So too is a feeling of helplessness or powerlessness in the face of the school machine. For teachers, as Schneider and Dimito (2008) illustrated, a lack of guidance and a lack of access to resources can result in a school seeming impotent when faced with incidents of homophobic bullying. This was perhaps the central issue in the story of Laura Rhodes. The school had exhausted all avenues open to it to support Laura, and actually what teachers at that school needed more than anything else was information on how to support young people dealing with the complex issue of sexuality in adolescence. Nevertheless, failure by a school to respond appropriately when homophobic bullying occurs can have dire consequences for all involved. As the cases of Megan Donovan and Joseph Ramelli illustrate, local authorities, administrators, and educators may be held liable where there is evidence that they failed to take sufficient action to stop bullying from taking place. There can be no excuse for letting young people suffer abuse at school, whatever the reason underlying that abuse. In the following chapter I introduce some of my findings that demonstrate why homophobic bullying should be taken seriously.

7

The Legacy of Homophobic Bullying
at School

Previously I suggested that researchers in the field of developmental psychopathology argued that traumatic events experienced in childhood and adolescence have a long-term and debilitating effect upon the quality of adult life. While Rutter (1989, 1996) provided a caveat to this argument, suggesting that the process of growing up has a moderating influence upon the severity of the long-term outcomes associated with trauma, he also argued that it was impossible to eliminate entirely the impact of early experience from the psychological schema of the adult.

I also suggested that the fact that homophobia can be found within most of the institutions that make up society means that for most lesbians, gay men, and bisexual men and women the opportunity to put their experiences of victimisation behind them is rarely realised, and, consequently, demonstrations of resilience and/or recovery are more likely to be linked to individual coping styles and strategies rather than the result of the process of maturity. To assess the psychosocial correlates of school-based bullying (in all its forms), it is not only necessary to consider the relative impact of factors such as suicidal ideation, bullying in adulthood, social support, and relationship status upon affective state and self-acceptance, it is also necessary to consider the personal accounts of participants, and, as Mason-Schrock (1996) has shown, to use their narratives to explore the ways in which they have interpreted and coped with their experiences of victimisation.

In this chapter, the results will be presented from the second (quantitative) and third (qualitative) studies I conducted on the nature and long-term correlates of homophobic bullying. Data are presented from a follow-up study of 119 men and women who participated in my original retrospective study of the nature of homophobic bullying. Comparable with the previous chapter, I have opted to include extracts from the interviews I conducted with 16 participants, to provide a rich picture of

the long-term impact that participants believed school-based homophobic bullying had upon their lives.

Key Issues to Consider

Self-harming Behaviour

In their study of suicidal ideation and parasuicidal behaviour among a
random sample of 750 young males living in Calgary, Bagley and Tremblay
(1997) found that gay and bisexual young men were 14 times more likely
to engage in self-destructive behaviours than the heterosexual young men
who participated in their study. They attributed this to family and community reactions to participants' emerging gay or bisexual identities.
Although Hershberger and D'Augelli (1995) were cautious about making
a link between suicidal ideation and peer, family, and community intolerance, much of the existing research focusing upon self-harming behaviours among sexual minority youth (lesbian, gay, bisexual, and transgendered)
has suggested that both personal and societal negative appraisals of homosexuality and/or bisexuality have an impact upon a young person's mental
health and his or her susceptibility to self-harming behaviour.

In my follow-up study with 119 former victims of homophobic
bullying, I thought it likely that participants would not only report self-
harming behaviours in adolescence as a result of their experiences of
intolerance at school, but also that self-harming behaviour could be
compounded by the difficulties they had faced in coming to terms with
their sexual orientation. Indeed, as I found in a matched control study
I conducted with Nathalie Noret (Rivers & Noret, 2008) among a
sample of same-sex- and opposite-sex-attracted secondary school students (N = 106), after controlling for exposure to bullying behaviour,
same-sex-attracted youth were more likely to report having symptoms of
negative affects than their opposite-sex-attracted peers.

Bullying in Adulthood

Within the general work-based population, Rayner and Hoel (1997)
proposed that workplace bullying should be considered in terms of five
indirect behaviours: threats to professional status, threats to personal

standing, isolation, overwork, and destabilisation. While incidents of physical aggression should not be discounted, Rayner and Hoel's assessment of the behaviours that constituted workplace bullying encompassed a number of scenarios that workers may have experienced on a daily basis but not necessarily construed as bullying per se (e.g., work overload).

In her study of the incidence of workplace bullying in the U.K., Rayner (1997) explored the nature of employee harassment and victimisation with a sample of 1,137 part-time students enrolled on courses at Staffordshire University. She found that over half of her sample reported having been bullied within the working environment and that over three quarters had witnessed similar incidents. Although gender-wise comparisons found no significant differences in the number of men and women who said they were bullied at work, more women said they had been bullied by men as well as by women compared to the number of men who said they were bullied by members of the opposite sex.

Rayner's (1997) study also indicated that, for over half of her participants, bullying lasted for more than 11 weeks (15% reported it lasting upwards of two years). For those who reported being bullied frequently (once a week or more), the most common form of harassment they experienced was work overload, followed by intimidation and persistent criticism. While Rayner acknowledges that her sample was biased, both in terms of academic ability and age, her results suggested that workplace bullying was much more widespread than previous Scandinavian studies had implied.

Evans and D'Augelli (1996) also reported that lesbian, gay, and bisexual undergraduates reported having to negotiate their sexual identities at college or university. Not only did they have to decide whether or not to "come out"— particularly if they shared accommodation or decided to join a fraternity/sorority—but they also had to decide how they were going to manage their lives on and off campus to avoid threatening people and/or situations.

In this study, I opted to include questions on adult experiences of anti-lesbian/gay/bisexual victimisation to gather valuable information relating to the nature and frequency of such behaviour at work or at university/college. Furthermore, to assess the psychosocial correlates and long-term effects of homophobic bullying, the incorporation of a measure of victimisation in adulthood allowed for a much more sensitive analysis of the data, partialling out the possible effects of adult victimisation from the outcome measures of negative affect and post-traumatic stress disorder (PTSD).

The Psychosocial Correlates of Agonic and Hedonic Aggression at School

Hawker's (1997) study of social ranking theory and bullying behaviour proposed that the subordinate role victims play within the peer group was likely to have an impact upon their susceptibility to a depressive illness, especially where their subordination was constantly reinforced over a long period. Previously I argued that while agonic methods of intimidation are overt and provide the victim with an opportunity to defend himself or herself, where the method is covert the victim can be undermined without being given the opportunity to retaliate. While both Gilbert (1997) and Hawker (1997) proposed that any long-term outcomes (e.g., depression) would be the same regardless of the nature of the bullying experienced by victims, significant emphasis has been placed on the impact of physical aggression upon victims' affective state, playing down the impact of both verbal and indirect aggression.

Consequently, I also wished to explore whether participants who were exposed to agonic (i.e., direct physical and verbal) methods of victimisation at school would fare better in the long term than those whose social status was eroded hedonically (i.e., indirectly) due to the fact that they were better able to retaliate against a direct assault.

Social Support Networks

King et al.'s (1998) study of PTSD among Vietnam War veterans found that social networks had a significant impact in promoting recovery from violence or trauma, especially where support was provided by peers, family members, and interested organisations. However, Frable et al. (1998) demonstrated that, in terms of supporting marginalised groups within society, the ability of a network to assist an individual in his or her development or recovery was reliant upon a certain degree of visibility or accessibility. They argued that if a client group was hidden from public view, social support networks could neither contact nor provide access for those who needed them most. Therefore, many marginalised individuals have been left to cope with the difficulties they have faced on their own.

It was also suggested that those who had concealable stigmas, such as being lesbian or gay, were more likely to suffer from negative self-perceptions of themselves because they were unable to seek similar others. As their results demonstrated, those with concealable stigmas were more likely to report higher rates of depression and anxiety than controls, although they were not found to show higher levels of hostility towards themselves or others.

This study set out to explore the relationship between the degree to which participants were visible within their communities and its impact upon self-acceptance and affective state.

Peer, Teacher, and Family Support at School

Various researchers have suggested that adolescents and young adults who were bereft of friendships during the early part of their development are more likely to suffer from low self-esteem, and are less likely than their more popular peers to be able to cope with various lifetime upheavals. In addition, young people who were without friends during middle childhood experienced difficulties in forming and maintaining romantic relationships during adolescence.

Although it seems unlikely that difficulties in forming or maintaining romantic relationships would be causally related to the absence of friendships at school, such an association is likely to reflect individual differences in self-esteem and social confidence, and these, in turn, may be linked to the absence of friends in middle childhood. However, Parker and Asher (1987) suggested that researchers should take a more dynamic approach in order to understand the nature of social interaction by "stepping out of the classroom" (p. 381). They argued that those who are unable to function effectively at school as a result of their social rejection may have been able to function more effectively in alternative environments where they are valued and accepted by others who were not their classmates. Consequently, young people who were popular outside school (with family members or alternative peers) were unlikely to exhibit many of the long-term sequelae of peer rejection. To this end, one of the objectives of the follow-up study was to determine whether or not the levels of social support reported by participants when they were at school had an effect upon measures of negative affect and internalised homophobia, and whether social interactions conducted outside school militated against potential long-term effects.

The Development of Intimate Relationships in Adulthood

Many adult survivors of child sexual abuse have reported experiencing a number of problems in terms of communicating their concerns, fears, and insecurities to their spouses/partners. Such problems include the inability to trust others, fear of emotional and physical intimacy, fear of being abused again, fear of suffering rejection, betrayal, or abandonment, and feelings of unworthiness or dependence. In addition, Gilmartin (1987) found that experiences of victimisation at school and unpopularity among peers were not only associated with an inability to form or maintain lasting intimate relationships, they were also associated with an inability to form platonic relationships with members of the same and opposite sex.

Both Gilmartin's (1987) study and Cahill et al.'s (1991) review of literature had significant ramifications for the present study. Based upon their findings, it was conjectured that participants in this study not only would show indices of insecurity within relationships, but would also show that those who were more affected by their experiences of bullying at school would also demonstrate a number of difficulties in terms of forming and maintaining a long-term relationship with a significant other, and were likely to report a history of difficulties in maintaining platonic relationships with members of the same and opposite sex.

Symptoms of PTSD and their Correlates

Finally, linked to many of the issues raised above, the issue of PTSD arose. In King et al.'s (1998) study of PTSD among Vietnam War veterans, resilience and recovery were found to be associated with three particular factors: personal hardiness, social support, and the number of additional stressful life events veterans experienced on their return home. It was also suggested that coping strategies and personality types played a significant role in determining the likelihood of recovery following exposure to violence and trauma.

Although some Scandinavian researchers have associated PTSD with bullying behaviour at work, very little research has been conducted looking at the long-term impact of school-based bullying upon adult psychopathology. Leymann and Gustafsson's (1996) study found that over half of the participants with PTSD indicated that they had attempted to avoid situations that reminded them of work. In addition, over three quarters indicated that they had suffered from intrusive and uncontrollable recollections of bullying episodes that distressed them, and about two thirds indicated that they regularly ("at least once a week") suffered from sleep disturbances. In terms of depressive illness, three quarters suffered from moderate to severe depression, with some requiring medical treatment.

The limited research conducted on childhood and adolescent PTSD suggests that symptoms manifest themselves in a number of ways, varying from introversion to risk-taking behaviours and sexual recklessness. Interestingly, some of the symptoms considered indicative of PTSD in adolescents have also been found in young lesbians, gay men, and bisexual men and women experiencing difficulties coming to terms with their sexual orientation. For example, internalised homophobia has been associated with difficulties in forming and maintaining lasting intimate relationships, unsafe sexual practices, and avoidant coping strategies with AIDS among HIV seropositive gay men. Some researchers have argued that the combined effects of victimisation or alienation by peers, and difficulties in accepting one's sexual orientation, are correlated with the onset of a number of mental health problems among lesbian, gay, and bisexual youth. Such problems have included violent behaviour, alcoholism and substance abuse, eating disorders, and, most significantly, suicidal ideation.

One of the objectives of this follow-up study was then to explore the relationships between symptoms associated with PTSD and other measures of negative affect, paying particular attention to factors such as sexual recklessness, relationship security/insecurity, alcohol consumption, substance use/abuse, and suicidal ideation.

Methodology of the Follow-up Study

Participants

Participants in this study represented a subsample of those who participated in my first (and retrospective) study of homophobic bullying at school (N = 190). Overall, 142 questionnaires were returned by participants, of which 119 were eventually included in the analysis.

In terms of ethnic origin, this subsample consisted of 116 participants (90 men and 26 women) who were White European, 2 participants (1 man and 1 woman) who were Asian or Southeast Asian, and 1 man who was African-Caribbean.

The average age for the whole subsample was 28 years (28.5 years for men and 24 years for women). Ages ranged from 16 to 54 years (16 to 54 years for men and 16 to 44 years for women), with a standard deviation of 9 years (9.3 years for men and 7.3 years for women). 84% (101) had attended state/public schools (79 men and 22 women) and 16% (19) had been educated in either private or public school (14 men and 5 women).

At the time the survey was conducted 56% were in gainful employment, 26% were students in either sixth form or college/university, 10% were unemployed, and 8% were unable to work on the grounds of illness or disability.

Only 8% of participants had no formal academic qualifications. 81% held or were studying for certificates demonstrating proficiency in one or more subjects at the secondary/high school level. 52% held or were studying for at least one advanced school qualification. 30% held or were studying for a university/college degree and 37% held or were studying for professional or occupational qualifications (e.g., Diploma in Nursing, Counselling Certificate, Diploma in Psychotherapy).

Comparison Groups

Data were gathered from three different comparison groups for this study:

- Heterosexual adults who were not bullied at school: 33 male and 65 female undergraduates randomly selected from a number of lecture or tutorial groups in two British universities by myself and a third-year dissertation student from one of the universities sampled. Mean age was 24 years for both men and women (range 18 to 38 years, standard deviation 4.4 years [4.4 years for men, 4.5 years for women].

- Heterosexual adults who were bullied at school: 34 male undergraduates and 75 female undergraduates randomly selected by myself and a third-year dissertation student from two British universities sampled. Mean age was 24 years (25 years for men, 24 years for women), ranging from 19 to 44 years (standard deviation 5.0 years [4.4 years for men, 5.3 years for women]).

- Lesbian, gay, and bisexual adults who were not bullied at school: 76 gay or bisexual men and 40 lesbian or bisexual women selected from four British universities' lesbian, gay, and bisexual student associations sampled and community or support groups in London and the Southeast by myself and a third-year dissertation students from one of the universities sampled. Men age was 24 years (21 years for gay and bisexual men and 21 years for lesbian and bisexual women), ranging from 18 to 44 years (standard deviation 4.7 years [4.6 years for gay and bisexual men and 5.1 years for lesbian and bisexual women]).

The data from the undergraduate populations of four British universities, together with the participation of various community groups and support organisations for lesbians, gay men, and bisexual men and women were located in London and the Southeast.

Protocol and Measures

All participants completed a series of instruments included a bullying at work/college/university questionnaire very similar to the Olweus Bully/Victim Questionnaire, the Psychiatric Epidemiology Research Interview (PERI) Life Events Scale (Dohrenwend, Krasnoff, Askenasy, & Dohrenwend, 1978), a revised version of the Multiple Affect Adjective Check-List (Zuckerman & Lubin, 1965), the Revised Homosexual Attitudes Inventory (Shidlo, 1992), and a PTSD Symptom Questionnaire (Rivers, 1999).

PERI Life Events Scale

In their study of recovery and resilience among Vietnam War veterans, King et al. (1998) did not consider the impact of positive as well as negative life events upon affective state and coping potential. To determine whether scores on the measures were affected by recent events in the lives of former victims, they were asked to complete a revised version of the PERI Life Events Scale. This scale was favoured over others because it recognised that positive and negative life events would have a differential effect upon an individual's affective state. The scale consists of 10 subsections that identify both positive and negative life experiences (102 items in total). The 10 subsections are school/college/university, work and employment, personal relationships, having children and family issues, residence, crime and legal matters, personal finances, social activities and events, general issues, and health-related issues.

Several items on the scale were altered in order for the scale to be relevant to a British sample. For example, in the residence section, the item "Renovated a home" was replaced with "Redecorated a home." Similarly, in the section on personal finances, the term "foreclosure" was replaced with the term "repossession." Items relating to marriage were also revised to take into account the fact that, in the U.K., marriage between two members of the same sex is not allowed (though civil partnerships are). Thus, the item "Married" was changed to "Made a long-term commitment to a partner (e.g., marriage or equivalent)" and "Divorce" was changed to "Ended long-term relationship (e.g., divorce or equivalent)."

Multiple Affect Adjective Check-List

Zuckerman and Lubin's (1965) Multiple Affect Adjective Check-List (MAACL) was as a measure of negative affect. The MAACL consists of 132 adjectives (e.g., active, cautious, frank, irritated, outraged, wild) that do not lend themselves easily to interpretation by participants. Participants were asked to "tick" or "check" if each adjective reflected how they felt when they completed the questionnaire. Each of the affective scales was scored according to whether participants had ticked the plus (+) items or left blank the minus (–) items. Scores for all three scales were calculated by adding all the plus items ticked with all the minus items left blank.

Revised Homosexual Attitudes Inventory

To assess issues of self-image, fear of disclosure, and general attitudes towards homosexuality and bisexuality, a revised version of the Nungesser's Homosexual Attitudes Inventory (RHAI) was used (Nungesser, 1983; Shidlo, 1992). Shidlo's (1992) version of the Homosexual Attitudes Inventory was favoured over that of Nungesser (1983) and another published scale, the AIDS-Related Internalised Homonegativity Scale (ARIH), on a number of criteria. Firstly, Shidlo's version incorporated three subscales, allowing for a much more detailed analysis of participants' attitudes towards their homosexuality or bisexuality and homosexuality or bisexuality in general. Secondly, Shidlo's extended version (the RHAI) included six additional items relating to levels of personal homonegativity, a key measure in this study. Thirdly, Shidlo's comparative scale, the ARIH, focused specifically upon issues associated with HIV/AIDS and personal identity (see Shidlo, 1994).

Several empirical studies have shown that both Nungesser's (1983) and Shidlo's (1992) versions of the Homosexual Attitudes Inventory have good face, content, and construct validity (see Shidlo, 1994). Both versions obtained moderate to good measures of internal consistency for the total NHAI and RHAI (Nungesser α = .94; Shidlo α = .82), with the subscales ranging from .68 to .93 (Shidlo, 1992). The RHAI also shows good concurrent validity with other measures of internalised homophobia, with correlation coefficients ranging from .59 to .70 (all significant at $p \leq .001$) (see Alexander, 1986; Sbordone, 1993; Shidlo, 1992).

Several syntactical revisions were made to Shidlo's RHAI to make it applicable to lesbian and bisexual women and, as a result, two items that related specifically to gay men were removed. Each item in the RHAI is scored on a Likert-type scale. Nungesser's (1983) original version of the inventory was scored on a 5-point scale (SD = Strongly Disagree; D = Disagree; N = Neutral/No Opinion; A = Agree; SA = Strongly Agree). Shidlo's (1992, 1994) RHAI was scored on a 4-point scale (1 = Strongly Disagree; 2 = Mainly Disagree; 3 = Mainly Agree; 4 = Strongly Agree).

Both versions employed reverse scoring for some items. For this study, Nungesser's 1- to 5-point scale was used (SD = 1 and SA = 5).

PTSD Symptom Questionnaire

To assess whether or not participants continued to be affected by their experiences of being bullied at school, they completed a 24-item index of symptoms associated with PTSD. This questionnaire was constructed using the diagnostic criteria specified by the American Psychiatric Association (APA, 1994). It was favoured above other measures of PTSD for the following reasons. Firstly, it was not the intention of this study to diagnose PTSD directly but to gain insights into the residual effects experienced by participants (e.g., nightmares, flashbacks, panic attacks). Secondly, participants were asked to respond only if they could associate various features of the disorder directly with experiences of school (e.g., nightmares about being back at school, avoiding situations/events that reminded them of school, taking alcohol or prescription or nonprescription drugs to help them cope with memories of school). As a result, this questionnaire allows for a much more detailed picture of the long-term effects of bullying in school when compared to other scales that feature only one or two aspects of the disorder.

In terms of both face and content validity, the questionnaire may be considered a good indicator of the presence of symptoms of PTSD in participants as it adheres closely to the APA diagnostic criteria (1994). The questionnaire is divided into three sub-indexes: recollection, associative features, and day-to-day events.

Self-harming Behaviour

53% of former victims of homophobic bullying at school said that they had contemplated self-harm as a direct result of being bullied because of their actual or perceived sexual orientation (Fig. 7.1). 40% reported that they had attempted to self-harm or take their own lives on at least one occasion because of the bullying they experienced, and three quarters of those said that they had attempted on more than one occasion (the average number of attempts was four).

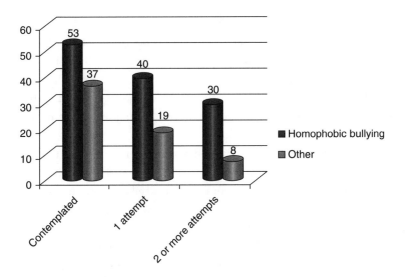

FIGURE 7.1   Self-harming behaviour among former victims of homophobic bullying

In addition, 37% also reported contemplating self-harm or suicide for reasons other than bullying. Reasons underlying such behaviour were primarily associated with feeling uncomfortable or unhappy with being lesbian, gay, or bisexual; emotional difficulties not associated with school; and family problems (including physical and/or sexual abuse by a primary care provider).

Bullying in Adulthood

In total, 66 (48 gay and bisexual men and 18 lesbian and bisexual women; 55%) participants reported having been bullied or harassed at some point either at work or at university/college because of their sexual orientation. Verbal harassment was the most frequently cited form of bullying experienced either at work or at university/college. Name-calling, teasing, and being ridiculed in public were reported by 24% of former victims overall. Indirect behaviours such as rumour-mongering or being frightened by a look/stare were found to be the next most common (19% and 17% respectively). Sexual assault or harassment was reported by 12% of the sample, followed by social isolation (11%) and having personal items or possessions taken (10%). Very few (4%) reported being physically assaulted (e.g., hit or kicked). Finally, 8% of the sample reported being bullied/harassed in other ways. These included having graffiti written about them in public places (e.g., lavatory walls) and receiving threatening telephone calls at home.

Significant associations were found between gender and the types of bullying/harassment experienced by participants at work/university/college: men recalled having had rumours spread about them much more than women, $\chi^2_{(1)} = 11.57, p \leq .0007$, while women were much more likely to recall being isolated by work colleagues, $\chi^2_{(1)} = 4.75, p \leq .03$. The following extract, taken from an interview with Simon, a successful lawyer, illustrates the total isolation some participants experienced at work:

> There was one person who I had a real problem with...a guy who was another lawyer who was within the legal team...who was also gay but very different to me. I mean *** [name given] was a real *Telegraph*-reading high Tory queen and we...we never saw eye to eye, but he was an extremely good networker within the office and consequently he had a "clique" built around him...which went out to lunch and, you know, did things in the evening. I felt very excluded from that. And, even though I was able to brush them aside suddenly feelings would emerge of, you know, not being...not being part of...of the gang and being on the outside, of being a loner, of being a person looking through the frosted glass window at the party inside. (Simon, aged 27)

37% said that they had been bullied/harassed by their coworkers or colleagues. 17% were bullied/harassed by a manager/supervisor or someone in authority, and one gay man said that he had been bullied/harassed by someone he managed/supervised. Comparable with school experiences, one quarter of those bullied at work reported it to a manager/supervisor or someone in authority. Only seven men and three women reported that the bullying/harassment stopped.

Mental Health of Former Victims of Homophobic Bullying

Participants' scores for the MAACL subscales for depression, anxiety, and hostility were compared to the scores gathered from the three comparative groups described earlier in this chapter (Fig. 7.2).

Depression

One-way analysis of covariance (ANCOVA), partialling out total scores for bullying in adulthood, and scores from Dohrenwend et al.'s (1978) PERI Life Events Scale showed that former victims of homophobic bullying scored significantly higher on the depression subscale when compared to heterosexuals who were not bullied at school, $F_{(1, 214)} = 30.16$, $p \leq .0001$, and lesbians, gay men, and bisexual men and women (LGBs) who were not bullied at school, $F_{(1, 201)} = 14.08$, $p \leq .0002$. However, no significant difference was found when the mean scores for participants were compared to those of the heterosexuals bullied at school.

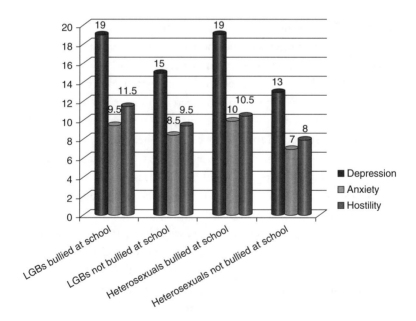

FIGURE 7.2   Mean scores for MAACL subscales

Anxiety

Scores for the former victims of homophobic bullying in this study were found to be significantly higher (using ANCOVA) when compared to those of heterosexuals not bullied at school, $F_{(1, 214)}$ = 23.49, $p \leq$ .05. When their scores were then compared to those of the heterosexuals who were bullied at school, and LGBs not bullied at school, no significant differences were found.

Hostility

ANCOVA found a significant difference between the mean scores of former victims of bullying behaviour when compared to heterosexuals not bullied at school, $F_{(1, 214)}$ = 19.95, $p \leq$ .0001, only. All other comparisons were not significant.

Agonic and Hedonic Aggression and Negative Affect

To explore the relationship between participants' susceptibility to a number of affective disorders and the nature of the bullying they experienced at school, responses provided by the question "In what way were you bullied at school?" were used to allocate participants to one of two groups: those who were primarily subjected to direct physical or direct verbal bullying (agonic-n = 56; 50 men and 6 women) and those who were primarily subjected to indirect bullying (hedonic-n = 21; 15 men and 6 women). All other victims indicated that they had been bullied both directly and indirectly in roughly equal measure.

Comparisons were then made between the two groups to determine constancy of effect in terms of experiences of bullying in adulthood (using a composite severity score; see Rivers, 1999), and in terms of their exposure to positive and negative life events. One-way analysis of variance indicated that both groups did not differ significantly in terms of their experiences of bullying in adulthood, or in terms of their exposure to positive or negative life events.

In terms of negative affect, mean scores for MAACL subscales were not found to vary significantly between groups in terms of depression, anxiety, and hostility. In addition, the total score for negative affect was not found to differ significantly between the groups.

Comparisons between the victims of agonic and hedonic bullying at school were also made for scores of internalised homophobia. Total scores for the RHAI were not found to differ significantly between the groups. Similar results were found when considering each of the subscales.

Being Hidden

To determine the degree to which being open had an effect upon our outcome measures, participants were grouped according to the ages at which they disclosed their sexual orientation to another person. The three groups consisted of those who disclosed their sexual orientation to another before the age of 16 years (n = 37), those who disclosed their sexual orientation after the age of 16 (n = 68), and those who have never disclosed their sexual orientation (n = 14).

In terms of negative affect, mean scores for MAACL subscales were not found to vary significantly between all three groups. However, total scores for the RHAI were found to differ significantly between the groups, with those who have never disclosed their sexual orientation displaying significantly more indices of internalised homophobia than those who disclosed before and after 16 years of age, $F_{(2, 112)} = 11.24$, $p \leq .0001$.

Peer, Teacher, and Family Support at School

For this analysis, I recoded variables according to the degree of support former victims indicated they had received when they were being bullied at school. In the end three groups were identified: those who received no support from family and teachers but did have a friend at school (n = 38), those who had some support from family and teachers at school and had two or three friends (n = 68), and those who had sought out support regularly and had a large circle of friends when they were young (n = 15).

Effect constancy was assessed to determine whether or not members differed significantly in terms of experiences of bullying in adulthood, or in terms of their exposure to positive and negative life events. One-way analysis of variance indicated that all three groups did not differ significantly in terms of their experiences of bullying in adulthood or in terms of their exposure to positive or negative life events.

Mean scores for MAACL subscales were found to vary significantly between all three groups in terms of depression and hostility, but not for anxiety. In terms of depression in adulthood, significant differences were found between those who received no support when they were at school and those who received some support, $F_{(2, 111)} = 6.25, p \leq .01$. In terms of hostility, significant differences were found between those who received no support when they were at school, and those who received a great deal of support, $F_{(2, 112)} = 3.27, p \leq .05$.

In terms of internalised homophobia, mean scores for the total RHAI were not found to differ significantly between groups, nor did they differ significantly on the subscales.

Parker and Asher (1987) argued that in order to understand the dynamics of children's social relationships it was also necessary to take some measure of their socialisation experiences outside the school grounds. They argued that it would be unlikely that children who were popular outside school would exhibit many of the long-term sequelae of peer rejection. To explore the potential effects that social interactions conducted outside of school had upon the various measures used in this study, former victims were allocated to one of two groups based upon their responses to questions about their social networks outside school. Seventy former victims of homophobic bullying reported spending their free time either alone or, perhaps, with one friend. Twenty-one said they spent their free time with several friends.

> I played on my bike a lot and then around 14 or 15, I used to go and stay with my best friend...it was often lonely...miserable. (Catherine, aged 23)
>
> It was quite sad in a way because as I said I felt left out from everyone else. (Alex, aged 19)
>
> A feeling of missing out...a feeling of hearing people in school talking about these wild parties and their...the sexual decathlons

that they were…they were involved in. And, the…the fun playing… playing in the park after…after school with their friends from home. A feeling that I was being deprived of this. (Simon, aged 27)

Despite the isolation participants experienced, mean scores for MAACL subscales were not found to vary significantly between groups. Similarly, no significant differences were found between groups in terms of internalised homophobia (total scores and subscales).

The Development of Intimate Relationships in Adulthood

At the time the follow-up study was conducted, 76% of participants were or had recently been in a relationship where there had been an emotional involvement and/or they had lived with someone. The average length of time participants who were in a relationship at the time had been together with their partner was 3.3 years (3.2 years for men and 3.6 years for women).

When asked to estimate the average duration of a relationship, more men indicated that their relationships lasted longer than two years (25%) than women (17%). However, more women reported relationships lasting between 6 months and 1 year (25%) than men (18%). Notwithstanding, as the following extracts demonstrate, participants expressed a great deal of concern about forming relationships. Their responses showed a great deal of hesitancy in allowing others to become close, and as Michael's comment reveals, some participants expressed the concern that they did not know how to initiate a relationship with another person.

> I developed a great deal of aloofness which means that I do keep people at arm's length until I'm really safe on my ground which means that can be hard work for the other party to break that down. (Simon, aged 27)
> I'm not prepared to give people much room for manoeuvre. Either I like them or I don't like them. If I don't like them, I don't really want to be around them. I don't want them in my life; I don't want to know them. I'm not prepared to make halfway house friendships with people…and so, consequently, the small group of friends that I've got are people that I'm very very close to,

that I have sort of invested a lot of emotional time in and who invest a lot of emotional time in myself. (Tom, aged 32)

I certainly feel...certainly feel that having had to internalise my feelings I...I don't know how to go about getting into a relationship. (Michael, aged 26)

Symptoms of PTSD

One of the objectives of this study was to explore whether or not former victims of homophobic bullying experienced any of the symptoms associated with PTSD. For PTSD to be diagnosed, usually the following criteria have to be met: an individual has experienced an event that it outside the range of usual human experience and that would be markedly distressing to almost anyone; the traumatic event is persistently re-experienced in one of five different ways (Table 7.1); an individual persistently avoids stimuli associated with the trauma or reports a numbing of general responsiveness since its occurrence as indicated by the presence of at least three symptoms (Table 7.2); an individual reports at least two persistent symptoms of increased arousal not present before the trauma (Table 7.3); and the duration of the disturbance extends beyond one calendar month.

Analysis of the results was broken down into three distinct sections corresponding to APA (1994) diagnostic criteria. Table 7.1 illustrates the

TABLE 7.1   Number of participants (as percentages) reporting frequent and persistent recollections of homophobic bullying according to estimated duration

	Duration					
	0–6 months	1–2 yrs	2–3 yrs	3–4 yrs	5 yrs +	Total %
Recollection/Re-experience						
Distressing memories	0	2	2	1	16	21
Dreams/nightmares	0	1	1	0	2	4
Reliving events	3	1	1	0	4	9
Flashbacks	0	2	1	2	4	9
Situation/event distress	2	3	2	4	15	26

TABLE 7.2   Number of participants (as percentages) reporting a current and persistent avoidance of stimuli or numbing of general responsiveness

			Frequency		
	Never	Not often	Sometimes	Often	Always
Features					
Do you find yourself trying to avoid thoughts and feelings which remind you of the event(s)?	34	17	29	14	5
Do you avoid activities or situations which may remind you of the event(s)?	34	17	26	14	9
Do you find it difficult to recall important aspects of the event(s)?	37	20	28	9	6
Do you find it difficult to continue being interested in things you did before the event(s) took place?	60	9	21	6	4
Do you ever feel like an outsider in social situations?	6	10	38	33	13
Do you find it difficult to show emotions to others?	15	15	37	26	7
Do you ever feel as if you have no real future (i.e. no prospect of having a partner, career or long life)?	21	19	27	21	13

number of participants (as percentages) who reported experiencing persistent recollections of being bullied at school on a frequent basis (i.e., "often" or "always") over a period of at least six months.

26% of former victims said they continued to be distressed regularly by recollections of bullying. 21% said they experienced distressing or intrusive memories. Very few (only 4%) reported having dreams or nightmares about being bullied at school, but slightly more (9%) recalled having experienced flashbacks (hallucinations and dissociative episodes) or a feeling of reliving events while awake.

Table 7.2 illustrates the number of participants (as percentages) who reported current and persistent avoidance of certain stimuli or a feeling of numbness in responding to people or events surrounding them that they associated with being bullied at school.

Nearly half of the participants in the follow-up study (46%) said they regularly ("often" and "always") felt like an outsider in social

TABLE 7.3   Number of participants (as percentages) reporting symptoms of arousal not present before being bullied at school

	Never	Not often	Sometimes	Often	Always
			Frequency		
Symptoms of arousal					
Do you ever have difficulty going to sleep or staying asleep?	16	14	38	22	10
Do you feel irritable?	4	11	43	36	6
Do you ever have outbursts of anger?	8	26	44	21	2
Do you ever feel as if you cannot express yourself?	13	20	33	30	5
Do you ever feel as if you are losing control?	13	23	35	22	7
Do you ever have difficulty concentrating on what you are doing?	3	18	40	35	4
Do you become very wary of meeting new people or facing new situations?	10	20	31	21	18
Do you ever over react?	6	22	39	27	6
Do you become nervous in situations which remind you of event(s)?	27	15	27	18	13
Do you ever take alcohol to help you cope with memories of the events?	61	12	19	4	3
Do you ever take prescription drugs to help you cope with memories of the event(s)?	81	9	6	1	3
Do you ever take non–prescription drugs to help you cope with memories of the event(s)?	80	7	8	4	1

situations and 34% said they regularly felt as if they had no real future. 33% also said they often or always found it difficult to show emotion to others, while slightly fewer (23%) said they actively avoided social situations that reminded them of events at school. 19% said they actively avoided thinking about school on a regular basis, and 15% had difficulty recalling particular incidents associated with being bullied at school. Only 10% said that they found it difficult to continue with any interests they had at school, although this result is to be expected, as interests/recreational activities/hobbies can change with age.

Former victims of homophobic bullying reported that irritability was the most common symptom they experienced (42%) on a regular basis ("often" or "always"), followed by poor concentration (39%), a wariness of meeting new people or facing new situations (39%), and difficulties in self-expression (35%). 33% felt that they often or always overreacted to situations or events that caused them discomfort, and 32% said that they suffered from dyssomnia on a regular basis. 31% reported regularly feeling nervous in situations that reminded them of being at school, and 29% reported they often did not feel in control of their lives. Just under one quarter (23%) said they often had outbursts of anger. 7% said they drank alcohol on a regular basis to help them cope with memories of being bullied at school, while 5% said they also took nonprescription drugs. Finally, 4% said they were regularly prescribed prescription drugs that helped them cope with memories of being bullied at school.

Understanding the Potential Legacy of Homophobic Bullying

The results demonstrated just over half of the participants in this study reported contemplating self-harm as a result of the homophobic bullying they experienced at school, while 40% said they had attempted at least once, and three quarters of those more than once. While these results suggest that participants were particularly at risk from self-destructive behaviours when they were at school, a number of methodological considerations relating to the reliability and validity of these findings require some discussion before conclusions can be drawn.

One of the first considerations that must be taken into account when assessing the results from this study relates to its retrospective nature and the fact that I required participants to unravel the causal features of their self-harming behaviour—a very difficult task. A second consideration relates to current estimates of suicidal ideation among adolescents when they were at school. Data suggest that between 8% and 13% of all young people attempt suicide on at least on occasion (see Mehan, Lamb, Saltzman, & O'Carroll, 1992), and it has been argued that where such ideation is related to issues of sexual orientation, estimates can rise substantially, ranging from 30% to 62.5%. However, in Warren's

(1984) study, while about one third of participants indicated that they had been bullied at school or pressurised to conform in some way, only one fifth of the total sample indicated that they had attempted suicide because they were lesbian or gay. Although very little information was offered relating to the reasons underpinning such behaviour, comparison of Warren's data with those of Mehan et al. (1992) suggested that lesbian, gay, and bisexual youth are more likely to engage in self-harming behaviour and suicidal ideation than their heterosexual peers because of the difficulties they face growing up in a heterosexual world. Therefore, by limiting participation in the present study to those who had experienced victimisation at school as a result of their actual or perceived sexual orientation, it was likely that reported rates of self-harming behaviour and suicidal ideation would be considerably higher than the 20% reported by Warren.

A third and related consideration derives from Muehrer's (1995) assertion that it is difficult to separate out the impact of one antecedent from that of another when considering self-harming behaviour among young lesbians, gay men, and bisexual men and women. Comparable with Hershberger and D'Augelli (1995), he has argued that the combined effects of familial as well as societal homophobia have be taken into account when attempting to establish a causative link between certain environmental influences and self-destructive behaviours. Indeed, it should be recalled that participants in the present study were also asked to answer a series of questions relating to self-harming behaviours that they believed were the result of factors other than bullying at school. While 37% said they had contemplated self-harming behaviour or suicide for a number of other reasons (including sexual abuse), just over half of that number (19%) said that they had attempted to hurt themselves or take their own lives at least once, with 8% reporting having engaged in such behaviour more than once. In a similar vein, in their study of the prevalence of suicidal ideation among lesbian, gay, and bisexual youth, Remafedi, Farrow, and Deisher (1991) found that those who attempted suicide were much more likely to have a history of family dysfunction, sexual abuse, substance abuse, antisocial behaviour, and criminal misconduct, and this, they argued, had an impact upon their propensity to engage in self-harming behaviour.

While there were no direct measures of family functioning contained within the present study, some inferences may be drawn from this study. For example, very few participants (15%) reported telling someone at home why they were being bullied, which suggests that, while the majority of families may not necessarily have reacted negatively if participants had disclosed the reason for their victimisation, they were not given the opportunity to be supportive. Indeed, the overall degree of social support participants received (from family members, peers, and/or teachers) when they were being bullied at school was found to have a differential effect upon scores for negative affect, with those receiving no support scoring high on measures of depression and, more pertinently, hostility than those who received some or a great deal of support.

The above findings suggest that while participants may have found it difficult to separate out the reasons underpinning their attempts to self-harm, this may have been due, in part, to a layering effect whereby the effects of bullying at school were exacerbated by their (the participants') perceptions of potential intolerance or hostility from within the community or, indeed, from within the family. This is likely to have resulted in both their alienation and further isolation, thus reducing their chances of seeking or receiving support. Indeed, this is a view shared by Frable et al. (1998), who argued that students with concealable stigmas (e.g., being lesbian or gay) were not only more likely to lack social support, but were also more likely to lack expert knowledge about their social group because of (i) their isolation and (ii) their perception of the mores of the society or culture in which they lived. And, as Frable et al. pointed out, such isolation resulted in students negatively appraising themselves, their stigma, and those who were similarly stigmatised.

Bullying in Adulthood

Comparable to their experiences of bullying at school, participants who reported being bullied in adulthood (either at work or at university/college) indicated that verbal harassment was used by their peers most frequently as a method of intimidation. Indirect methods of victimisation such as rumour-mongering were also frequently cited, as was being frightened by a person's look or stare. Sexual assault or harassment was reported by some participants, and, surprisingly, it preceded both social isolation and physical assault in terms of its frequency. While significantly more men than women reported having rumours spread about them, the results also indicated that women were more likely to report being isolated by their peers or coworkers than men, and this is worthy of further consideration.

Pilkington and D'Augelli (1995) found a higher rate of physical violence directed against young lesbian and bisexual women compared to young gay and bisexual men. They suggested that such a finding may have been linked to the differing nature of social relationships among young men and young women. They maintained that young women are far more likely to disclose personal information to their friends than young men, and because of this they have argued that the young women in their survey experienced more physical abuse because peers knew they were lesbian or bisexual, whereas they only perceived or suspected the young men of being gay. In the survey of bullying at school, the background data provided by 190 men and women showed that while 50% of women had disclosed their sexual orientation to at least one other person by 16 years of age, only 21% of men said they had similarly done so.

If, as Pilkington and D'Augelli (1995) suggested, women are more likely to disclose their sexual orientation to their peers than men, this may also provide an explanation as to why lesbian and bisexual women in the present study reported slightly more direct verbal abuse at work or at university/college, and significantly more social isolation when compared to gay and bisexual men. Based upon the findings from the survey of bullying at school, the fact that lesbian and bisexual women were more likely to be open about their sexual orientation with colleagues than gay or bisexual men would have rendered them much more vulnerable to criticism and abuse. Yet, at the time this study was conducted, I found very few differences between women and men in terms of the number who said they were open about their sexual orientation, although no measure was taken of the degree to which participants disclosed personal information to colleagues at work or at university/college during data collection.

Having said that, the fact that participants tended to be bullied by their peers at work or at university/college, rather than by those in authority, or older colleagues, suggests that the dynamics of victimisation were very similar to those found in the earlier study of bullying at school. According to Askew and Ross (1988) one of the ways in which such discriminatory practices are reinforced is through banter, particularly among men, whereby a prejudicial statement is expressed through the medium of supposed humour:

Backs to the wall lads, here comes Gary. (Moriarty, 1997, p. 126)

Ridgeway and Balkwell's (1997) discussion of status construction theory also provides an insight into the nature of the bullying experienced by participants either at work or at university/college. Status construction theory relates to the process whereby a group arrives at a series of consensual beliefs about its order or structure and the value it places upon certain individuals and their behaviour through the application of a three-stage model that asserts that social structure is organised according to the distribution of resources, the distribution of the population on individual/difference variables, and he relationship between these distributions. Where interaction occurs between groups with nominal characteristics (e.g., race, ethnicity, or sexuality) that are also found to correlate with resource characteristics (e.g., wealth or poverty, or success or failure) estimations of esteem and worthiness follow. Thus, access to resources is perceived as a competence, and those groups with access to resources (i.e., wealth) perceive themselves to be more competent than those without. Where access to resources (i.e., perceived competence) is found to correlate with factors such as race, ethnicity, or, indeed, sexuality, the group with greater access to those resources evaluates itself more favourably than others, and promulgates stereotypes that portray those with fewer resources as less worthy.

A corollary of this tension between these groups vying for access to resources is that those who see themselves to be unjustly barred from access will effectively seek to remedy the situation by attempting to change their devalued status through a series of coping strategies that challenge any perceived threat to their social identity, or their interpretation of the social order. Thus, it follows that any individual or group who constitute a threat to the social identity of others will, potentially, face discrimination or harassment by those who perceive themselves or their social status to be under attack. For those participants in the follow-up study who experienced victimisation at the hands of their peers, it is argued that they may have been bullied because they were seen as a threat to the status quo. By discriminating against a lesbian, gay, or bisexual colleague, coworkers and fellow students not only made a statement about their own sexual orientation, but they may also have made a wider social statement about the acceptability of those who do not conform to the majority's way of life.

Therefore, on the one hand, homophobia becomes the expression of an individual's or group's negative appraisal of those who are attracted to members of their own gender: it is, in essence, an *active* form of discrimination that can take many forms. Alternatively, rather than homophobia being an expression of anti-lesbian/gay/bisexual feeling, it can also be viewed as an expression of pro-heterosexual sentiment: a restatement of the predominance and commonality of heterosexuality among humankind. In this respect is ceases to be active homophobia and becomes, as Rothblum and Bond (1996) have argued, heterosexism: the unwillingness to recognise the salience of any state other than that of heterosexuality.

Agonic and Hedonic Aggression at School

Hawker's (1997) study of social ranking theory and bullying behaviour proposed that the subordinate role victims play within the peer group was likely to have an impact upon their susceptibility to a depressive illness, especially if their subordination was constantly reinforced over a long period. Building upon this proposition, I suggested that, unlike agonic methods of intimidation, which are overt and provide the victim with an opportunity to defend himself or herself, if the method is covert the victim can be undermined without being given the opportunity to retaliate. While both Gilbert (1997) and Hawker (1997) proposed that any long-term outcomes (e.g., depression) would be the same regardless of the nature of the bullying experienced by victims, other researchers have placed significant emphasis on the impact of physical aggression upon the victims' affective state, playing down the impact of both verbal and indirect aggression.

However, I also argued that if an individual had the opportunity to defend himself or herself against physical and verbal attack, regardless of the success of the venture, the very act of defence may have guarded against a total loss of status and self-respect. Consequently, the present study suggested that participants who were exposed to agonic (i.e., direct physical and verbal) methods of victimisation at school would fare better in the long term than those whose social status was eroded hedonically (i.e., indirectly) due to the fact that they were better able to retaliate against a direct assault. As the results illustrated, scores on various measures of negative affect and internalised homophobia did not differ significantly on the basis of exposure to primarily either agonic or hedonic aggression at school.

The study of both agonic and hedonic aggressive behaviour arose from Hawker's (1997) study of social ranking theory and its association with the onset of depression. Based upon the ethological principle of involuntary subordination, Gilbert (1992) proposed that depression is causally related to the power dynamic found between individuals in a social situation. For example, rather than the interaction between the weaker and stronger person ending when the dominance of the latter is established, involuntary subordination may not always succeed in pacifying the winner or in eliciting appropriate behavioural signals from the loser (i.e., a change in behaviour). If this occurs, it results in the "intense and prolonged" suffering of the loser, which manifests itself as a depressive illness (Hawker, 1997, p. 21).

In this study, the nature of the bullying experienced by participants may have been irrelevant. Comparable with the Aaron Fricke's story, which he recounted in his autobiography, *Confessions of a Rock Lobster*, for some young people a look or stare is all that is needed to instil fear.

Social Support Mechanisms

The results offered in this chapter suggest that, in terms of negative affect, social support has an effect upon scores for both depression and hostility, although not for anxiety. It was also interesting to note that, in terms of internalised homophobia, those who received little support at school were not found to differ significantly from those who received some or a great deal of support.

Having said that, it was also found that participants who received considerable support from peers, family members, and/or teachers had "come out" earlier (mean = 15.5 years) than those who received some support (mean = 19.3 years) or no support (mean = 18.1 years). While I argued earlier that those who disclosed their sexual orientation when they were at school were likely to experience much more harassment by peers, these results suggested that if participants received social support from peers, family members, and/or teachers, it militated against the onset of depression and hostility.

With respect to friendships outside of school, participants who spent much of their free time either alone or with one friend did not differ significantly from those who spent their free time with a small group of friends or many friends. Bagwell et al.'s (1996) 12-year longitudinal study found that sociometric status in childhood (i.e., being popular vs. rejected) was a predictor of school performance, career success, personal aspirations, and sociability in adulthood, whereas simply having friends was not. However, Bagwell et al. also found that childhood friendships not only predicted positive attitudes towards family members and feelings of self-worth, but, surprisingly, they also predicted depressive symptoms, thus implying that friendship may not always act as a buffer against the impact of violence or trauma.

Inevitably, friendships vary as a function of those with whom an individual is friendly, and the level of intimacy an individual shares with each person. Thus, friendship is multidimensional, and to assess the efficacy of friendships as buffers against adversity it is necessary to assess their strength in terms of their content (e.g., what friends do together), constructiveness (e.g., how disputes between friends are resolved), closeness (e.g., willingness to disclose), symmetry (i.e., do friends exert the same amount of influence on each other in terms of "social power"?), and affective character or attachment style (i.e., secure or insecure attachment).

In effect, the number of friends an individual has is immaterial in determining the level of functional support a person receives. Rather, it is the quality of the individual's relationship with another that has a differential effect upon the efficacy of any support he or she receives. Therefore, participants who may only have had one friend could have received a greater degree of social support than those who reported having a number of friends.

An alternative explanation relating to the discussion of friendship derives from Bem's (1996) developmental theory of sexual orientation, which he called Exotic Becomes Erotic (EBE), and is very closely allied to the discussion of social identity theory found in Chapter 1. According to Bem, the development of sexual orientation occurs as a result of an individual's erotic or romantic attraction to those who were either dissimilar or unfamiliar to him or her during childhood. In the case of heterosexuals, he has argued that erotic and romantic attachments are formed towards members of the opposite sex; among lesbians and gay men, such attachments are formed towards members of their own sex. Thus, EBE theory suggests that the exclusion experienced by lesbians and gay men from their same-sex peer groups in childhood will actually facilitate same-sex eroticisation in adolescence. However, because not all lesbians and gay men report being isolated by their peers in childhood, were Bem's theory solely about the issue of proximity, its relevance to the findings from the present study are called into question.

While Bem (1996) placed considerable emphasis upon gender nonconformity in childhood as an antecedent of peer isolation and homosexual orientation, his theory also suggests that identification with same-sex peers may play a role in defining sexual orientation. Thus, if a child or young person feels emotionally alienated from his or her same-sex peer group, he or she is likely to identify more closely with others who are similarly alienated (i.e., members of the opposite sex), although he or she may never express such feelings for fear of being ostracised. Consequently, a young person can be physically a member of one per group, although secretly identify and empathise with members of an alternative peer group. Therefore, it can be argued that participants' recollections of the number of friendships they had as children/adolescents may not have been a useful discriminating variable as they did not take in account the degree to which they (the participants) identified with those they called their friends.

Intimate Relationships in Adulthood

Both Gilmartin's (1987) study and Cahill et al.'s (1991) review of literature had significant ramifications for the present study. Based upon their findings, it was argued that participants who were more affected by their experiences of bullying at school would also demonstrate a number of difficulties in terms of forming and maintaining a long-term relationship with a significant other, and were likely to report a history of difficulties in maintaining platonic relationships with members of the same and opposite sex.

In this study many of the issues that have been highlighted were not found. The majority of participants had been in relationships that had lasted approximately 3 years, suggesting that they were able to maintain those relationships with members of the same sex, although the quality of those relationships was not explored fully.

However, some participants expressed concerns about their ability to maintain such relationships successfully, and they also commented on the permissive nature of those relationships, particularly those of gay and bisexual men, which they felt undermined the level of commitment one or other partner brought to it.

In the interviews, some participants expressed fears about being too possessive, being trapped, or being hurt. One participant felt that the presence of a partner brought with it a loss of independence and a sense of being held back. Another (Paul; see below) described how such feelings eventually led him to separate from his boyfriend and embark upon a series of casual sexual encounters. Interestingly, he described this period in his life in terms of a belated adolescence in which he had hoped to experience all those things he believed he should have experienced as a teenager:

> I wanted my freedom. I wanted what other people did in their teenage years and early twenties, you know.

As Cahill et al. (1991) pointed out, issues such as feeling trapped or being overly possessive have been cited in several research reports exploring the nature of intimate relationships among participants who have suffered abuse or experienced trauma in childhood. Consequently, it is inadvisable to draw too many conclusions based upon the data in this study.

Symptoms of PTSD

About 40% of participants reported the regular occurrence of one or more symptoms associated with PTSD. While it is impossible to make a diagnosis with the tool used in this study, the frequency of reports of symptoms is indicative of potential long-term mental health problems resulting from prolonged homophobic bullying.

Reports of individual symptoms suggested that the participants in this study continued to be troubled by their recollections of homophobic bullying long after they had left secondary/high school. Indeed, D'Augelli, Grossman, and Starks (2006) found that 9% of their sample of 528 lesbian, gay, and bisexual youth met the criteria for PTSD based upon their previous experiences of victimisation; thus, the presence of symptoms several years after the victimisation ended should not be a surprise. As the data in Table 7.3 illustrate, a very small number used both prescription and nonprescription drugs as a coping strategy, and in some cases the regular use of alcohol suggests that experiences of bullying at school may be a contributory factor in a number of chronic conditions not normally associated with bullying behaviour.

Also, as the data in Table 7.2 illustrate, issues associated with confidence in social situations were a significant factor in the lives of many participants, adding further support to the argument that the development of social relationships in childhood is pivotal to a successful transition into adulthood. Such issues (which may manifest themselves as an inability to trust others, fear of emotional and physical intimacy, fear of being abused again, fear of suffering rejection, betrayal, or abandonment, and feelings of unworthiness or dependence) are central to Gilmartin's (1987) thesis on the long-term effects of bullying. Furthermore, as I mentioned earlier, he argued that experiences of victimisation and unpopularity among peers results in the inability to form platonic relationships, promoting a desire to withdraw from such social interactions and close off any emotional investment in new relationships with potential friends and even loved ones. In the end, some former victims of homophobic bullying become adept at avoiding social situations in order to ensure that they limit the opportunities to be hurt again.

> I need to feel that I really like the person and that I really understand the person before I'm prepared to get involved with them, which is why I'm very slow to make friends generally. It takes me a very long time to trust. It's usually about trust and how much I do trust people. (Tom, aged 32)

8

Summary and General Conclusions

In this chapter, I am ultimately left with the questions: what have we learned and where do we go from here? In the following pages I summarise the key findings from the studies I have detailed in this book, and then look at some of the changes that are being reported in cutting-edge research with lesbian, gay, and bisexual young people in schools, colleges, and universities today. My aim here is to demonstrate both the continuities and discontinuities in behaviour and practise among students, and the successes and challenges that lesbian, gay, and bisexual youth now face. I have also returned to social psychological explanations of prejudice and look at some recent experimental work that leads the way in providing a framework for breaking down the barriers between groups. Finally, I consider what there is yet to learn about the lives of lesbian, gay, and bisexual youth, and where future research should be focused.

What We Have Learned So Far

Name-calling and being ridiculed in front of others were the most frequently cited forms of homophobic bullying experienced at school by participants in my retrospective study. These findings reinforce both Allport's (1954) and Gallup's (1995) stereotyping hypotheses, in that the men and women I surveyed were, for the most part, called names that related specifically to their perceived sexual orientation at school. Furthermore, among males, these names tended to focus upon perceived homosexual sexual practises, gender atypicality, and presumptions of illness/abnormality. Many of the names and labels men were called also reinforced Mac an Ghaill's (1994) suggestion that schools were masculinising agents, which required boys and young men to earn their masculinity through a process of conformity.

The analyses revealed that participants' recollections of being bullied indirectly at school were associated with recollections of it occurring within the school building. For example, being frightened by a look or stare and rumour-mongering were associated with bullying taking place in corridors, classrooms, and changing rooms. As the results in Table 5.6 demonstrate, significant associations were found between participants' recollections of being bullied in the corridors, classrooms, and school-yard, and being bullied by groups of young men and young women, rather than by individuals or groups of same-sex peers. In effect, there was partial support for some of the arguments postulated by Postmes and Spears (1998) in that the acceptability of anti-homosexual attitudes most likely had an effect upon the expression of aggression. Reported fre-quencies of bullying were high, with 69% of all the participants report-ing being bullied once a week or more. However, in Chapter 5 participants also recalled significantly more peers coming to their assistance than teachers. Indeed, two thirds of the men and women I surveyed recalled peers intervening on at least one occasion, with just under a half recalling intervention occasionally and one quarter receiving assistance sometimes or more often. While this suggested that participants were not as estranged from their peers as those lesbians, gay men, and bisexual men and women portrayed in other studies, this may have been a result of the fact that many (79% of men and 50% of women) had not "come out" at school. Indeed, it is plausible to assume that the number of peers who were will-ing to intervene when participants were being bullied at school would have been negatively affected had their sexual orientation become a matter of fact rather than one of speculation.

The results provided in Chapter 5 demonstrate that, unlike other studies of bullying behaviour, much of the bullying participants were exposed to was localised within their own class or year group. Of con-siderable concern in the retrospective study was the fact that 21 partici-pants (19 men and 2 women) recalled being sexually assaulted at school. Indeed, additional analyses indicated that there was a significant associa-tion between reports of sexual assault at school and bullying taking place in the changing rooms before or after sports lessons, suggesting that this was the most likely venue for such behaviour (see Rivers, 1999). Indeed, this finding reinforced Rigby's (1997) comments relating to the central role that sports play in the definition of those who are members of the in-group and those who are relegated to out-group status, particularly among men.

Very few participants recalled having told a teacher about being bullied at school. While more women reported that they had felt able to tell a teacher compared to the men in this study, only 16% said they disclosed the reason for their bullying. However, considering that 26% reported having been bullied by a teacher because of their actual or perceived sexual orientation, approaching a member of staff for help may have been seen as an unquantifiable risk especially in schools where sex or religious education presented homosexuality as sinful, or where teachers either used or failed to sanction homophobic language in class. This view is also supported in the story provided by the mother of a gay son who was bullied by a senior member of school staff.

As I discussed in Chapter 4, much of the current research focusing upon the psychosocial correlates and long-term effects of both personal and societal negative appraisals of homosexuality and/or bisexuality suggests that they have an impact upon mental health and susceptibility to self-harm among lesbians, gay men, and bisexual men and women. Indeed, the study detailed in Chapter 7 set out to explore the relationship between bullying at school and mental health issues among a subsample of 119 lesbians, gay men, and bisexual men and women.

One of the first issues addressed in Chapter 7 related to the reported incidence of suicide or self-harm in adolescence as a result of being bullied at school and the difficulties participants had faced in coming to terms with their sexual orientation. Taking Warren's (1984) reported level of suicidal ideation (20%) as a baseline for comparison, it was expected that participants' reports of self-destructive behaviours in adolescence would be higher than those reported in Warren's study.

Overall, 53% of participants reported having contemplated self-harm as a result of bullying at school, while 40% said they had attempted at least once, and 30% more than once. Although these results suggested that participants were particularly at risk from self-destructive behaviours when they were at school, there were a number of methodological limitations relating to the reliability and validity of these findings. For example, participants may have found it difficult to separate out the reasons underpinning their attempts to self-harm. They were also asked to answer a series of questions relating to self-harming behaviours that they believed were the result of factors other than bullying at school, and as the results demonstrated 19% reported attempting to self-harm at least once, with 8% reporting such behaviour more than once. Concordant with the findings of Hershberger and D'Augelli (1995), the combined effects of familial as well as societal homophobia may have had contributory influences upon participants' predisposition toward self-harming behaviours, and while an episode of bullying may have precipitated an episode of self-harm, there may have also been a number of underlying factors (including internalised homophobia) that may affected participants' affective states, and these may not have been recalled with any clarity.

55% of participants had also been bullied or harassed either at work or at university/college ostensibly on the grounds of their actual or perceived sexual orientation. Comparable with their experiences of bullying at school, those who reported being bullied in adulthood indicated that verbal harassment was used by their peers most frequently as a method of intimidation. Interestingly, the dynamics of victimisation were very similar to those found in the earlier study of bullying at school in that participants tended to be bullied by their peers rather than by those in authority, or older colleagues. Indeed, these findings reinforce Postmes and Spears' (1998) argument that where discriminatory attitudes, beliefs, or behaviours are perceived to be a situational norm by the group, members will identify with or participate in the resultant antinormative behaviour in order to ensure that they will either retain or augment their social status within the peer group, and deflect attention away from themselves (cf. Klein, 1946).

With respect to Hawker's (1997) social ranking theory, participants' scores for self-harm, negative affect, and internalised homophobia were not found to differ significantly on the basis of exposure primarily to either agonic or hedonic aggression at school. In line with both Frable et al.'s (1998) and King et al.'s (1998) findings, participants who were either visible within their communities or supported to some degree by friends, family members, or teachers were likely to fare better than those who were hidden or recalled receiving little, if any, support when they were at school. Furthermore, those who had not disclosed their sexual orientation were also found to be more uncomfortable about being lesbian, gay, or bisexual than those who had disclosed, and they expressed greater discomfort at the possibility of disclosing to another person.

In terms of internalised homophobia, those who received little support at school were not found to differ significantly from those who received some or a great deal of support. With respect to friendships enacted outside school, the results indicated that, in terms of negative affect and internalised homophobia, those who spent much of their free time either alone or with one friend did not differ significantly from those who spent their free time with a small group of friends or many friends. Interestingly, this suggests that that the number of friends participants had when they were at school was immaterial in determining the level of functional support they received; rather, the quality of those relationships was more important (cf. Hartup, 1996).

In the follow-up study, 40% of participants reported the regular occurrence ("often" or "always") of one or more symptoms associated with PTSD. While no evidence was found suggesting a relationship between PTSD and revictimisation in adulthood, concomitant with Helzer et al.'s (1987) observations, my research suggests that there were, and continue to be, a number of people who were and are hidden from medical and psychiatric services despite living with the effects of experiences of victimisation and harassment on a daily basis.

Ultimately, much of the data from my studies have relied upon an element of retrospection. Concerns about the reliability of retrospective data were of primary importance in data collection, and to offset those concerns I undertook a small study with 60 participants from my first study of homophobic bullying at school to assess the stability of memories for past events (see Rivers, 2001a). In their meta-analytical reassessment of research using retrospective data collection techniques, Brewin, Andrews, and Gotlib (1993) concluded that "adults asked to recall salient factual details of their own childhoods are generally accurate, especially concerning experiences that fulfil the criteria of having been unique, consequential, and unexpected. Their agreement with independent sources is likely to vary from fair to excellent, depending on the concreteness of the item recalled, the provision of recognition cues, the length of time elapsed, and their awareness of the relevant facts at the time" (p. 87).

In my own reliability study, using a subsample of 60 men and women who received two copies of the same questionnaire 12 to 14 months apart, my intention was to demonstrate that recollections were not only relatively stable across time, but were also not affected by their understanding of the aims and objectives of the study (thus providing an additional index of reliability in the absence of a social desirability rating scale).

Although the Olweus Bully/Victim Questionnaire was not entirely suited to retrospective research, especially in recalling the incidence of indirect or relational bullying, generally I found that memories of school events were relatively stable across time. However, in addition to questions relating to the stability of those memories also comes the question of factual reliability. Without peer or teacher nomination strategies to identify the bully/victim status of participants when they were at school, it was impossible to assess the reliability of participants' retrospective reports. Yet this is a criticism that can be levied at any research asking participants to recall experiences, whether recent or long past. Although some studies of contemporary bullying have provided a measure of reliability in terms of assessing the degree of concordance between participants' perceptions of their own bully/victim status and peer/teacher nominations, the majority of researchers studying bullying continue to rely upon self-reports without necessarily assessing the reliability of those reports. In the end, bullying is very much a subjective experience, and as I have concluded elsewhere (see Rivers et al., 2007) while a student's intention may not be to bully another, if the purported victim feels that the behaviour can be construed as bullying, then it becomes bullying. This may account for the significant discrepancies we find in self-reports of bully and victim status among students. Nevertheless, an important question remains: do young people today face the same level of discrimination as they did in the past?

Today's Students: The Gay Teen and the Postgay Era

With the coming of the twenty-first century, various authors have noted something of a sea change in the way lesbian, gay, and bisexual youth experience education. Savin-Williams (2005), in his controversial book *The New Gay Teenager*, argues that the deficit model of research that has so preoccupied researchers (including this author) has, to a significant degree, distorted the successes that sexual minority youth experience. Savin-Williams argues that since the early research of the 1980s and

1990s, experiences of growing up for lesbian, gay, and bisexual youth have changed and no longer differ dramatically from those of their heterosexual counterparts. He describes such young people as moving from a position of exceptionality to one of banality. In what he describes as "a postgay era," these youth can "pursue diverse personal and political goals whether they be a desire to blend into mainstream society or a fight to radically restructure modern discourse about sexuality" (p. 222). Thus, we should no longer view lesbian, gay, and bisexual young people as potentially damaged or particularly vulnerable when compared to heterosexual youth, but rather accept them as self-actualised, with the ability to forge their own future without fear of reprisal. However, what evidence do we have for this dramatic turnabout in the fortunes of lesbian, gay, and bisexual youth?

In a more recent study I conducted with Nathalie Noret (Rivers & Noret, 2008), 53 students (average age 13.6 years) who reported being solely or primarily attracted to members of the same sex were matched with 53 peers who reported being attracted solely to members of the opposite sex and were compared on six demographic factors as well as exposure to bullying at school. Using data on tobacco and alcohol use, drug use, health risk behaviours, concerns and sources of social support, interpersonal sensitivity, depression, anxiety, hostility, suicidal ideation, loneliness, and concentration, we found that same-sex-attracted youth were still more likely to engage in some health risk behaviours when compared to their opposite-sex-attracted peers. For example, same-sex-attracted students reported drinking alcohol alone more than opposite-sex-attracted peers; however, they were no more likely to use Class 1 and 2 drugs. They were more likely to report being worried about their sexual orientation, and were more likely to seek support from a member of school staff than opposite-sex-attracted peers. In terms of mental health issues, same-sex-attracted youths were also more likely to report feeling lonely, and exhibited some of the classic symptoms associated with enforced isolation.

While our study suggests that perhaps the picture Savin-Williams (2005) paints of the new gay teenager is not one that resonates with the young people with whom Nathalie and I worked, increasingly there is empirical support for Savin-Williams' observations among older teenagers, particularly those between the ages of 16 and 18 years.

In his study of male students attending three sixth-form colleges in the U.K., McCormack (forthcoming) presents data demonstrating that many of the students he interviewed intellectualise and espouse pro-gay attitudes and support openly gay students in their midst. McCormack further demonstrates that the unofficial hierarchies within these sixth-form colleges are no longer based upon the marginalisation and subordination of particular individuals and groups. Thus, homophobia in school settings is both temporally and spatially situated, and unlike many of the studies conducted in the 1980s and 1990s, today's male students are not uniformly homophobic. Although McCormack acknowledges that heterosexuality is still esteemed in the school setting, lesbian, gay, and bisexual students are increasingly supported and valued by their peers and by schools.

In a related article, McCormack (2010) further argues that in two of the three sixth-form colleges in which he collected data, there was no tangible evidence of homophobia. In the third, although homophobic epithets were reported, they were used by a minority of boys, and words such as "poof" were not part of the everyday heterosexual male student discourse. However, comparable with the findings from the studies I conducted, McCormack argues that even when homophobia is not part of everyday discourse and is shunned by many students, when it occurs little is done to support the victim: the majority of students do not change their behaviours or respond when they hear a homophobic name being called. Thus, while homophobia may be condemned within the context of an interview with a researcher, the reality in the classroom or schoolyard may be different. The reticence McCormack found suggests that the 'gay" label is not one that many young men feel they can challenge openly, even when it is not directed at them.

However, McCormack and Anderson (in press) have argued that, unlike the boys in Mac an Ghaill's (1994) study, today's teenagers no longer wish to project an image of homophobic heterosexuality. They argue that heterosexual identities are consolidated through a discourse of (hetero)sexual potency and, somewhat ironically, a willingness to articulate same-sex desire, albeit in safe contexts (i.e., where banter and horseplay are common). Today's young heterosexual male is, in many ways, a complex individual, with a sense of morality that challenges inequality and a desire to express platonic love for his same-sex friends; but at the same time, he is wary about the ways in which such love is expressed. So, rather than the gay teenager being a force for change in society, it can equally be argued that the heterosexual teenager has driven this change. But how can this change be explained?

Despite the large amount of research conducted in the field of bullying behaviour, as I have previously argued, little attention has been paid to the theoretical understandings of this phenomenon. While some researchers have suggested that a primary motivator for bullying behaviour is low self-esteem, other researchers have shown that so-called bullies display well-developed social skills (Sutton, Smith, & Swettenham, 1999). For victims, bullying reinforces a sense of worthlessness and a sense of missing out particularly in terms of the everyday experiences that heterosexual youths encounter.

In previous chapters, I have argued that the official and unofficial hierarchies that exist within schools value some traits and actively denigrate others. Furthermore, an individual's self-esteem is intrinsically linked to group membership. Greater self-esteem is experienced by those who are members of the in-group and lower self-esteem is experienced by members of the out-group. Perpetrators of bullying may have moderate to low social status, and may also be isolates among their own peers, but they may gain heightened status and self-esteem by drawing together an in-group consisting of younger or less able confederates who are willing to assist him or her in bullying others. I have also argued in Chapter 3 that if victims have very low social status within their own peer group and, as a consequence, low self-esteem, they are also unlikely to be able to raise their self-esteem, because their social networks are being continually eroded by peers. In such situations, even with the sense of social justice displayed by the young men in McCormack's (2010) study, the decision not to intervene or to ignore the plight of a victim of homophobic bullying can be seen as a defence mechanism ensuring that the observer does not become a target for the bullies.

In essence, McCormack's (2010) research highlights the fact that, even when we wish to intervene, bystander apathy continues to be the *modus operandi* for the majority, but why is this the case?

Research conducted by Dovidio, Kawakami, and Beech (2001) can help us understand why many of us do not intervene in situations that outrage us. They have shown that there is very weak convergence between explicit attitudes that we purport to hold and those we hold implicitly. While prejudices can be explicitly rejected and statements of support can be made (particularly in the face of social criticism), prejudicial attitudes or beliefs can still be retained. Thus, while an individual may espouse pro-gay attitudes, he or she may act in ways that betray a more indifferent view. Concomitantly, Rudman, Phellan, and Heppen (2007) have shown that there is a learned component to the development of explicit and implicit attitudes that, if not challenged, can promote unhealthy or problematic behaviour.

Inevitably this means that teachers and parents need to understand the prevailing attitudes and beliefs among young people in order to effectively combat any form of bullying behaviour. They also need to understand how those prejudices, beliefs, and dislikes arise and how students engage with them on a daily basis (either online or among peers). However, as social psychologists Turner and Crisp (2010) have shown in their experimental studies, educational mechanisms such as using imagined experiences or scenarios (similar to the class activities provided in Chapter 6), can result in a reduction in both implicit and explicit prejudices. Furthermore, in a related study, Hall, Crisp and Suen (2009) have argued that an ability to blur boundaries between groups also has the effect of reducing implicit prejudice. In effect, they suggest that, within the classroom context, activities that downplay inter-group differences also have the potential to promote inter-group relations. However, greater tolerance of lesbians, gay men, and bisexual men and women within society and the introduction of equality legislation, civil partnerships, adoption rights, and gay marriage are also likely to have an impact upon the way in which young people (particularly those over the age of 16 years) appraise and understand homosexuality. Indeed, as Taulke-Johnson (2009) has shown in his study of young gay men at university, being "gay" was not a central part of university life or experience, and with each generation of undergraduates it has increasingly been downplayed, becoming only one facet of multifaceted lives, as this interview extract illustrates (p. 75):

> It hasn't really played a huge part in my life to be honest since I've been here [at university]... I don't really think it really played a part in kind of how I felt or how I socialised or how I got on with

other people… It hasn't played a very large role at all in where I've chosen to live or who I've chosen to live with or how comfortable I've been living there. (Eli)

Overview and General Conclusions

Despite their experiences of bullying, it was clear that many of the people I have surveyed or interviewed have overcome their experiences of homophobic bullying and have gone on to build successful full lives. While there was some evidence supporting the assertion that lesbian, gay, and bisexual former victims of homophobia are prone to depression when compared to other groups, this was only one result from a battery of measures showing that there is little evidence of long-term anxiety among participants or, indeed, insecurity in forming relationships that has previously been reported. Although some of the men and women I interviewed expressed concerns about forming relationships, there is little evidence to suggest that these concerns became realities. Having said that, participants did comment that they felt they had missed out on a significant part of their social and sexual development during adolescence, and this may have had a detrimental effect upon their early attempts to initiate both social and sexual relationships in later life.

One of the most significant results to emerge from this study is undoubtedly the number of participants who contemplated or attempted self-harm when they were being bullied at school. However, while one should not dismiss the gravity of these findings, a note of caution must be added. As Bagley and Tremblay (1997) pointed out in their study of suicidal ideation and parasuicidal behaviour among 18- to 27-year-old Canadian males, gay and bisexual men accounted for no less than 62.5% of suicide attempters. This suggests that, in addition to homophobia in the classroom, experiences of societal heterosexism were also likely to play a significant role in decision-making processes. As I argue above, where changes have occurred in society's attitudes towards lesbians, gay men, and bisexual men and women, we should also see a reduction in the incidence of self-harming behaviour.

While the findings from the studies I have conducted do not necessarily paint a picture of long-term trauma for the majority of lesbians, gay men, and bisexual men and women bullied at school, they do represent a considerable body of evidence identifying the nature and correlates of homophobia that has occurred within educational institutions. Given some of the positive outcomes found in these studies, future researchers should begin to focus more intently upon the strategies and resilience strategies used by marginalised groups to successfully negotiate their way into adulthood. Furthermore, we perhaps need to explore more widely the changing nature of the school environment and the impact social and legal recognition of the salience of lesbian and gay relationships have for young people in our educational systems. Finally, we should not underestimate the value of those who support lesbian, gay, and bisexual youths and their families as they negotiate their way into adulthood. The value of social support cannot be underestimated in overcoming difficult transitional periods, and it is important that we explore more closely the qualities associated with that support.

References

Achenbach, T. M., & Edelbrock, C. S. (1981). Behavioral problems and competencies reported by parents of normal and disturbed children aged four through sixteen. *Monographs of the Society for Research in Child Development,* 46 (1, No. 188).

Adams, A. (1992). *Bullying at work: How to confront it and overcome it.* London: Virago.

Ahmad, Y., & Smith, P. K. (1994). Bullying in schools and the issue of sex differences. In J. Archer (Ed.), *Male violence* (pp. 70–83). London: Routledge.

Ahmad, Y., Whitney, I., & Smith, P. K. (1991). A survey service for schools on bully/victim problems. In P. K. Smith & D. A. Thompson (Eds.), *Practical approaches to bullying* (pp. 103–111). London: David Fulton.

Alexander, R. A. (1986). *The relationship between internalized homophobia and depression and low self-esteem in gay men.* Unpublished doctoral dissertation, University of California at Santa Barbara.

Allen, R. E. (1992) (Ed.). *Oxford English dictionary* (8th ed.). Oxford: Clarendon Press.

Allport, G. W. (1954). *The nature of prejudice.* London: Addison-Wesley.

American Psychiatric Association (1994). *The diagnostic and statistical manual of mental disorders (DSM IV).* Washington, DC: American Psychiatric Association.

Anderson, E. (2008). Inclusive masculinities in fraternal settings. *Men and Masculinities, 10,* 604–620.

Anderson, E. (2009). *Inclusive masculinity: The changing nature of masculinities.* New York: Routledge.

Anderson, E. M., Clarke, L., & Spain, B. (1982). *Disability in adolescence.* London: Methuen.

Angell, E. (2003). *Judaism and homosexuality. The Psychologist,* 16, 9.

Aronson, E. (1980). *The social animal.* San Francisco: Freeman.

Arora, C. M. J. (1996). Defining bullying: towards a clearer understanding and more effective intervention strategies. *School Psychology International,* 17, 317–329.

Arnot, M. (1994). Male hegemony, social class and women's education. In L. Stone (Ed.), *The education feminist reader* (pp. 84–104). London: Routledge.

Askew, S., & Ross, C. (1988). *Boys don't cry: Boys and sexism in education.* Milton Keynes: Open University Press.

Atria, M., Strohmeier, D., & Spiel, C. (2007). The relevance of the school class as social unit for the prevalence of bullying and victimization. *European Journal of Developmental Psychology,* 4, 372–387.

Aurand, S. K., Adessa, R., & Bush, C. (1985). *Violence and discrimination against Philadelphia lesbian and gay people.* Unpublished report, Philadelphia Lesbian and Gay Task Force.

Bagley, C., & Ramsay, R. (1986). Sexual abuse in childhood: psychological outcomes and implications for social work practice. *Journal of Social Work and Human Sexuality,* 5, 33–47.

Bagley, C., & Tremblay, P. (1997). Suicidal behaviors in homosexual and bisexual males. *Crisis,* 18, 24–34.

Bagwell, C. L., Newcomb, A. F., & Bukowski, W. M. (1996). *Pre-adolescent friendship and peer rejection as predictors of adult adjustment.* Unpublished manuscript, University of Richmond.

Bailey, M. J., Bobrow, D., Wolfe, M., & Mikach, S. (1995). Sexual orientation of adult sons of gay fathers. *Developmental Psychology,* 31, 124–129.

Ball, H. A., Arseneault, L., Taylor, A., Maughan, B., & Moffitt, T. E. (2008). Genetic and environmental influences on victims, bullies and bully-victims in childhood. *Journal of Child Psychology and Psychiatry,* 49, 104–112.

Bem, D. J. (1996). Exotic becomes erotic: a developmental theory of sexual orientation. *Psychological Review,* 103, 320–335.

Berrill, K.T. (1992). Anti-gay violence and victimization in the United States: an overview. In G. M. Herek & K. T. Berrill (Eds.), *Hate crimes: Confronting violence against lesbians and gay men* (pp. 19–45). Newbury Park, CA: Sage.

Besag, V. E. (1989). *Bullies and victims in schools.* Milton Keynes: Open University Press.

Biblarz, T. J., & Stacey, J. (2010). How does the gender of parents matter? *Journal of Marriage & Family,* 72, 3–22.

Bigner, J. J., & Bozett, F. W. (1990). Parenting by gay fathers. In F. W. Bozett & M. B. Sussman (Eds.), *Homosexuality and family relations* (pp. 155–176). New York: Harrington Park Press.

Bjerregaard, B. (2002). Self-definitions of gang membership and involvement in delinquent activities. *Youth Society, 34,* 31–54.

Björkqvist, K. L., Ekman, K., & Lagerspetz, K. M. J. (1982). Bullies and victims: their ego picture, ideal ego picture, and normative ego picture. *Scandinavian Journal of Psychology, 23,* 281–290.

Björkqvist, K. L., Lagerspetz, K. M. J., & Kaukiainen, A. (1992). Do girls manipulate and boys fight? Developmental trends in regard to direct and indirect aggression. *Aggressive Behavior, 18,* 117–127.

Boswell, J. (1996). *The marriage of likeness: Same-sex unions in pre-modern Europe.* London: Fontana.

Boulton, M. J. (1995). Patterns of bully/victim problems in mixed race groups of children. *Social Development, 4,* 277–293.

Boulton, M. J., & Smith, P. K. (1992). Ethnic preferences and perceptions among Asian and White middle school children. *Social Development, 1,* 55–66.

Boulton, M. J., & Smith, P.K. (1994). Bully/victim problems in middle-school children: stability, self-perceived competence, peer perceptions and peer acceptance. *British Journal of Developmental Psychology, 12,* 315–329

Brewin, C. R., Andrews, B., & Gotlib, I. H. (1993). Psychopathology and early experience: a reappraisal of retrospective reports. *Psychological Bulletin, 113,* 82–98.

Briere, J., & Runtz, M. (1987). Post sexual abuse trauma: data and implications for clinical practice. *Journal of Interpersonal Violence, 2,* 367–379.

Bronfenbrenner, U. (1977). Toward an experimental ecology of human development. *American Psychologist, 32,* 513–531.

Brown, R. (1995). *Prejudice: It's social psychology.* Oxford: Blackwell.

Browne, A., & Finkelhor, D. (1986). Impact of childhood sexual abuse: a review of the research. *Psychological Bulletin, 99,* 66–77.

Bushnell, J. A., Wells, J. E., & Oakley-Browne, M. A. (2007). Long-term effects of intrafamilial sexual abuse in childhood. *Acta Psychiatrica Scandinavica, 85,* 136–142.

Byrne, B. J. (1987). *A study of the incidence and nature of bullies and whipping boys (victims) in a Dublin City post primary school for boys.* Unpublished MEd thesis, Trinity College Dublin.

Byrne, B. J. (1994). Bullies and victims in a school setting with reference to some Dublin schools. *Irish Journal of Psychology, 15,* 574–586.

Cahill, C., Llewelyn, S. P., & Pearson, C. (1991). Long-term effects of sexual abuse which occurred in childhood: a review. *British Journal of Clinical Psychology, 30,* 117–130.

California Safe Schools Coalition & 4-H Center for Youth Development, University of California, Davis. (2004). *Consequences of harassment based on actual or perceived sexual orientation and gender non-conformity and step to making schools safer.* San Francisco & Davis: Authors.

Cohn, T. (1988). Sambo: a study in name-calling. In E. Kelly & T. Cohn (Eds.), *Racism in schools: New research evidence* (pp. 29–63). Stoke-on-Trent: Trentham.

Congregation for the Doctrine of the Faith (1986). *Letter to the bishops of the Catholic Church on the pastoral care of homosexual persons.* Retrieved 14 May 2010 from: http://www.vatican.va/roman_curia/congregations/cfaith/documents/rc_con_cfaith_doc_19861001_homosexual-persons_en.html.

Connell, R. W. (1992). A very straight gay: masculinity, homosexual experience and the dynamics of gender. *American Sociological Review*, 57, 735–751.

Craig, W. M., & Pepler, D. J. (1995). Peer processes in bullying and victimization: an observational study. *Exceptionality Education Canada*, 5, 81–95.

Craig, W. M., & Pepler, D. (1997). Observations of bullying and victimization in the school years. *Canadian Journal of School Psychology*, 2, 41–60.

Cramer, D. (1986). Gay parents and their children: a review of research and practical implications. *Journal of Counseling and Development*, 64, 504–507.

D'Augelli, A. R. (1992). Lesbian and gay male undergraduates' experiences of harassment and fear on campus. *Journal of Interpersonal Violence*, 7, 383–395.

D'Augelli, A. R., Grossman, A. H., & Starks, M. T. (2006). Childhood gender atypicality, victimization, and PTSD among lesbian, gay, and bisexual youth. *Journal of Interpersonal Violence*, 21, 1462–1482.

Darwin, C. (1859). *On the origin of species by means of natural selection.* London: Murray.

Davey, A. G. (1983). *Learning to be prejudiced: Growing up in a multiethnic Britain.* London: Edward Arnold.

Decker, S. H., & Curry, G. D. (2000). Addressing key features of gang membership: Measuring the involvement of young members. *Journal of Criminal Justice*, 28, 473–482.

Derogatis, L. R. (1993). *Brief Symptom Inventory: Administration, Scoring, and Procedures Manual.* Minneapolis: National Computer Systems Inc.

Deschamps, J-C., & Devos, T. (1998). Regarding the relationship between social identity and personal identity. In S. Worchel, J. F. Morales, D. Páez, & J-C. Deschamps (Eds.), *Social identity: International perspectives* (pp. 1–12). London: Sage.

Diener, E. (1976). Effects of prior destructive behavior, anonymity, and group presence on deindividuation and aggression. *Journal of Personality and Social Psychology*, 33, 497–507.

Diener, E. (1980). Deindividuation: the absence of self-awareness and self-regulation in group members. In P. B. Paulus (Ed.), *Psychology of group influence* (pp. 209–242). Hillsdale: Erlbaum.

Diener, E., Westford, K. L., Dineen, J., & Fraser, S. C. (1973). Beat the pacifist: the deindividuation effects of anonymity and group presence. *Proceedings of the 81st Annual Convention of the American Psychological Association*, 8, 221–222.

Dohrenwend, B. S., Krasnoff, L., Askenasy, A. R., & Dohrenwend, B. P. (1978). Exemplification of a method of scaling life-events: the PERI Life Events Scale. *Journal of Health and Social Behavior, 19*, 205–229.

Doise, W. (1976). *L'Articulation psychosociologique et les relations entre groupes.* Brussels: De Boeck.

Douglas, T. (1995). *Scapegoats: Transferring blame.* London: Routledge.

Dovidio, J. F., Kawakami, K., & Beach, K. R. (2001). Implicit and explicit attitudes: Examination of the relationship between measures of intergroup bias. In R. Brown & S. L. Gaertner (Eds.), *Blackwell handbook of social psychology: Intergroup processes* (pp. 175–197). Oxford: Blackwell.

Dressler, J. (1978). Gay teachers: a disesteemed minority in an overly esteemed profession. *Rutgers/Camden Law Journal, 9*, 399–445.

Dukes, R. L., Martinez, R. O., & Stein, J. A. (1997). Precursors and consequences of membership in youth gangs. *Youth and Society, 29*, 139–165.

Duncan, N. (1999). *Sexual bullying.* London: Routledge.

Duveen, G., & Lloyd, B. (1986). The significance of social identities. *British Journal of Social Psychology, 25*, 219–230.

Earnshaw, J., & Cooper, C. L. (1996). *Stress and employer liability.* London: Institute of Personnel and Development.

Einarsen, S. (2000). Harassment and bullying at work: A review of the Scandinavian approach. *Aggression and Violent Behavior, 5*, 379–401.

Einarsen, S., Raknes, B. I., & Matthiesen, S. B. (1994). Bullying and its relationship to work and environment quality: an exploratory study. *European Work and Organizational Psychologist, 4*, 381–401.

Ellason, J. W., & Ross, C. A. (1997). Childhood trauma and psychiatric symptoms. *Psychological Reports, 80*, 447–450.

Ellis, A. (1997). *Workplace bullying.* Unpublished report, Ruskin College, Oxford.

Ellis, V., & High, S. (2004). Something more to tell you: Gay, lesbian or bisexual young people's experiences of secondary schooling. *British Educational Research Journal, 30*, 213–225.

Epstein, D. (1994) (Ed.). *Challenging lesbian and gay inequalities in education.* Buckingham: Open University Press.

Espelage, D. L., & Holt, M. L. (2001). Bullying and victimization during early adolescence: Peer influences and psychosocial correlates. *Journal of Emotional Abuse, 2*, 123–142.

Espelage, D. L., Holt, M. K., & Henkel, R. R. (2003). Examination of peer-group contextual effects on aggression during early adolescence. *Child Development, 74*, 205–220.

Espelage, D. L., & Swearer, S. M. (2003). Research on school bullying and victimization: What have we learned and where do we go from here? *School Psychology Review, 32*, 365–383.

Evans, N. J., & D'Augelli, A. R. (1996). Lesbians, gay men and bisexual people in college. In R. C. Savin-Williams & K. M. Cohen (Eds.), *The lives of lesbians, gays, and bisexuals: Children to adults* (pp. 201–226). Fort Worth: Harcourt-Brace.

Eysenck, H. J. (1976). Genetic factors in personality development. In A. R. Kaplan (Ed.), *Human behavior genetics* (pp. 245–282). Springfield: Charles C. Thomas.

Eysenck, H. J., & Eysenck, S. B. (1975). *Manual: Eysenck Personality Questionnaire.* San Diego: EdITS.

Farrington, D. P. (1993). Childhood origins of teenage antisocial behaviour and adult social dysfunction. *Journal of the Royal Society of Medicine, 86,* 13–17.

Farrington, D. P. (1995). The development of offending and antisocial behaviour from childhood: key findings from the Cambridge Study in Delinquent Behaviour. *Journal of Child Psychology and Psychiatry, 36,* 929–964.

Festinger, L., Pepitone, A., & Newcomb, T. (1952). Some consequences of de-individuation in a group. *Journal of Abnormal and Social Psychology, 47,* 382–389.

Finkelhor, S., Mitchell, K., & Wolak, J. (2000) *Online victimization: A report on the nation's youth.* Available online from http://www.unh.edu/ccrc/Youth_Internet_info_page.html (accessed 12 April 2009).

Fonagy, P., Steele, M., Steele, H., Higgitt, A., & Target, M. (1994). The theory and practice of resilience. *Journal of Child Psychology and Psychiatry, 35,* 231–257.

Fox, S., & Stallworth, L.E. (2005). Racial/ethnic bullying: Exploring links between bullying and racism in the US workplace. *Journal of Vocational Behavior, 66,* 438–456.

Frable, D. E. S., Platt, L., & Hoey, S. (1998). Concealable stigmas and positive self-perceptions: feeling better around similar others. *Journal of Personality and Social Psychology, 74,* 909–922.

Frazer, J. G. (1923). *The golden bough.* London: Macmillan.

Frey, K. S., Hirschstein, M. K., Snell, J. L., Edstrom, L. V. S., MacKenzie, E. P., & Broderick, C. J. (2005). Reducing playground bullying and supporting beliefs: An experimental trail of the Steps to Respect Program. *Developmental Psychology, 41,* 479–491.

Fricke, A. (1981). *Confessions of a rock lobster.* Boston: Alyson.

Frodi, A., Macauley, J., & Thome, P.R. (1977). Are women always less aggressive than men? A review of the experimental literature. *Psychological Bulletin, 84,* 634–660.

Gallup, G. G. (1995). Have attitudes towards homosexual been shaped by natural selection? *Ethology and Sociobiology, 16,* 53–70.

Gallup, G. G., & Suarez, S. D. (1983). Homosexuality as a byproduct of selection for optimal heterosexual strategies. *Perspectives in Biology and Medicine, 26,* 315–321.

Garcia-Reid, P., Reid, R., & Peterson, N. A. (2005). School engagement among Latino youth in an urban middle school context: Valuing the role of social support. *Education and Urban Society, 37,* 257–275.

Gentry, S. E. (1992). Caring for lesbians in a homophobic society. *Health Care for Women International*, 13, 173–180.

Gilbert, P. (1989). *Human nature and suffering*. Hove: Erlbaum.

Gilbert, P. (1992). *Depression: The evolution of powerlessness*. Chichester: Wiley.

Gilbert, P. (1997). The evolution of social attractiveness and its role in shame, humiliation, guilt and therapy. *British Journal of Medical Psychology*, 70, 113–147.

Gilmartin, B. G. (1987). Peer group antecedents of severe love-shyness in males. *Journal of Personality*, 55, 467–489.

Gladstone, G. L., Parker, G. B., & Mahli, G. S. (2006). Do bullied children become anxious or depressed adults? A cross sectional investigation of the correlates of bullying and anxious depression. *Journal of Nervous and Mental Disease*, 194, 201–208.

Goffman, E. (1968). *Stigma: Notes on the management of spoiled identity*. Harmondsworth: Penguin (Pelican Edition).

Goffman, E. (1969). *The presentation of the self in everyday life*. Harmondsworth: Penguin.

Golombok, S., & Tasker, F. (1996). Do parents influence the sexual orientation of their children? Findings from a longitudinal study of lesbian families. *Developmental Psychology*, 32, 3–11.

Gottman, J. S. (1990). Children of gay and lesbian parents. In F. W. Bozett & M. B. Sussman (Eds.), *Homosexuality and family relations* (pp. 177–196). New York: Harrington Park Press.

Griffin, C. (1985). *Typical girls? Young women from school to the job market*. London: Routledge and Kegan Paul.

Griffin, P. (1995). Homophobia in sport: addressing the needs of lesbian and gay high school athletes. In G. Unks (Ed.), *The gay teen: Educational practice and theory for lesbian, gay and bisexual adolescents* (pp. 53–65). New York: Routledge.

Gross, L., Aurand, S., & Adessa, R. (1988). *Violence and discrimination against lesbian and gay people in Philadelphia and the Commonwealth of Pennsylvania*. Unpublished report, Philadelphia Lesbian and Gay Task Force.

Hall, N. R., Crisp, R. J., & Suen, M-W. (2009). Reducing implicit prejudice by blurring intergroup boundaries. *Basic & Applied Social Psychology*, 31, 244–254.

Hamner, K. M. (1992). Gay-bashing: a social identity analysis of violence against lesbians and gay men. In G. M. Herek & K. T. Berrill (Eds.), *Hate crimes: Confronting violence against lesbians and gay men* (pp. 179–190). Newbury Park: Sage.

Hartup, W. W., & Stevens, N. (1997). Friendships and adaptation in the life course. *Psychological Bulletin*, 121, 355–370.

Hartup, W. W. (1996). The company they keep: friendships and their developmental significance. *Child Development*, 67, 1–13.

Haugaard, J. J., & Tilly, C. (1988). Characteristics predicting children's responses to sexual encounters with other children. *Child Abuse and Neglect*, 12, 209–218.

Hawker, D. S. J. (1997). *Socioemotional maladjustment among victims of different forms of peer aggression.* Unpublished PhD thesis, Keele University.

Hawkins, D. L., Pepler, D. J., & Craig, W. M. (2001). Naturalistic observations of peer intervention in bullying. *Social Development*, 10, 512–527.

Heinemann, P. P. (1972). *Mobbning - gruppvåld bland barn och vuxna.* Stockholm: Natur och Kultur.

Helzer, J. E., Robins, L. N., & McEvoy, L. (1987). Post-traumatic stress disorder in the general population: findings of the epidemiologic catchment area survey. *New England Journal of Medicine*, 317, 1630–1634.

Henderson-King, E. I., & Nisbett, R. E. (1996). Anti-black prejudice as a function of exposure to the negative behaviour of a single black person. *Journal of Personality and Social Psychology*, 71, 654–664.

Henry, D. B., Cartland, J., Ruchross, H., & Monahan, K. (2004). A return potential measure of setting norms for aggression. *American Journal of Community Psychology*, 33, 131–149.

Herbert, M. (1998). *Clinical child psychology: Social learning, development and behaviour.* Chichester: Wiley.

Herdt, G. H., & Boxer, A. (1996). *Children of horizons: How gay and lesbian teens are leading a new way out of the closet.* Boston: Beacon.

Herek, G. M. (1984). Beyond 'homophobia': a social psychological perspective on attitudes towards lesbians and gay men. *Journal of Homosexuality*, 10, 1–21.

Herek, G. M. (1986). The social psychology of homophobia: towards a practical theory. *Journal of Law and Social Change*, 14, 923–934.

Herek, G. M. (1992). Psychological heterosexism and anti-gay violence: the social psychology of bigotry and bashing. In G. M. Herek & K. T. Berrill (Eds.), *Hate crimes: Confronting violence against lesbians and gay men* (pp. 149–169). Newbury Park: Sage.

Herman, J., & Hirschman, L. (1981). *Father-daughter incest.* Cambridge: Harvard University Press.

Hershberger, S. L., & D'Augelli, A. R. (1995). The impact of victimization on the mental health and suicidality of lesbian, gay and bisexual youths. *Developmental Psychology*, 31, 65–74.

Hinde, R. A., Titmus, G., Easton, D., & Tamplin, A. (1985). Incidence of 'friendship' and behavior with strong associates versus non-associates in preschoolers. *Child Development*, 54, 1041–1053.

Hinduja, S., & Patchin, J. W. (2008). Cyberbullying: An exploratory analysis of factors related to offending and victimization. *Deviant Behavior*, 29, 129–156.

Hoover, J. H., Oliver, R., & Hazler, R. J. (1992). Bullying: perceptions of adolescent victims in the Midwestern USA. *School Psychology International*, 13, 5–16.

Howes, C. (1989). Peer interaction of young children. *Monographs of the Society for Research in Child Development*, 54 (No. 217).

Hunt, R., & Jensen, J. (2007). *The school report: The experiences of young gay people in Britain's schools*. London: Stonewall.

Hunter, J. (1990). Violence against lesbian and gay male youths. *Journal of Interpersonal Violence, 5,* 295–300.

Juvonen, J., Graham, S., & Schuster, M. A. (2003). Bullying among young adolescents: The strong, the weak, and the troubled. *Pediatrics, 112,* 1231–1237.

Kelly, E., & Cohn, T. (1988). *Racism in schools: New research evidence*. Stoke-on-Trent: Trentham.

Kilpatrick, D. G., Saunders, B. E., Veronen, L. J., Best, C. L., & Von, J. M. (1987). Criminal victimization: lifetime prevalence, reporting to police, and psychological impact. *Crime and Deliquency, 33,* 479–489.

King, L. A., King, D. A., Fairbank, J. A., Keane, T. M., & Adams, G. A. (1998). Resilience-recovery factors in post-traumatic stress disroder among female and male Vietnam veterans: hardiness, postwar social support and additional stressful life events. *Journal of Personality and Social Psychology, 74,* 420–434.

Klein, A. M. (1989). Managing deviance: hustling, homophobia and the bodybuilding subculture. *Deviant Behaviour, 10,* 11–27.

Klein, M. (1946). *Writings: Notes on some schizoid mechanisms* (Vol. 3). London: Hogarth.

Klinger, E. (1977). *Meaning and void: Inner experience and the incentives in people's lives*. Minneapolis: University of Minnesota Press.

Kobasa, S. C. (1979). Stressful life events, personality and health: An enquiry into hardiness. *Journal of Personality and Social Psychology, 37,* 1–11.

Kohlberg, L., LaCross, I., & Ricks, D. (1972). The predictability of adult mental health from childhood behavior. In B. B. Wolman (Ed.), *Manual of child psychopathology* (pp. 1217–1284). New York: McGraw Hill.

Kovacs, M., & Devlin, B. (1998). Internalizing disorders in childhood. *Journal of Child Psychology and Psychiatry, 39,* 47–63.

Kowalski, R. M., Limber, S. P., & Agatston, P. W. (2008). *Cyberbullying: Bullying in the digital age*. Malden, MA: Wiley/Blackwell.

Kupersmidt, J. B. (1983, April). *Predicting delinquency and academic problems from childhood peer status*. Paper presented at the Biennial Meeting of the Society for Research in Child Development, Detroit, MI, USA.

Lagerspetz, K. M. J., Björkqvist, K. L., & Peltonen, T. (1988). Is indirect aggression typical in females? Gender differences in aggressiveness in 11- to 12-year-old children. *Aggressive Behavior, 14,* 403–414.

Lagerspetz, K. M. J., Björkqvist, K. L., Berts, M., & King, E. (1982). Group aggression among school children in three schools. *Scandinavian Journal of Psychology, 23,* 45–52.

Lansford, J. E., Dodge, K. A., Pettit, G. S., Bates, J. E., Crozier, J., & Kaplow, J. (2002). A 12-year prospective study of the long-term effects of early childhood physical maltreatment on psychological, behavioral, and academic problems in adolescence. *Archives of Pediatric and Adolescent Medicine,* 156, 824–830.

Larsen, H., Branje, S. J. T., van der Valk, I., & Meeus, W. H. J. (2007). Friendship quality as a moderator between perception of interparental conflicts and maladjustment in adolescence. *International Journal of Behavioral Development,* 31, 549–558.

Le Bon, G. (1895). *The crowd: A study of the popular mind.* London: Transaction.

Lemert, E. M. (1967). *Human deviance, social problems and social control.* Englewood Cliffs, NJ: Prentice–Hall.

Leymann, H., & Gustafsson, A. (1996). Mobbing at work and the development of post-traumatic stress disorder. *European Journal of Work and Organizational Psychology,* 5, 251–275.

Li, Q. (2005, April) *Cyberbullying in schools: Nature and extent of adolescents' experience.* Paper presented at the Annual American Educational Research Association Conference, Montreal.

Li, Q. (2006). Cyberbullying in schools: A research of gender differences. *School Psychology International,* 27, 157–170.

Li, Q. (2007). New bottle but old wine: A research of cyberbullying in schools. *Computers in Human Behavior,* 23(4), 1777–1791.

Limber, S. P., & Small, M. A. (2003). State laws and policies to address bullying in schools. *School Psychology Review,* 32, 445–455.

Ma, X. (2001). Bullying and being bullied: To what extent are bullies also victims? *American Educational Research Journal,* 38, 351–370.

Mac an Ghaill, M. (1994). *The making of men: Masculinities, sexualities and schooling.* Buckingham: Open University Press.

Malik, G. (1990). *Bullying: An investigation of race and gender aspects.* Unpublished MSc thesis, University of Sheffield.

Mar, M. (1995). Blue collar, crimson blazer. *Harvard Magazine,* 11, 47–51.

Maras, P. F. (1993). *The integration of children with disabilities into the mainstream.* Unpublished PhD thesis, University of Kent at Canterbury.

Marsella, A. J., & Snyder, K. K. (1981). Stress, social supports and schizophrenic disorders: towards an interaction model. *Schizophrenia Bulletin,* 7, 152–163.

Martin, A. D. (1982). Learning to hide: the socialisation of the gay adolescent. In S. Feinstein, J. Looney, A. Schwartzberg, & A. Sorosky (Eds.), *Adolescent psychiatry* (pp. 52–65). Chicago: University of Chicago Press.

Martlew, M., & Hodson, J. (1991). Children with mild learning difficulties in an integrated and in a special school: comparisons of behaviour, teasing and teachers' attitudes. *British Journal of Educational Psychology,* 61, 355–372.

Mason, A., & Palmer, A. (1996). *Queer bashing: A national survey of hate crimes against lesbians and gay men.* London: Stonewall.

Mason-Schrock, D. (1996). Transsexuals' narrative construction of the 'true self'. *Social Psychology Quarterly,* 59, 176–192.

Matsui, T., Tsuzuki, Y., Kakuyama, T., & Louonglatco, M. (1996). Long-term outcomes of early victimization by peers among Japanese male university students: model of a vicious cycle. *Psychological Reports*, 79, 711–720.

McCann, P. D., Minichiello, V., & Plummer, D. (2009). Is homophobia inevitable? Evidence that explores the constructed nature of homophobia, and the techniques through which men unlearn it. *Journal of Sociology*, 45, 201–220.

McCormack, M. (2010). The declining significance of homohysteria for male students in three sixth forms in the south of England. *British Educational Research Journal*, iFirst, 1–17.

McCormack, M. (forthcoming). *School boys, sexuality and friendship: The emergence of the gay friendly high school*. New York: Oxford University Press.

McCormack, M., & Anderson, E. (in press). "It's just not acceptable anymore": The erosion of homophobia and the softening of masculinity at an English state school. *Sociology*.

McLaughlin, C., Arnold, R., & Boyd, E. (2005). Bystanders in schools: What do they do and what do they think? Factors influencing the behaviour of English students as bystanders. *Pastoral Care in Education*, 23, 17–22.

Mehan, P. J., Lamb, J. A., Saltzman, L. E., & O'Carroll, P. W. (1992). Attempted suicide among young adults: progress towards a meaningful estimate of prevalence. *American Journal of Psychiatry*, 149, 41–44.

Meiselman, K. (1978). *Incest: A psychological study of causes and effects with treatment recommendations*. San Francisco: Jossey–Bass.

Mikkelsen, E. G., & Einarsen, S. (2008). Relationships between exposure to bullying at work and psychological and psychosomatic health complaints: The role of state negative affectivity and generalized self-efficacy. *Scandinavian Journal of Psychology*, 43, 397–405.

Miller, B. (1979). Gay fathers and their children. *Family Coordinator*, 28, 544–552.

Mondimore, F. M. (1996). *A natural history of homosexuality*. Baltimore: The Johns Hopkins Press.

Moran, S., Smith, P. K., Thompson, D., & Whitney, I. (1993). Ethnic differences in experiences of bullying in Asian and White Children. *British Journal of Educational Psychology*, 63, 431–440.

Moriarty, M. (1997). *Working in UNISON for lesbian and gay rights*. London: UNISON.

Morrison, T. G., McLeod, L. D., Morrison, M. A., Anderson, D., & O'Connor, W. E. (1997). Gender stereotyping, homonegativity, and misconceptions about sexually coercive behavior among adolescents. *Youth and Society*, 28, 351–382.

Muehrer, P. (1995). Suicide and sexual orientation: a critical summary of recent research and direction for future research. *Suicide and Life Threatening Behavior*, 25, 72–81.

Murphy, S. M., Kilpatrick, D. G., Amick-McMullan, A., Veronen, L. J., Paduhovich, J., Best, C. L., Villeponteaux, L. A., & Saunders, B. E. (1988). Current psychological functioning of child sexual assault survivors: a community study. *Journal of Interpersonal Violence, 3,* 55–79.

Nabuzoka, D., & Smith, P.K. (1993). Sociometric status and social behaviour of children with and without learning difficulties. *Journal of Child Psychology and Psychiatry, 34,* 1435–1448.

Nansel, T. R., Overpeck, M., Pilla, R. S., Ruan, W. J., Simons-Morton, B. G., & Scheidt, P. (2001). Bullying behaviors among U.S. youth: Prevalence and association with psychosocial adjustment. *Journal of the American Medical Association, 285,* 2094–2100.

NCH (2002). *NCH national survey 2002: Bullying.* Available from http://www.nch.org.uk/itok/showquestion.asp?faq=9&fldAuto=145 (accessed 1 September 2003).

New Jersey Department of Education. *Model Policy and Guidance for Prohibiting Harassment, Intimidation and Bullying on School Property, at School-Sponsored Functions and on School Buses, Revised April 2006.* Retrieved 10 October 2006 from http://www.state.nj.us/njded/parents/bully.htm.

Newman, D. L., Moffit, T. E., Caspi, A., Magdol, L. Silva, P. A., & Stanton, W. R. (1996). Psychiatric disorder in a birth cohort of young adults: prevalence, comorbidity, clinical significance, and new case incidence from ages 11 to 21. *Journal of Consulting and Clinical Psychology, 64,* 552–562.

Norwich, B., & Kelly, N. (2004). Pupils' view of inclusion: moderate learning difficulties and bullying in mainstream and special schools. *British Educational Research Journal, 30,* 43–65.

Nungesser, L. G. (1983). *Homosexual acts, actors and identities.* New York: Praeger.

O'Moore, A. M., & Hillery, B. (1989). Bullying in Dublin Schools. *Irish Journal of Psychology, 10,* 426–441.

OfSTED (2002). *Sex and relationships (HMI443).* London: Author.

Oldmeadow, J., & Fiske, S.Y. (2007). System-justifying ideologies moderate status = competence stereotypes: Roles for belief in a just world and social dominance orientation. *European Journal of Social Psychology, 37,* 1135–1148.

Olweus, D. (1973). *Hackkycklingar och oversittare: Forskning om skolmobbning.* Stockholm: Almqvist och Wicksell.

Olweus, D. (1977). Aggression and peer acceptance in adolescent boys: two short-term longitudinal studies of ratings. *Child Development, 48,* 1301–1313.

Olweus, D. (1978). *Aggression in schools: Bullies and whipping boys.* New York: Wiley.

Olweus, D. (1984). Aggressors and their victims: bullying at school. In N. Frude & H. Gault (Eds.), *Disruptive behaviour in schools* (pp. 57–76). Chichester: Wiley.

Olweus, D. (1985). 80,000 barn er innblandet i mobbing. *Norsk Skoleblad, 2,* 18–23.

Olweus, D. (1987). Bully/victim problems among schoolchildren in Scandinavia. In J. P. Mykelbust & R. Ommundsen (Eds.), *Psykologprofesjonen mot år 2000* (pp. 395–413). Oslo: Universitetsforlaget.

Olweus, D. (1991). Bully/victim problems among schoolchildren: basic facts and effects of a school based intervention program. In D. Pepler & K. H. Rubin (Eds.), *The development and treatment of childhood aggression* (pp. 411–448). Hillsdale: Erlbaum.

Olweus, D. (1993a). *Bullying at school: What we know and what we can do.* Oxford: Blackwell.

Olweus, D. (1993b). Victimization by peers: antecedents and long-term outcomes. In K. H. Rubin & J. B. Asendorf (Eds.), *Social withdrawal, inhibition and shyness* (pp. 315–341). Hillsdale: Erlbaum.

Olweus, D. (1994). Annotation: Bullying at school: basic facts and effects of a school based intervention program. *Journal of Child Psychology and Psychiatry, 35,* 1171–1190.

Ortega, R., & Lera, M. J. (2000). The Seville Anti-Bullying School Project. *Aggressive Behaviour, 26,* 113–124.

Parker, J. G., & Asher, S. R. (1987). Peer relationships and later personal adjustment: are low-accepted children at risk? *Psychological Bulletin, 102,* 357–389.

Parkhurst, J. T., & Asher, S. R. (1987, April). *The social concerns of aggressive-rejected children.* Paper presented at the Biennial Meeting of the Society for Research on Child Development, Baltimore, MD, USA.

Patchin, J., & Hinduja, S. (2006). Bullies move beyond the schoolyard: A preliminary look at cyberbullying. *Youth Violence and Juvenile Justice, 4,* 148–169.

Patterson, C. J. (1992). Children of lesbian and gay parents. *Child Development, 63,* 1025–1042.

Perry, D. G., Kusel, S. J., & Perry, L. C. (1988). Victims of peer aggression. *Developmental Psychology, 24,* 807–814.

Pilkington, N. W., & D'Augelli, A. R. (1995). Victimization of lesbian, gay and bisexual youth in community settings. *Journal of Community Psychology, 23,* 33–56.

Postmes, T., & Spears, R. (1998). Deindividuation and antinormative behavior: a meta-analysis. *Psychological Bulletin, 123,* 238–259.

Poteat, V. P. (2007). Peer group socialization of homophobic attitudes and behavior during adolescence. *Child Development, 78,* 1830–1842.

Poteat, V. P., Espelage, D. L., & Koenig, B. W. (2009). Willingness to remain friends and attend school with lesbian and gay peers: Relational expressions of prejudice among heterosexual youth. *Journal of Youth and Adolescence, 38,* 952–962.

Poteat, V. P., & Rivers, I. (2010). Bullying roles and the use of homophobic epithets toward students. *Journal of Applied Developmental Psychology, 31,* 166–172.

Prentice-Dunn, S., & Rogers, R. W. (1982). Effects of public and private self-awareness on deindividuation and aggression. *Journal of Personality and Social Psychology*, 43, 503–513.

Prentice-Dunn, S. & Rogers, R. W. (1989). Deindividuation and the self-regulation of behavior. In P. B. Paulus (Ed.), *The psychology of group influence* (pp. 86–109). New York: Erlbaum.

Preston, J. (1991). *The big gay book*. New York: Plume.

Price, D. A. (2004, September). *No needs to fear: Ending bullying in U.S. schools*. Presented at International Policy and Research Conference on School Bullying and Violence, Stavanger, Norway.

Price, J. H. (1982). High school students' attitudes towards homosexuality. *Journal of School Health*, 52, 469–474.

Randall, P. (1997). *Adult bullying: Perpetrators and victims*. London: Routledge.

Rayner, C., & Hoel, H. (1997). A summary review of literature relating to workplace bullying. *Journal of Community and Applied Social Psychology*, 7, 181–191.

Rayner, C. (1997). The incidence of workplace bullying. *Journal of Community and Applied Social Psychology*, 7, 199–208.

Reicher, S., Spears, R., & Postmes, S. (1995). A social identity model of deindividuation phenomena. In W. Stroebe & M. Hewstone (Eds.), *European review of social psychology* (pp. 161–198). Chichester: Wiley.

Remafedi, G. (1987). Male homosexuality: the adolescent's perspective. *Pediatrics*, 79, 326–330.

Remafedi, G., Farrow, J., & Deisher, R. (1991). Risk factors for attempted suicide in gay and bisexual youth. *Pediatrics*, 87, 869–876.

Ridgeway, C. L., & Balkwell, J. W. (1997). Group processes and the diffusion of status beliefs. *Social Psychology Quarterly*, 60, 14–31.

Ridgeway, C. L., & Correll, S. J. (2006). Consensus and the creation of status beliefs. *Social Forces*, 85, 431–454.

Rigby, K., & Slee, P. (1993). Dimensions of interpersonal relating among Australian secondary school children and their implications for psychological well-being. *Journal of Social Psychology*, 133, 33–42.

Rigby, K. (1997). *Bullying in schools and what to do about it*. London: Jessica Kingsley Press.

Rivers, I. (1997a). Lesbian, gay and bisexual development: theory, research and social issues. *Journal of Community and Applied Social Psychology*, 7, 329–343.

Rivers, I. (1997b). Violence against lesbian and gay youth and its impact. In M. Schneider (Ed.), *Pride and prejudice: Working with lesbian, gay and bisexual youth* (pp. 31–48). Toronto: Central Toronto Youth Services.

Rivers, I. (1998). Psychological perspectives on human sexuality. In M. V. Morrissey (Ed.), *Sexuality and healthcare: A human dilemma* (pp. 61–74). Dinton: Mark Allen (Quay Books).

Rivers, I. (1999). *The psycho-social correlates and long-term implications of bullying at school for lesbians, gay men and bisexual men and women.* Unpublished PhD thesis, University of Surrey (Roehampton Institute, London).

Rivers, I. (2001a). The bullying of sexual minorities at school: Its nature and long-term correlates. *Educational and Child Psychology,* 18, 33–46.

Rivers, I. (2001b). Retrospective reports of school bullying: Recall stability and its implications for research. *British Journal of Developmental Psychology,* 19, 129–142.

Rivers, I., Duncan, N., & Besag, V. E. (2007). *Bullying: A handbook for educators and parents.* Westport: Greenwood/Praeger.

Rivers, I., & Noret, N. (2008). The mental health well-being of sexual minority youth: An assessment of school-based risk. *School Psychology Review,* 37, 174–187.

Rivers, I., & Noret, N. (2010). 'I h 8 u': Findings from a five-year study of text and e-mail bullying. *British Educational Research Journal,* 36, 543–671.

Rivers, I., Poteat, V. P., Noret, N., & Ashurst, N. (2009). Observing bullying at school: The mental health implications of witness status. *School Psychology Quarterly,* 24, 211–223.

Rivers, I., & Smith, P. K. (1994). Types of bullying behavior and their correlates. *Aggressive Behavior,* 20, 359–368.

Rogers, C. A., & Frantz, C. (1962). *Racial themes in Southern Rhodesia.* New Haven, CT: Yale University Press.

Ross, M. W. (1996). Societal reaction and homosexuality: culture, acculturation, life events, and social supports as mediators of response to homonegative attitudes. In E. D. Rothblum & L. A. Bond (Eds.), *Preventing heterosexism and homophobia* (pp. 205–218). Thousand Oaks, CA: Sage.

Rothblum, E. D., & Bond, L. A. (1996). Introduction: approaches to the prevention of heterosexism and homophobia. In E. D. Rothblum & L. A. Bond (Eds.), *Preventing heterosexism and homophobia* (pp. ix–xix). Thousand Oaks, CA: Sage.

Rubin, K. H., LeMare, L. J., & Lollis, S. (1990). Social withdrawal in childhood: developmental pathways to peer rejection. In S. R. Asher & J. D. Coie (Eds.), *Peer rejection in childhood* (pp. 217–249). New York: Cambridge University Press.

Rudman, L. A., Phelan, J. E., & Heppen, J. (2007). Developmental sources of implicit attitudes. *Personality and Social Psychology Bulletin,* 33, 1700–1713.

Rutter, M. (1989). Pathways from childhood to adult life. *Journal of Child Psychology and Psychiatry,* 30, 23–51.

Rutter, M. (1996). Transitions and turning points in developmental psychopathology: as applied to the age span between childhood and mid-adulthood. *International Journal of Behavioral Development,* 19, 603–626.

Salmivalli, C., Huttunen, A., & Lagerspetz, K. M. J. (1997). Peer networks and bullying in schools. *Scandinavian Journal of Psychology,* 38, 305–312.

Salmivalli, C., Lagerspetz, K. M. J., Björkqvist, K. L., Österman, K., & Kaukiainen, A. (1996). Bullying as a group process: participant roles and their relation to social status within the group. *Aggressive Behavior, 22,* 1–15.

Salmivalli, C., & Voeten, M. (2004). Connections between attitudes, group norms, and behaviour in bullying situations. *International Journal of Behavioral Development, 28,* 246–258.

Savin-Williams, R. C. (2005). *The new gay teeanger.* Cambridge: Harvard.

Sbordone, A. J. (1993). *Gay men choosing fatherhood.* Unpublished dissertation, City University of New York.

Schneider, M (1997) (Ed.). *Pride and prejudice: Working with lesbian, gay and bisexual youth.* Toronto: Central Toronto Youth Services.

Schneider, M. S., & Dimito A. (2008). Educators' beliefs about raising lesbian, gay, bisexual, and transgender issues in the schools: The experiences in Ontario, Canada. *Journal of LGBT Youth, 5,* 49–71.

Sears, J. T. (1991). *Growing up gay in the south: Race, gender, and journeys of the spirit.* New York: Harrington Park Press.

Sedgwick, E. K. (1990). *The epistemology of the closet.* Harmondsworth: Penguin.

Shapiro, W. (1998). Ideology, 'history of religions', and hunter-gatherer studies. *Journal of the Royal Anthropological Institute: Incorporating Man, 4,* 489–510.

Shidlo, A. (1992). *AIDS related health behaviour: Psychosocial correlates in gay men.* Unpublished doctoral dissertation, State University of New York at Buffalo.

Shidlo, A. (1994). Internalized homophobia: conceptual and empirical issues in measurement. In B. Greene & G. M. Herek (Eds.), *Lesbian and gay psychology: Theory, research and clinical applications* (pp. 176–205). Thousand Oaks: Sage.

Smith, P. K. (1991). The silent nightmare: bullying and victimisation in school peer groups. *The Psychologist, 4,* 243–248.

Smith, P. K., Mahdavi, J., Carvalho, M., Fisher, S., Russell, S., & Tippett, N. (2008). Cyberbullying: Its nature and impact on secondary school pupils. *Journal of Child Psychology and Psychiatry, 49,* 376–385.

Smith, P. K., Mahdavi, J., Carvalho, M., & Tippett, N. (2006). *An investigation into cyberbullying, its forms, awareness and impact, and the relationship between age and gender in cyberbullying.* London: Department for Education and Skills Research Brief No. RBX03–06.

Smith, P. K., Morita, Y., Junger-Tas, J., Olweus, D., Catalano, R., & Slee, P. (1999). *The nature of school bullying: A cross-national perspective.* London: Routledge.

Smith, P. K., & Sharp, S. (1994). The problem of school bullying. In P. K. Smith & S. Sharp (Eds.), *School bullying: Insights and perspectives* (pp. 1–19). London: Routledge.

Smith, P. K., & Shu, S. (2000). What good schools can do about bullying: Findings from a survey in English schools after a decade of research and action. *Childhood, 7,* 193–212.

Smith-Khuri, E., Iachan, R., Scheidt, P. C., Overpeck, M. D., Nic Gabhainn, S., Pickett, W., & Harel, Y. (2004). A cross-national study of violence-related behaviors in adolescents. *Archives of Pediatrics and Adolescent Medicine,* 158, 539–544.

Solberg, M. E., Olweus, D., & Endresen, I. M. (2007). Bullies and victims at school: Are they the same pupils? *British Journal of Educational Psychology,* 77, 441–464.

Spears, R., & Lea, M. (1992). Social influence and the influence of the 'social' in computer-mediated communication. In M. Lea (Ed.), *Contexts of computer-mediated communication* (pp. 30–65). Hemel Hempstead: Harvester Wheatsheaf.

Spears, R., & Lea, M. (1994). Panacea or panopticon? The hidden power in computer-mediated communication. *British Journal of Social Psychology,* 29, 121–134.

Spriggs, A. L., Iannotti, R. J., Nansel, R. J., & Haynie, D. L. (2007). Adolescent bullying involvement and perceived family, peer and school relations: commonalities and differences across race/ethnicity. *Journal of Adolescent Health,* 41, 283–293.

Stacey, J., & Biblarz, T. J. (2001). (How) Does the sexual orientation of parents matter? *American Sociological Review,* 66, 159–183.

Stein, B. D., Elliott, M. N., Jaycox, L. H., Collins, R. L., Berry, S. H., Klein, D. J., & Schuster, M. A. (2004). A national longitudinal study of the psychological consequences of the September 11, 2001 terrorist attacks: Reactions, impairment, and help seeking. *Psychiatry: Interpersonal and Biological Processes,* 67, 105–117.

Stott, C. J., & Adang, O. M. J. (2004). 'Disorderly' conduct: social psychology and the control of football hooliganism at 'Euro2004'. *The Psychologist,* 17, 318–319.

Sturman, E. D., & Mongrain, M. (2008). The role of personality in defeat: a revised social rank model. *European Journal of Personality,* 22, 55–79.

Sutton, J., Smith, P. K., & Swettenham, J. (1999). Bullying and theory of mind: A critique of the social skills deficit view of antisocial behaviour. *Social Development,* 8, 117–127.

Tajfel, H. (1972). La catégorisation sociale. In S. Moscovici (Ed.), *Introduction à la psychologie sociale* (pp. 272–302). Paris: Larousse.

Tajfel, H., & Turner, J. C. (1986). The social identity theory of intergroup behaviour. In S. Worchel & W.G. Austin (Eds.), *Psychology of intergroup relations* (pp. 7–24). Chicago: Nelson-Hall.

Tasker, F., & Bigner, J. (2007) (Eds.). *Gay and lesbian parenting: new directions.* Binghamton: Haworth.

Tasker, F., & Patterson, C. J. (2007). Research on gay and lesbian parenting: Retrospect and prospect. *Journal of Gay, Lesbian, Bisexual and Transgender Family Issues,* 3, 9–34.

Taulke-Johnson, R. A. (2008). Moving beyond homophobia, harassment and intolerance: gay male university students' alternative narratives. *Discourse: Studies in the Cultural Politics of Education, 29,* 121–133.

Taulke-Johnson, R. A. (2009). *Living differently: gay male undergraduates' student experiences.* Unpublished PhD thesis, Cardiff University.

Telingator, C., & Patterson, C. J. (2008). Children and adolescents of lesbian and gay parents. *Journal of the American Academy of Child and Adolescent Psychiatry, 47,* 1364–1368.

Thomashausen, A. E. A. M. (1987). *The dismantling of apartheid.* Cape Town: Printpak Books.

Thompson, D. A., Whitney, I., & Smith, P. K. (1994). Bullying of children with special needs in mainstream schools. *Support and Learning, 9,* 103–106.

Tierney, W. G. (1997). *Academic outlaws: Queer theory and cultural studies in the academy.* Thousand Oaks, CA: Sage.

Tolan, P. H., & Guerra, N. G. (1994). Prevention of delinquency: current status and issues. *Applied and Preventive Psychology, 3,* 251–273.

Trenchard, L. (1984). *Talking about young lesbians.* London: London Gay Teenage Group.

Trenchard, L., & Warren, H. (1984). *Something to tell you.* London: London Gay Teenage Group.

Troyna, B., & Hatcher, R. (1992). *Racism in children's lives: A study of mainly-white primary schools.* London: Routledge.

Turner, R. N., & Crisp, R. J. (2010). Imagining intergroup contact reduces implicit prejudice. *British Journal of Social Psychology, 49,* 129–142.

Unks, G. (1995) (Ed.). *The gay teen: Educational practice and theory for lesbian, gay, and bisexual adolescents.* New York: Routledge.

Van Cleave, J., & Davis, M. M. (2006). Bullying and peer victimization among children with special health care needs. *Pediatrics, 118,* 1212–1219.

Van der Linden, F. J., & Dijkman, T. A. (1989). *Jong zijn en volwassen worden in Nederland.* Nijmegen: Hooveld.

Vitaro, F., Tremblay, R. E., Kerr, M., Pagani, L., & Bukowski, W. M. (1997). Disruptiveness, friends' characteristics, and delinquency in early adolescence: A test of two competing models of development. *Child Development, 68,* 676–689.

Vollebergh, W. (1991). *The limits of tolerance.* Utrecht: Rijksuniversitait te Utrecht.

Wainright, J. L., & Patterson, C. J. (2008). Peer relations among adolescents with female same-sex parents. *Developmental Psychology, 44,* 117–126.

Warren, H. (1984). *Talking about school.* London: London Gay Teenage Group.

Werner, N. E., & Crick, N. R. (2004). Maladaptive peer relationships and the development of relational and physical aggression during middle childhood. *Social Development, 13,* 495–514.

Whitney, I., Nabuzoka, D., & Smith, P. K. (1992). Bullying in schools: mainstream and special needs. *Support and Learning, 7,* 3–7.

Whitney, I., & Smith, P. K. (1993). A survey of nature and extent of bullying in junior/middle and secondary schools. *Educational Research, 35,* 3–25.

Whitney, I., Smith, P. K., & Thompson, D. A. (1994). Bullying and children with special educational needs. In P. K. Smith & S. Sharp (Eds.), *School bullying: Insights and perspectives* (pp. 213–240). London: Routledge.

Williams, J. E., & Morland, J. K. (1976). *Race, color, and the young child.* Chapel Hill: University of North Carolina Press.

Williams, G. A., & Asher, S. R. (1987, April). *Peer and self-perceptions of peer rejected children: Issues in classification and subgrouping.* Paper presented at the Biennial Meeting of the Society for Research in Child Development, Baltimore, MD, USA.

Williams, K. R., & Guerra, N. G. (2007). Prevalence and predictors of internet bullying. *Journal of Adolescent Health, 41,* 14–21.

Williams, W. L. (1992). *The spirit and the flesh: Sexual diversity in American Indian culture.* Boston: Beacon.

Wright, P. H. (1989). Gender differences in adults' same- and cross-gender friendships. In R. G. Adams & B. A. Winstead (Eds.), *Older adult friendship* (pp. 197–221). Newbury Park: Sage.

Xie, H., Cairns, R. B., & Cairns, B. D. (1999). Social networks and configurations in inner-city schools: Aggression, popularity, and implications for students with EBD. *Journal of Emotional and Behavioral Disorders, 7,* 147–155.

Yule, W., & Udwin, O. (1991). Screening child survivors for post-traumatic stress disorder: experiences from the 'Jupiter' sinking. *British Journal of Clinical Psychology, 30,* 131–138.

Yule, W., & Williams, R. (1990). Post-traumatic stress reactions in children. *Journal of Traumatic Stress, 3,* 279–295.

Zimbardo, P. G. (1969). The human choice: individuation, reason, and order vs. deindividuation, impulse, and chaos. In W. J. Arnold & D. Levine (Eds.), *Nebraska Symposium on Motivation* (pp. 237–307). Lincoln: University of Nebraska Press.

Zuckerman, M., & Lubin, B. (1965). *Manual for the Multiple Affect Adjective Check List.* San Diego: EdITS.

Author Index

Achenbach, T. M., 65
Adams, A., 79
Adams, G. A., 68–70, 75, 76, 154, 156, 160, 188
Adang, O. M. J., 49
Adessa, R., 32
Agatston, P. W., 17
Ahmad, Y., 5, 7, 22
Alexander, R. A., 161
Allen, R. E., 5
Allport, G. W., 52, 53, 94, 105, 106, 185
American Psychiatric Association, 162, 170
Amick-McMullan, A., 66
Anderson, D., 59, 60
Anderson, E., 30, 192
Anderson, E. M., 24–26
Andrews, B., 189
Angell, E., 122
Arnold, R., 13
Arnot, M., 30
Arora, C. M. J., 8
Arseneault, L., 13
Asher, S. R., 64, 65, 74, 155, 168

Ashurst, N., 14, 15, 47
Askenasy, A. R., 159, 165
Askew, S., 29, 177
Atria, M., 13
Aurand, S. K., 32

Bagley, C., 66, 81–82, 86, 87, 152, 195
Bagwell, C. L., 73, 180
Bailey, M. J., 60–61
Balkwell, J. W., 57–59, 177
Ball, H. A., 13
Bates, J. E., 67
Beach, K. R., 193
Bem, D. J., 180–81
Berrill, K. T., 32
Berry, S. H., 67
Berts, M., 28, 42
Besag, V. E., 4, 5, 7, 30, 42–44, 47, 108, 131, 190
Best, C. L., 66, 67
Biblarz, T. J., 61
Bigner, J. J., 61
Bjerregaard, B., 50

Subject Index

Note: Page numbers followed by "*f*" and "*t*" denote figures and tables, respectively.